SWAMPED

Interdisciplinary Teaching Approaches for New Faculty

Edited by Justin M. Carroll

UNG

UNIVERSITY *of*
NORTH GEORGIA™
UNIVERSITY PRESS

Blue Ridge | Cumming | Dahlonega | Gainesville | Oconee

Published by:
University of North Georgia Press
Dahlonega, Georgia

Printing Support by:
Lightning Source Inc.
La Vergne, Tennessee

Cover and book design by Corey Parson.

ISBN: 978-1-959203-08-7

For more information, please visit: http://ung.edu/university-press
Or e-mail: ungpress@ung.edu

Table of Contents

Building Relationships and Deeper Connections
in the Classroom

Introduction

Justin M. Carroll

When I defended my dissertation in the early 2010s, I had a quiet confidence that belied a chasm of self-doubt. When Indiana University East (IUE) hired me soon after entering the job market, I felt insecure and scared instead of proud and happy. I thought I had tricked them somehow. Given time, they would know me as a fraud. Over ten years later, I still feel intense flashes of this old insecurity, and I know I am not alone. Given the pressures of landing a tenure-track position and, if hired, the pressures of securing tenure and promotion, the initial years as a new professor can often feel like a Hobbesian nightmare: "solitary, poor, nasty, brutish, and short" (Leviathan, i, xiii, 9).

Luckily for me, I had great colleagues. Many of whom featured in this book were among the first people I met on campus. They impressed me with the quality of their research and absolute dedication to teaching. They were supportive and kind. They took a lonely profession, where people tend to research, write, and step into the classroom alone, and transformed the experience into a space of collaboration, innovation, and affirmation.[1] Their

---

1   For a discussion of student-centered learning environments and their development over time, see: Sabine Hoiden, Kurt Reusser, "Foundations of Student-Centered Learning and Teaching," *The Routledge International Handbook of Student-Centered Learning and Teaching in Higher Education* (New York: Routledge, 2021), 17–46. Likewise, in the context of this book, active learning plays a vital role in how we conceptualize many of our efforts. Active learning is a difficult pedagogical approach to define. Still, we understand it to be a movement away from the passive consumption of knowledge and towards creating space for students to shape, comment, direct, and decide what and how they might learn.

example and mentorship proved to be a boon for my career; they helped me clear a path toward something better and served as an impetus for this work.[2]

Academia creates and maintains these problems across graduating cohorts because doctoral programs in the United States still privilege research over the craft of teaching. As a result, many new humanities faculty members from graduate school may feel underprepared for their outstanding teaching commitments. They may enter the classroom feeling forced to reinvent the wheel, develop robust teaching agendas from whole cloth, or master necessary teaching skills without sufficient pedagogical grounding.[3] I certainly did. I still recall the embarrassment of not knowing what Bloom's Taxonomy was or what a colleague meant by "constructivism."[4] I can remember the intense consternation of my first year on the job, where I went home every day feeling like I had let my students, colleagues, and myself down.

See: David Mello, Colleen A. Less, "Effective Active Learning in the Arts and Sciences," Humanities Faculty Publications & Research, Page 45 (2013). http://scholarsarchive.jwu.edu/huannities_fac/45 Accessed October 13, 2022. In this regard, each chapter draws upon and incorporates insights from various pedagogical traditions, namely, constructivism, social constructivism, and liberationism. For examples of how constructivism operates across disciplines, see: *Constructivism: Theory, Perspectives, and Practice*, edited by Catherine Twomey Fosnot, editor. (New York: Teachers College, 2005); James Pelech, *The Comprehensive Handbook of Constructivist Teaching: From Theory to Practice*, Gail Pieper, editor. (Charlotte: Information Age Publishing, 2010); Yvon Cano-Fullido, "Constructivism Learning Theory: A Paradigm for Teaching and Learning," *IOSR Journal of Research and Method in Education, Volume 5, Issue 6* (November–December, 2015), 66–70. In discussing this project with the authors, several mentioned Paulo Freire and the legacy of liberationist/critical pedagogy as being an influence on their teaching. See: Paulo Freire, *Pedagogy of the Oppressed*. (New York: Bloomsbury Academic, 2018).

2   For a discussion of the importance mentorship plays in higher education and the growth of junior faculty members, see: Sharan B. Merriam, et. al, "Mentoring in Higher Education: What We Know Now." *The Review of Higher Education* 11, no. 2 (1987): 199–210; Roberta G. Sands, L. Alayne Parson, & Josann Duane (1991) "Faculty Mentoring Faculty in a Public University," *The Journal of Higher Education*, 62:2, 174–193; Joselynn Fountain & Kathryn E. Newcomer (2016) *Developing and Sustaining Effective Faculty Mentoring Programs, Journal of Public Affairs Education*, 22:4, 483–506; Hallie E. Savage, Rashelle S. Karp, & Rose Logue (2004) "Faculty Mentorship At Colleges And Universities," *College Teaching*, 52:1, 21–24.

3   For an extended conversation about the many failings of graduate schools, and their failures to guide new faculty in terms of teaching, see: Leonard Cassuto, *The Graduate School Mess: What Caused It and How We Can Fix It* (Cambridge: Harvard University Press, 2015).

4   Later in my office, I googled Bloom's Taxonomy, and found this website: Patricia Armstrong, Bloom's Taxonomy. Vanderbilt University Center for Teaching. Retrieved [October 2, 2022)] from https://cft.vanderbilt.edu/guides-sub-pages/blooms-taxonomy/.

Given the increasing pressures of publication for new faculty members, the decreasing resources and budgets of publishers, and the often ballooning requirement of service (an area of academia often hidden or obscured from graduate students), the first two or three years of a new faculty member's life is fraught.[5] Set against the ticking tenure clock or, increasingly, the instability of adjuncting, many new faculty members experience imposter syndrome. Given the avalanche of new responsibilities on their shoulders, how could they not?

In February 2020, I went to dinner with Dr. Daron Olson, my colleague in the IUE History program, and I outlined a vision for a book. Over dinner, I described a monograph that offered a series of actionable semester-long projects, assignments, or practices that new faculty members could use to build, develop, and articulate a continuing teaching agenda.

I explained how I wanted this monograph to give new faculty members materials to create engaging, informative, and transformative learning experiences as quickly as possible for their students. In this regard, I suggested that each chapter incorporate pedagogical practices geared towards active and deep learning. Each chapter would demonstrate how these projects, assignments, and practices encourage students to reflect on their efforts, think about their thought processes and how/why they thought that way, participate democratically and transparently in the development of their learning environments, and help them apply their learning efforts or new skills in unique or lateral contexts.[6]

---

5   For a recent study about faculty mental health and the fears and confusions attached to mental health issues, see: Margaret Price, Mark S. Salzer, Amber O'Shea, and Stephanie L. Kerschaum, "Disclosure of Mental Disability by College and University Faculty: The Negotiation of Accommodations, Support, and Barriers." *Disability Studies Quarterly*, Vol. 37, No. 2 (2017).

6   For discussions of various strategies and practices for developing active, equitable, and reflective learning practices in the classroom, see: John C. Bean, Dan Melzer, *Engaging Ideas: The Professor's Guide to Integrating Writing, Critical Thinking, and Active Learning in the Classroom.* (New Jersey: John Wiley & Sons, 2021); Joe Feldman, *Grading for Equity: What It Is, Why It Matters, and How It Can Transform Schools and Classrooms.* (Thousand Oaks, CA: Corwin, 2019); *Transparent Design in Higher Education and Leadership: A Guide to Implementing the Transparency Framework Institution-Wide to Improve Learning and Retention*, edited by Mary-Ann Winkelmes, Allison Boye, and Suzanne Tapp. (Sterling, VA: Stylus Publishing, 2019); *Using Reflection and Metacognition to Improve Student Learning*, edited by Matthew Kaplan, Naomi Silver, Danielle LaVaque-Manty, and Deborah Meizlish. (Sterling, VA: Stylus Publishing, 2013).

I wanted a clear, readable, and engaging volume. To the best of my ability, I wanted to recreate the conversations in most faculty hallways. The unofficial and unmediated sites and spaces at IUE, where faculty share, sometimes quite colorfully, their experiences and observations, helped me feel like a part of a larger community, a peer among equals, and uniquely engaged in a lively culture. When I asked Dr. Olson to participate, he immediately said yes. I asked others, and they agreed.

As a group, we all believe in making something new from what is already there and that faculty members learn best from each other. As such, each chapter offers a range of projects/assignments/processes immediately actionable in any collegiate classroom, allowing the reader to adapt, modify, or reuse this material to fit any academic context or need. The goal is not to be possessive or precious about our work or experiences at our regional public university but to share and disseminate them as widely as possible so that others might use them, make them better, and share them further. In an era where co- and multi-disciplinary teaching is increasingly common across higher education classrooms, both in disciplinary and SOTL (Scholarship of Teaching and Learning) research, these chapters work to lower the barriers between academic disciplines and faculty, particularly within the humanities, and to create the conditions for more dynamic, inclusive, and multifaceted learning experiences for our students.[7]

Each project/assignment/process highlighted in this book has been field-tested, assessed, rethought, revised, and often reworked by various authors over multiple semesters. They are high quality. Each chapter offers a detailed narrative about the different projects/assignments/processes and how they worked and operated over an entire semester. The authors provide concrete examples, comments, and student feedback, and highlight the pitfalls and missteps that occurred along the way. In highlighting the good and bad in these approaches, we want the reader to see our work's limits and horizons so they can judge appropriately and modify our work to fit their unique needs, well beyond the numerous suggestions, examples, and adaptations

---

7   See: Mary Beth Doyle and Donna Bozzone, "Multidisciplinary Teaching Providing Undergraduates with the Skills to Integrate Knowledge and Tackle 'Big' Questions," *The Journal of the Center for Interdisciplinary Teaching & Learning*, vol. 7, no. 1, 12–17.

offered by each author within the course of their narratives. Each chapter will explain how we did it and how it might also be used in your classrooms.

Furthermore, these projects/assignments helped students master new skills and ways of seeing the world and acquire personal agency in their educations and beyond. Since many of these projects are extensive and semester-long, and some span multiple semesters, students become part of something more significant and permanent; their work is more than a "one-off" grade quickly forgotten, but a lasting memory and real legacy that will influence subsequent students.

Finally, these projects/assignments/processes can create freedom and academic space for new faculty members early in their careers to work on their vital research, focus on innovative service opportunities, or help mitigate teaching fears and uncertainties that often accompany the transition from graduate student to professor.[8] These projects, assignments, and processes are modular, adaptable, and fit into any teaching agenda. They allow new and tenured faculty members to quickly and consistently incorporate unique, well-developed, high-impact learning experiences into their classrooms without sacrificing time and effort, fostering exceptional learning environments and experiences for their students.

For ease of use and clarity, the chapters in this volume fall into three sections that reflect their general purpose and value. Section #1, "Learning Experiences and Opportunities Outside of the Classroom," features two chapters written by World Language Professor Dianne Moneypenny and History Professor Christine Nemcik, respectively, both focusing on issues related to designing meaningful study-abroad experiences that connect abstract classroom material with the lived reality

---

8   In some ways, our monograph was inspired by Maggie Berg's and Barbara K. Seeber's "Slow Professor Manifesto" and serves to help faculty members recover some time and balance in their own lives. Berg and Seeber write poignantly, "We need . . . to protect a time and a place for timeless time, and to remind ourselves continually that this is not self-indulgent but rather crucial to intellectual work. If we don't find timeless time, there is evidence that not only our work but also our brains will suffer." They articulate how crisis administrating affects faculty, students, and universities throughout their narrative. Sharing and borrowing from each other—small acts of grace and charity—can be a strategy in combating what often feels like a long defeat for faculty members. See: Maggie Berg, Barbara K. Seeber, *The Slow Professor: Challenging the Culture of Speed in the Academy.* (Toronto: University of Toronto Press, 2016), 28.

of day-to-day life abroad. Another chapter by History Professor Justin M. Carroll focuses on documentary filmmaking and fostering collaborative student/community partnerships outside the history classroom. A final chapter, written by Education Professor James Barbre, explores the value of service-learning opportunities for students and how to define and embed them within courses.

Section #2, "Immersive Assignments and Learning Experiences in the Classroom," features chapters written by History Professor Daron W. Olson, which focus on putting students in the shoes of past historical actors through collaborative role-playing games in the classroom and the creation and workshopping of student-driven plays based around historical themes. Likewise, History Professor Justin M. Carroll's chapter focuses on the production and craft of history and creating a collaborative open-source U.S. history textbook. History Professor Christine Nemcik's work explores cross-cultural encounters and historical research by creating Mexican Day of the Dead altars in her introductory courses.

Finally, Section #3, "Building Relationships and Deeper Connections in the Classroom," offers two chapters. English Professor Kelly Blewett's work explores how she uses feedback to build trust and establish productive relationships with students that promote success outside the classroom. And in the last chapter of the book, World Language Professor Félix Burgos uses historical memory and assignments related to personal memory to help students better understand themselves and each other.

All told, the projects/assignments/processes described in these chapters span across semesters, evolve year after year and grow to allow faculty members to establish unique niches, teaching agendas, and long-term strategies that build toward a compelling argument for tenure and promotion. We hope our chapters help faculty members, new and old, maintain exciting and multifaceted learning environments for their students and foster greater collaboration with their colleagues. Finally, we hope our work saves time, effort, and heartache for our colleagues and, in doing so, helps restore a better work-life balance and creates space for us to be genuinely better.

Learning Experiences and Opportunities Outside of the Classroom

"I Never Knew That Was Here":

Microhistories, Short Documentaries, and Collaborative History Making

Justin M. Carroll

History comes in unexpected guises. As a new faculty member at Indiana University East in the fall of 2011, I encountered one of the strongest and most engaged cohorts of History majors I had ever seen. They were a diverse mix of traditional and non-traditional students and included a robust military veteran contingent. They steeped themselves in History and, more interestingly, in popular cultural representations of History. Their knowledge came from an increasingly global array of sources: online videos, comic books, memes, gifs, films, music, and games. I watched *Epic Rap Battles*, remixes of Bruno Ganz's performance of Hitler in *The Downfall*, and a detailed description of Assassin's Creed III gameplay.[1] These students impressed upon me the degree to which modern Americans encountered historical knowledge, narratives, and arguments largely outside academic classrooms and primarily outside of books, articles, and other kinds of text. Inspired by these students, I endeavored to re-think my courses, reimagine what I wanted my students to know, and explore new ways to help them communicate their knowledge of the past through various media.

---

1   For an example of Epic Rap Battles, see: Nice Peter, EpicLLOYD, "Steve Jobs vs. Bill Gates," YouTube video, 2:47 minutes, June 14, 2012, https://www.youtube.com/watch?v=njos57IJf-0 (Accessed 7-31-2021); For a recent example of the remixes of Bruno Ganz's Hitler performance in *The Downfall*, see: Ethancushing, "Trump Loses Election (Downfall Meme)," 3:49 minutes, November 6, 2020, https://www.youtube.com/watch?v=Jj7P4FUxu7k (Accessed 7-31-2021); Ubisoft Montreal, *Assassin's Creed III*, Ubisoft, Multiplatform, October 30, 2012.

Over my career at IUE, I have tried to use this student-driven insight to create unique course assignments that find students where they live, which, fair to say, is increasingly online. I worked towards giving them skills to communicate their love of History in non-traditional ways and better appreciate how non-textual forms of communication create arguments and develop points of view. As an adjunct to these skills, I hoped they would become critical consumers by making non-traditional historical narratives. Starting with a 200-level course I created in 2012 called "The Wild West and American Identity," filmmaking and documentary-making played essential roles in my pedagogy. In general, across my courses, I try to employ student-centered constructivist approaches, in which I foster learning environments where students can take active ownership and responsibility for their learning and create space for them to practice preexisting skills or develop transferable ones.[2] As such, I made course content and a series of assignments geared towards bridging traditional Historical research methods with hands-on, collaborative filmmaking and documentary techniques. In 2018, after securing tenure at IUE, I took charge of HIST-H217: The Nature of History. This course is a bottleneck experience for sophomore History and Education majors. In 2019, my efforts culminated in an ambitious project that merged local History, museum studies, and documentary-making into a transformative learning experience.

This chapter will provide an overview of this course and how its documentary-making project operated over IUE's 15-week semester. I will pay particular attention to how the students formed groups, developed topics, mastered skills, engaged in research, and planned, shot, and edited their films. I will also discuss the significant missteps, pitfalls, and mistakes the students and I encountered throughout this semester and how we collectively addressed them. By way of an appendix, I have included a shell syllabus, course handouts, and course readings, which I will refer

2   For a discussion and overview of constructivism and the works I consulted when I started teaching at Indiana University East, see: *Constructivism: Theory, Perspectives, and Practice*, Catherine Twomey Fosnot, editor. (New York: Teacher College Press, 2005); James Pelech, *The Comprehensive Handbook of Constructivist Teaching: From Theory to Practice*, Gail Pieper, editor. (Charlotte: Information Age Publishing, 2010); Yvon Cano-Fullido, "Constructivism Learning Theory: A Paradigm for Teaching and Learning," *IOSR Journal of Research and Method in Education*, Volume 5, Issue 6 (November–December, 2015), 66–70.

to throughout the chapter. I will discuss the project's overall success and whether the students developed a clear sense of historical methodology through their documentaries. Finally, when applicable and appropriate, I will explore how this project can be modified or re-developed to work or operate in other humanities/social science-centered courses and classrooms, largely within the context of transferable skills and cross-discipline applications.

Course Overview

I introduced the documentary project to my students in HIST-H217: The Nature of History by telling them: "Your projects may fail, and that's okay. Honestly, you'd be surprised by how often your professors start projects and invest considerable time into them, only to see them fall apart. That's how we learn to do better." Because non-traditional assignments are prominent in my courses, I have always found it advantageous to be honest, open, and reassuring about the process. "We are here to learn about the research *process*," I announced, "the documentary-making *process*, the creative *process*, and how these *processes* help guide our thinking and workflow. We go where they take us, and sometimes that means new directions, and sometimes that means brick walls. We mustn't be afraid of that." Years of "grade-training," the ubiquitous belief that grades matter or that some grade in a random class will define the rest of a student's life, often create risk-averse behaviors. From how I teach, worrying about grades fundamentally destroys effective learning environments and negates students' intellectual growth. I belabored this point on the first day of class and repeated it often over the semester, culminating in a group contract.

I had spent the summer talking to Karen Shank-Chapman, the executive director of the Wayne County Historical Museum (WCHM) in Richmond, Indiana. Founded in the 1930s, the WCHM grew out of the private collection of a wealthy socialite and philanthropist, Julia Meek Gaar. A world traveler, she collected art, artifacts, manuscripts, and other ephemera from all over. For example, Gaar's Egyptian mummy, nearly 3,000 years old, is surrounded by its grave goods and plays a prominent role in the collection. Shank-Chapman and her excellent staff permitted me to bring my students to the museum and gave us carte blanche to use, film, and explore many of the artifacts in the production of our documentaries.

I thought having students work at the museum to handle, analyze, film, and conduct research into these artifacts would be a fascinating and transformative experience, especially for undergraduates. Moreover, this non-academic classroom experience would have the added value of helping students think critically about local museums, the stories they tell, the way they come into existence, and the various roles they play within the larger community.

Former students expressed genuine interest in exploring local history in prior class iterations. As such, I wanted students to leave the course with a clearer sense of how the landscapes and communities they lived in linked to more extensive national and global processes. I banned the use of non-US, non-Indiana artifacts in their documentaries. I also hoped this limitation would help with their projects' overall quality and effectiveness. I did not want them to be overwhelmed by choice. And it would be easier, I thought, for the students to find footage, sources, interviewees, and access locally.

By the second class of the first week, the students sorted themselves into groups of three or four. Unfortunately, I let them choose their partners, which may have been a mistake, as one group struggled to hold each other accountable or prove critical of the quality of each other's work efforts. After the students self-grouped, I talked to them about research, writing, filming, editing, and the general processes involved with each. For example, editing was slow and laborious but essential to storytelling, while filming required a clear sense of what the documentary should look like and how to capture that on screen. All these roles collaborated. We talked about software and cameras, oral interviews and notetaking, and I promised that we would practice these skills over the semester. Finally, before ending class, I asked them to consider what they imagined their role in producing their short documentaries would be and why. I asked them to be honest about their interests and passions.

Early in the semester, I needed to give my students a clearer sense of how they could tell historical narratives about the past through local objects. As a graduate student, I listened to a BBC Radio series called *A History of the World in 100 Objects* that I thought could serve as a viable and accessible model.[3] In a 15-minute segment, Neil MacGregor, the director of

3   For an example of this podcast, see: Neil MacGregor, "Credit Card," *A History of the World in*

the British Museum, explored how a particular object shaped history and modern society. Luckily, the series produced a companion book, which I bought for the course. Using selected examples from MacGregor's *A History of the World in 100 Objects*, the students and I discussed how they could use artifacts to frame exciting and compelling stories of the past.[4] For example, we explored how an old coin could center multiple historical accounts about commerce or the evolution of exchange, as well as how metal-based currency could allow students to delve into the lives of those who made it. MacGregor's work proved fruitful and valuable, and the students enjoyed reading the various vignettes. Aspects of these discussions showed up in the final short documentaries, and several students, in subsequent history courses, continued to explore the idea of "microhistories" in different formats and contexts.

The MacGregor readings and subsequent discussions framed our first visit to the museum during week two of the course. The students came to the museum armed with pens, paper, and a short, guided assignment; they each had 25 minutes to explore the museum and choose some objects of interest. By limiting the time, I hoped they would latch onto artifacts that best stood out or spoke to them. From there, in their groups, they discussed which artifact they liked best and then had to narrow down their choices and come up with a single consensus object they would want to spend the remainder of the semester researching. The groups chose a surprisingly eclectic assortment of artifacts. They sidestepped the more iconic examples of American and Indiana history in the museum's collections, such as the massive Conestoga Wagon or the various cars built in early 20th-century Richmond, Indiana. Instead, they picked a Civil War musket, an old schoolhouse, evidence of a significant disaster from the 1960s, a long-established bakery, and a reel lawnmower.

After their group discussion, each member had 15 minutes to draw and write down their observations. They had to illustrate their objects from three different angles and develop a list of eight to 10 potential ideas, associations, references, or exciting aspects of their artifact. Again, by limiting their time, I wanted the students to focus on and explore what drew their attention; why

100 Objects, BBC Radio 4, Podcast Audio, October 21, 2010, https://www.bbc.co.uk/programmes/b00vcqcz (Accessed 7-15, 2021).

4   Neil MacGregor, *A History of the World in 100 Objects* (New York: Penguin Books, 2013).

did this artifact inspire them? I wanted them to generate lists of potentialities that might later be useful as shots, narrative angles, or storytelling devices. These lists became helpful in the short documentary projects' later research and writing stages.

We ended our museum visit in the community room. The groups talked about how their object made them feel or think and what kind of stories their artifact might help them tell about the history of Wayne County, Indiana. These conversations were free-flowing and far-ranging; it was a spitballing session. The groups left the museum with a finalized object for their documentaries and a series of drawings and associations. They had notes from our group conversation and were armed with various comments from the professor and their classmates.

This material became the grist for a reflection and brainstorming assignment due a week or so later. First, as individuals, they had to think about what information they needed to tell the story of their object, for example, the relevant people, places, things, or ideas. Next, they had to think about who they could interview about their object—experts or professors, community members, or other voices that could provide relevant insight. Finally, they had to reflect on what they would need to film to tell the story of their object visually—maps, paintings, photos, footage, etc. Much of the success of the short documentaries came from this initial period of planning and conceptualization.

The groups worked inside and outside the classroom on their short documentaries—some had weekly meetings, others met online or discussed the material over email and text. By the fourth week of the course, they had to turn in a group contract that detailed the overall conception of their projects, responsibilities, and outlined documentary pitch. For this assignment, I explained to the students that I would grade their work based on how well they executed their overall vision and, outside of the formal assignment requirements, i.e., total length, quality primary/secondary sources, and other elements that define solid historical research, explained how they had a tremendous opportunity to define what success and excellence looked like in the context of their work.[5] Moreover, through this contractual approach,

---

5   My shift from a traditional grading approach towards contract grading and other methods was influenced by the following texts: Alfie Kohn, *Ungrading: Why Rating Students Undermines Learning*

I wanted them to have a clear structure and long-term planning in place so that, should trouble arise, they could negotiate any obstacle. I also wanted them to state what they wanted to say about their artifact clearly; this meant considering a potential title, explaining how the object would anchor their documentary, and stating why they thought the story they were telling had merit. With these two components in place, I hoped the groups would have touchstones that would guide them through the research, writing, filming, and editing processes and the complications that would come later. Finally, in the development of these contracts, I hoped my students would practice learning how to learn in a simulated real-world context, in which they would often be asked to negotiate multiple competing perspectives, integrate new with preexisting knowledge, and produce tangible, quality results at the direction of, while also largely independent of, their managers or bosses.[6]

The students had to turn in in-group status reports during weeks six, week nine, and 11. For example, in Group Status Report #1, they had to read a section of Steven Stockman's book, *How to Shoot Video that Doesn't Suck*, which I chose as a course text to help them work through filmmaking.[7] Moreover, because of my university's digital contracts, our students have free access to the full suite of Adobe products. In this course, we focused on Adobe Premiere. I incorporated free and accessible tutorials found on the Adobe website and YouTube.[8] With this material in mind,

(and What to Do Instead), Susan D. Blum, editor. (Morgantown: West Virginia University Press, 2020); Joe Feldman, *Grading for Equity: What It Is, Why It Matters, and How it Can Transform Schools and Classrooms.* (Thousand Oaks: Corwin, 2019); Linda B. Nilson, *Specifications Grading: Restoring Rigor, Motivating Students, and Saving Faculty Time.* (Sterling, Stylus Publishing, 2015); Asao B. Inoue, *Labor-Based Grading Contracts: Building Equity and Inclusion in the Compassionate Writing Classroom.* (Denver: University Press of Colorado, 2019).

6   Dorit Alt, "Contemporary Constructivist Practices in Higher Education Settings and Academic Motivational Factors," *Australian Journal of Adult Learning*, Vol. 53, Number 3, November 2016, pgs. 376–379. Self-directed learning, digital learning, self-motivated labor is an increasingly important part of the modern economy, and more importantly, seems connected to higher rates of pay, job satisfaction, and security. See: "AWS Global Digital Skills Study: The Economic Benefits of a Tech-Savvy Workforce." *Gallup*. Accessed October 30, 2022. https://www.gallup.com/analytics/402284/aws-digital-skills-study.aspx.

7   Steve Stockman, *How to Shoot Video That Doesn't Suck: Advice to Make Any Amateur Look Like a Pro* (New York: Workman Publishing Company, 2011).

8   For examples of the kinds of resources we employed in the course, see: "Premiere Pro Tutorials," Adobe.com. Accessed: September 2, 2022. https://helpx.adobe.com/premiere-pro/tutorials.html;

the groups turned in short reports where they detailed the shape of their documentaries, what research they accomplished, and what kinds of scenes or shots they needed, interviews they lined up, and resources they had on hand. Moreover, each group member had to write a short status report on their work within the group. For example, if their job was to research for the script, they documented what they accomplished in that area, what they planned next, how much work they had left, and how their work fit into the group's master plan. The final two Group Status Reports required them to upload footage, scripts, images, and other material on hand to a collaborative cloud storage space, where I could examine their progress and check their quality. Because of the labor-intensive nature of this project, I feared any group that fell behind would be unable to catch up or thrive. These reports mitigated such concerns. However, groups still fell behind.

In conjunction with *How to Shoot Video that Doesn't Suck* and the Group Status Reports, I developed a series of mini workshops in class. These workshops were practical demonstrations related to the basics and rudiments of filmmaking. For example, we explored how to interview a subject in an open-ended way or the best way to frame and light a subject for their documentaries. Moreover, I showed them how to use Adobe Premiere—namely, importing footage, cutting, assembling, incorporating music, and exporting their final cut as a high-definition file.

During these demonstrations, I learned the limitations of my students' technological savvy and quickly concluded that the "digital natives" rhetoric is fundamentally flawed.[9] In a context where my freshman and sophomore students were quite happy to show me their own YouTube and TikTok videos, I assumed they had a baseline competency in general computer usage and digital production. That was not the case. Most had smartphones with fantastic hi-def cameras, but few had computers with enough ram to process footage. One student admitted that they wrote their papers on their phones. Many lacked WiFi at home or in their apartments. These admissions

Olufemmi, "Learn Premiere Pro in 30 Minutes," Youtube.com. Accessed: September 2, 2022. https://www.youtube.com/watch?v=jVVVOo8LIlA.

9   For the destructive potential of this myth, see: Paul A. Kirschner, Pedro Bruyckere, "The Myths of the Digital Native and the Multitasker," *Teaching and Teacher Education*, Vol. 67, October 2017, pgs. 135–142.

surprised me. Although my university is considered an urban campus, our student body largely comes from a rural context; many commute daily, and most have full-time jobs. So, I opened my office computer for their use and brought in my personal computer as a backup. Likewise, I have found numerous online tutorials on YouTube related to filming, editing, shooting, etc. In subsequent iterations of the course, I plan to incorporate this material into guided modules that students must complete in the initial weeks of the semester to prepare them for the rigors and overall expectations of the assignment. Moreover, I plan on working with my campus Center for Teaching and Learning and our IT department to ensure students have complete access to the kinds of digital technologies this project and experience requires.

Concurrent with all the documentary work, I organized the courses' readings, assignments, and discussions in support. As a course on the nature of history, I chose two primary texts: Michael J. Salevouris' and Conal Furay's *The Methods and Skills of History: A Practical Guide* (2015) and Sarah Maza's *Thinking About History* (2017). *The Methods and Skills of History* introduced students to historical concepts, theories, and methods in an easily digestible manner through a series of well-designed assignments and practices.[10] Given the complexity of historical research and documentary making, this text helped us engage the daily practical, relevant, and usable skills that historians employ without too much trial or error. Likewise, Maza's work was an excellent and engaging undergraduate introduction to historiography and historiographical concerns. For example, she organized her book around questions like "The History of Whom?" and then traces how the field evolved from a focus on "Great Men" to social history and an ever-expanding cast of historical actors. These texts proved quite effective in helping students develop hands-on skills and a clearer understanding of History, but, more importantly, they helped center their focus amidst a complex project.

These readings and assignments framed our classroom discussions and created fascinating spaces to engage the groups on their projects. For example,

10   Michael J. Salevouris, Conal Furay, *The Methods and Skills of History: A Practical Guide.* (Oxford: John Wiley & Sons, Inc., 2015); Sarah Maza, *Thinking about History* (Chicago: University of Chicago Press, 2017).

during our class discussion of Chapter Three from Maza's *Thinking about History*, she discusses "the history of what," which sparked conversations about artifacts, micro-histories, and the concept of nature. One of the short documentary groups chose to explore the history of a reel lawnmower and its connection to Richmond, Indiana, which, at one time, was the "lawnmower capital of the world." Using the Maza reading and the group's research, we had more profound and complex conversations than usual. The students located the reel lawnmower within a matrix of evolving ideas about nature, industrialism, class, and capitalism. As a result of these exchanges, the short documentary group had the chance to discuss their project publicly with a knowledgeable audience. The class was able to connect the course readings to a tangible reality in an organic fashion. I found this moment thrilling because it happened without my planning. One of those happy accidents served as a springboard for future discussions, which I could plan carefully around the other group's projects.

The short documentary groups were in a full sprint by week 12, with only three weeks left in the semester. At this point, letting students pick their groups began to manifest problems in two of the five groups. One group, for example, failed to hold each other accountable. Despite advice and intervention, they had a relatively ramshackle project. They never developed a backup plan when their interviewee could not show up. All efforts to scaffold, chunk, keep tabs on, and encourage the group did not work, and what they turned in did not meet the assignment's standards. Another group lined up a great interview but failed to prepare adequately and frame or compose the subject well. As this interview was the set-piece of their short documentary, they hobbled the overall quality of their work.

In my courses, I try to view student missteps as my missteps. If a student struggles, I need to do something better to communicate what success would look like and how to get there. And these issues taught me several things that I found helpful later:

1. Group composition matters, and this step could have been better designed from the start. In response, I developed a skills inventory for the students to fill out, and I plan on using those to create balanced groups in the future.

2. At the beginning of the course, I was unsure if the students would have enough time to produce a rough cut of their documentaries, so instead, I opted to look at their rough footage and an edited scene. That was a mistake. In the future, I will create space to incorporate a rough-cut critique.

3. Finally, given the issues with interviewing and framing, I think more hands-on and practical demonstrations would be helpful. I will bring colleagues to sit for interviews in front of the class while each student group takes turns framing and filming them.

At the semester's end, I was relieved and overjoyed. I developed an extensive class project that required careful attention, planning, and negotiation. I stressed weekly, hoping I had not overburdened the students, raised the bar too high, or set them up to fail. There were hiccups and missteps. Some things could have been explained and conceptualized better. However, as the end of the semester came and the class turned in their final projects, I grew increasingly charmed, proud, and impressed by the quality of their work, the depths of their research, and the spirit they brought to their short documentaries.

We ended the semester with a premiere party and short film festival and watched, commented, and critiqued the films. Visually, the documentaries ran the gamut. One took the form of a Ken Burns-style documentary that explored Southeastern Indiana's history and the Civil War through a musket rifle. Another opted for a humorous approach and filmed a modern-day infomercial about a late 19th-century lawnmower. Finally, one student used footage her grandfather shot about a significant disaster in Richmond, Indiana, to tell a uniquely personal history of the event. These documentaries weren't perfect.[11] However, they showed care, effort, and attention. They used the skills of a historian alongside the language of cinema and filmmaking to reimagine the past. In doing so, they developed new ways of communicating with and understanding the world around them.

---

11 In my courses, I give students the right to decide what happens to their material; if they would like to share their efforts publicly, they have that right and we discuss issues related to Creative Commons licensing, and the benefits and pitfalls of public engagement. In my experience, students hesitate to share their first efforts. When I talk about this project in other academic contexts, I talk about general issues that I saw or encountered in prior work.

Sample Syllabus Overview

Generic Course Description:

(This course was a sophomore seminar designed to teach the methods and skills of history; however, given its focus on transferable skills—digital filming, non-linear editing, interviewing, storytelling, team building, etc.—this material is broadly and infinitely transferable to other contexts. For example, looking at my Course Learning Objectives, the documentary project is the vehicle that carries the weight of these overall goals. In a traditional iteration of the course, this would have been a scaffolded research paper. In essence, the documentary project allowed students to engage in the practices of thinking historically, even as they leveraged this effort into developing a new skill set. Hypothetically, in an English class that explores creative non-fiction, students could easily practice the skills and expectations of the fourth genre in the creation of their documentary scripts even as they master the skills of digital filmmaking. They are not mutually exclusive and benefit from extending the learning experience to new contexts and adding value.)

"An introductory examination of (1) what history is, (2) modes of historical interpretation, (3) common problems historians encounter and why, and (4) the uses and misuses of history."

General Course Learning Objectives (CLOs):

Students who pass this course with a C grade or higher will be able to:
1. Explain what history is;
2. Describe different types or modes of historical interpretation;
3. Discuss common problems historians encounter and why;
4. Apply the uses of history to a variety of media;
5. Explore how history can be used in their career plans.

Suggested Course Reading Materials:

(Given the labor-intensive nature of digital filmmaking, I tried to limit the readings for this course to key and vital texts. I spent time considering texts that would give me "more bang for my buck," as it were. I assumed that developing new skills—and the discussions that would result from the development of these new skills—would fill in any potential gaps. Because this was a preexisting course that I modified to incorporate the documentary project, I often felt hyperaware of things I left out. However, given the results, I think sacrificing a book or several articles is worth the dislocation.)

1. Michael J. Salevouris, Conal Furay, *The Methods and Skills of History: A Practical Guide*. (New York: Wiley-Blackwell, 2015).
2. Sara Maza, *Thinking about History*. (Chicago: University of Chicago Press, 2017).
3. Steve Stockman, *How to Shoot Video that Doesn't Suck*. (New York: Workman Publishing, 2011).

Suggested Course Assignments:

(These assignments relate only to the documentary project and serve to scaffold the overall experience. Over the course of the semester, I used other traditional history assignments, such as primary source analyses, book reviews, and other short writings.)

1. Individual and Group Object Reflection Papers
2. Group Film Pitch, Contract, and Responsibility Details
3. Three Individual and Group Status Reports
4. Rough Cut of Short Documentary and Critique
5. Final Documentary and Exit Survey

Suggested Course Schedule:

(In my course, which is 15 weeks long, I organized the documentary project along the following lines. Please note that I tried to cut out ideas or readings that are not directly connected to the short documentary project. Moreover, I initially explained what I did each week and included new ideas from student feedback or my teaching observations. On average, I spent about 30 minutes a week on their projects.)

Week #1: Course Introduction, Short Documentary Project Discussion, and Group Formulation.

1. On the first day, hand out and conduct the *Individualized Skill Inventory*.

2. On the final day of the first week, form groups of three to four students and require them to share their contact information.

Week #2: Explore How Objects Can Tell History and Choice of Artifact

1. Choose three chapters from Neil MacGregor's *A History of the World in 100 Objects*. These readings demonstrate how objects can be used to frame and tell more extensive, complex stories.

2. At some point during the second week, the students need to choose an object for their documentaries. For example, the students traveled to a local museum.

Week #3: Individual and Group Museum Reflections and Follow-Up Questions

1. After the groups picked their objects, they reflected on what kinds of stories their things could tell and created a list of possible angles. Task them to begin the research project; go to the library's website and start searching. Google their objects. Have them get a sense of what is out there. Let them ask all follow-up questions about the short documentary assignment.

2. Assign Individual and Group Object Reflection Papers.

Week #4: History Telling with Objects and Films

1. History and Filmmaking are both vehicles for story. This week, use some class time to show students examples of short documentaries under 10 minutes and how they work to tell unique stories. Have them discuss what caught their attention, what kept their attention, and why some examples might have worked better than others. Outside of class, the groups had to develop a film pitch, a contract, and a list of responsibilities.

2. Have students read Steven Stockman, *How to Shoot Video that Doesn't Suck.* (New York: Workman Publishing, 2011), pgs. 56–80.

3. Assign the Group Film Pitch, Contract, and Responsibility Assignment.

Week #5: Capturing and Framing Subjects

1. By this point, the students are deeply involved in their documentaries' research, writing, and production. As such, the groups work more outside of class. However, during this week, use class time to help students learn how to film and capture their objects or interviewees on film. For example, talk about the rule of thirds, upward and downward angles, etc.

Week #6: Interviewing and Engaging Subjects

1. As part of the short documentary project, the groups had to interview someone knowledgeable about their artifact. Ideally, I pushed them to interview experts, professors, or museum workers. As such, go over professionalism, interview preparation, questions, and consent forms. Have students practice interviewing the professor or bring in colleagues. Generally, the goal is to get the groups comfortable asking open-ended questions relevant to their projects. Moreover, the first status reports come due, which is an excellent point to intervene.

2. Have students read Steven Stockman, *How to Shoot Video that Doesn't Suck.* (New York: Workman Publishing, 2011), pgs. 82–156.

3. Assign Group Status Report #1

Week #7: Importing Footage and Editing their Documentary

1. By this week, the groups may have footage related to their documentaries. This week, use class time to help students learn how to import and edit their footage. Because there will be a range of applications, the best practice would be to do this demonstration generally or in the context of the readily available editing software. Moreover, the first status reports come due, which is an excellent point to intervene and provide hands-on support.

Week #8: Documentary Check-In and Follow-Up Questions

1. By this week, the groups are deep into the documentary-making process, and much of the work occurs outside the classroom.

However, create time and space for check-in and questions. For example, ask about research, writing, narration, editing, etc.

Week #9: Documentary Check-In and Follow-Up Questions

1. By this week, the groups are deep into the documentary-making process, and much of the work occurs outside the classroom. However, create time and space for check-in and questions. For example, ask about research, writing, narration, editing, etc. Moreover, the second status reports come due, which is an excellent point to intervene and provide hands-on support.

2. Have students read Steven Stockman, *How to Shoot Video that Doesn't Suck*. (New York: Workman Publishing, 2011), pgs. 196–226.

3. Assign Group Status Report #2

Week #10: Documentary Check-In and Follow-Up Questions

1. By this week, the groups are deep into the documentary-making process, and much of the work occurs outside the classroom. However, create time and space for check-in and questions. For example, ask about research, writing, narration, editing, etc.

Week #11: Documentary Check-In and Follow-Up Questions

1. By this week, the groups are deep into the documentary-making process, and much of the work occurs outside the classroom. However, create time and space for check-in and questions. For example, ask about research, writing, narration, editing, etc. Moreover, the third status reports come due, which is an excellent point to intervene and provide hands-on support. This report is a significant milestone; the groups should provide a clear sense of completeness.

2. Have students read Steven Stockman, *How to Shoot Video that Doesn't Suck*. (New York: Workman Publishing, 2011), pgs. 227–241.

3. Assign Group Status Report #3

Week #12: Documentary Check-In and Follow-Up Questions
1. By this week, the groups are deep into the documentary-making process, and much of the work occurs outside the classroom. However, create time and space for check-in and questions. For example, ask about research, writing, narration, editing, etc.

Week #13: Rough Cut of Documentary and Critiques
1. When I first taught the course, I left out a rough cut of the documentary assignment to give the students more time to work unfettered. I assumed that I would pick up issues through the group reports, and while I did, I also found that I did not get a clear sense of the state of their projects.
2. Assign Rough Cut of the Short Documentary

Week #14: Fall Break, Editing, and Finalizing Short Documentaries
1. Our university has a fall break that corresponds with Thanksgiving. This week, the groups should edit, finalize, and upload their short documentaries based on their rough-cut feedback and be prepared to turn them in by Sunday or Monday.

Week #15: Final Short Documentary Submissions and Class Film Presentations
1. During the course's final week, the groups must turn in their final short documentary projects. This week is a celebration, so organize a viewing/screening of their work and create space for each group to introduce and field questions about their work. In the end, I asked them to write short paragraphs of anonymous advice for future students. Incidentally, I found this material helpful in relating ways to support their efforts better.
2. Assign Final Cut of the Short Documentary

Assignment and Project Templates and Handouts:

Group Object Reflection Activity and Paper

(For this semester, I had access to a historical museum that allowed us to explore and utilize their collections. However, when I asked students about other potential documentary topics, they generated a range of potential ideas—a family heirloom, landscapes, lost buildings, forgotten spaces, forgotten "founders," etc. Upon reflection, these ideas and concepts would have been equally interesting and applicable. In subsequent iterations of the course, I might allow students to develop their documentary project topics. This change might be a useful exercise for non-history courses, as well as generate more intense student interest and help students explore a wider array of material and content.)

Activity:
- Object Selection for Short Documentary Project

Objectives:
- Identify an object that evokes empathy, curiosity, or a sense of merit individually and as a group.
- Explain why you chose your object and what you learned, felt, imagined, or appreciated about it during your observation period.

Preparatory Readings:
- Selection from Neil MacGregor in *A History of the World in 100 Objects*. (New York: Viking Press, 2008).

Onsite Activity:
- Individually examine the various assembled objects (for example, we were at a museum) for 15 minutes and make a list of three or four objects that stand out to you the most;
- In your short documentary groups, spend 15 minutes discussing your lists. What were the commonalities or overlaps?

- Afterward, spend 10 minutes deciding on an object for your short documentary project as a group. This object should be a consensus choice.
- As a group, spend 10 minutes brainstorming a list of 30 possible historical angles, stories, ideas, images, and associations related to your objects.
- As a class, we will spend 30 minutes discussing your group's object for your short documentary. As a group, you will need to explain why you chose your object, what you felt or thought about, and what kind of historical stories the object might allow you to tell.

Group Reflection Paper:
- Outside of class, as a group, you need to craft a short essay that provides thorough answers to the following questions/prompts:
  - Having chosen an object, what information do you need to tell a story about it? What concepts, keywords, backgrounds, peoples, places, things, or ideas might you need to explore?
  - Having chosen an object, who might you talk to about it? Think about resources in your own family, communities, and university. Do you think these people would be willing to be interviewed and recorded?
  - Having chosen an object, what other imagery might you need to help tell its story? Maps? Paintings? Photos? Footage?

Group Short Documentary Pitch, Contract, and Responsibility Details
(As a professor trained in a traditional manner, ceding authority made me anxious. However, I felt it was necessary for the overall success of the documentary projects and for fostering student learning and growth. I had to negotiate my desire to know what the students were doing and allow them to develop their projects as they saw fit. As discussed in the narrative, I explained to the class that this assignment served to give students space to decide major aspects of the project and asked them to spell out the central purpose of their work, the various roles and related responsibilities, their various and consistent work schedules, and what a successful project looked like to them as a group and as individuals.)

Activity:
- Develop a Group Short Documentary Pitch, Contract, and Responsibility Details

Objectives:
- Identify the significant roles your documentary might require (for example, researcher, narrator, editor, interviewer, camera person, etc.);
- Explain what those jobs are, what they are required to do, and who will be responsible for them;
- Condense the point of your project down into a one-sentence pitch.

Preparatory Readings:
- Selections from Steven Stockman's *How to Shoot Video that Doesn't Suck*. (New York: Workman Publishing, 2011).

Group Activity:
- As a group, you need to talk about the major roles your documentary might require and write out what you expect from that role—its purpose and a clear list of its responsibilities;
- As a group, you will need to decide who will be responsible for which role and how you plan to ensure that work gets done effectively;
- As a group, you will need to create a work schedule—a weekly meeting to discuss your project, any issues, needs, and worries;
- As a group, you will need to share contact information so you can communicate effectively;
- Once this material is squared away, as a group, you will need to discuss the kind of story you want to tell about your object and how you plan on telling your history;
- As a group, you will need to distill your idea into a short pitch: a possible title, the point of view of your project, and why your story matters;
- As a group, you want your pitch to grab people's attention.

<u>Assignment:</u>

- Please design, write, and sign your documentary pitch, contract, and responsibility detail assignment as a group. It needs to include the following information:
  - Your documentary pitch; a clear statement of what your short documentary will be about and what it will say/argue (no more than 150 words total);
  - List of documentary roles, their purpose, and their responsibilities;
  - The name and contact information of each person and what part they will play in the creation of your short film;
  - Arbitration process—what you will do if something or someone does not work out correctly. For example, how will the group solve problems, and when will you go to the professor for help if the group cannot resolve its issue(s);
  - Describe what a successful project looks like from the perspective of the group and from the perspective of your individualized roles. In other words, what does success look like to you and how do you think I should approach your work in terms of assessing its quality;
  - A group meeting schedule;
  - A signed statement from each member promising to fulfill their required roles.

Individual/Group Status Report #1 Template

(These individual/group status reports serve three basic functions: 1) they serve to keep the students on task and aware of their responsibilities outside of the classroom; 2) they serve to keep the professor informed of group and individual progress; and 3) they help the students see the interconnection between their own efforts and the larger goals of the group. Moreover, each report asks the groups to present their material and progress to the class, which allows for feedback, engagement, additional collaboration, and support. Because I used the entire 15 weeks of the semester to develop this project, three iterations of the assignment helped structure my course. They ensured students used their time as wisely as possible. However, in the future, I'm unsure if I would devote as much time to the project, and I might only use one or two individual/group status reports over a six to nine week time frame.

Activity:
- Inform your professor of your short documentary progress/status as a group and as individuals.

Objectives:
- Summarize the status of your documentary project;
- Explain what each member has done in the pursuit of their assigned roles.

Preparatory Readings:
- Selections from Steven Stockman's *How to Shoot Video that Doesn't Suck*. (New York: Workman Publishing, 2011).

Group Activity:
- Outside of class, as a group, write a tentative documentary outline—what kind of scenes you need, what kind of interviews you need, what variety of settings you want, and what type of research you need. You want this to be an outline to help with filming and a list of potential resources you might use—buildings, places, people, pictures, and footage.
- Outside of class, as individuals, write a status report based on your assigned role in the group—what have you done, what do you plan on doing, and how does this fit into the group's film goals.
- Outside of class, share your status reports with your group members—use this material to plan.
- In class, as a group, deliver your film pitch.
- In class, as individual members of the group, explain what you've done so far in your roles—where have you been successful, where have you met with difficulties, and what are your next steps forward?
- In class, as a group, ask for feedback and commentary.

Assignment:

- As a group, please design and write up a documentary outline. Please make this as complete as possible. It needs to include the following information:
    - The loose shape of your documentary—how do you plan on telling your story about the object? Remember, this might change, but it is best to have a shape in mind;
    - What research do you have? Remember, you will need to have at least four secondary sources and four additional primary sources as background research;
    - What kind of scenes do you imagine you will need to tell the story?
    - What kind of interviews do you want? Who do you plan on asking?
    - What resources do you have on hand to tell your story? Buildings, places, pictures, and other footage?
- As individual members of the group, please write up a status report based on your group role. It needs to include the following information:
    - What work/research have you done?
    - What work/research do you plan on doing?
    - What work/research do you have left?
    - How does this work fit into your group's overall plan and success?

Individual/Group Status Report #2 Template

Activity:

- Inform your professor of your short documentary progress status as a group and as individuals.

Objectives:

- Summarize the status of your documentary project;
- Explain what each member has done in the pursuit of their assigned roles.

Group Activity:
- Outside of class, as a group, you should have started filming interviews, filming your objects, writing scripts, and editing footage. You should be making your documentary.
- Outside of class, as individuals, write up a status report based on your assigned role in the group—what have you done, what do you plan on doing, and how does this fit into the group's film goals.
- Outside of class, share your status reports with your group members—use this material to plan.
- In class, as individual members of the group, explain what you've done so far in your roles—where have you been successful, where have you met with difficulties, and what are your next steps forward?
- In class, as a group, ask for feedback and commentary.

Assignment:
- As a group, please design and write up a documentary outline. Please make this as complete as possible. It needs to include the following information:
- Please upload your research, images, and footage to the online group folder. This material will let your professor look at your work in progress and create a shared space where your group can access it. It also serves as a digital backup.
- As individual members of the group, please write up a status report based on your group role. It needs to include the following information:
  - What work/research have you done?
  - What do you plan on doing with this work/research?
  - What work/research do you plan on doing?
  - What work/research do you have left?

Individual/Group Status Report #3 Template
Activity:
- Inform your professor of your short documentary progress status as a group and as individuals.

Objectives:
- Summarize the status of your documentary project;
- Explain what each member has done in the pursuit of their assigned roles.

Group Activity:
- Outside of class, as a group, you should have started filming interviews, filming your objects, writing scripts, and editing footage. You should be making your documentary.
- Outside of class, as individuals, write up a status report based on your assigned role in the group—what have you done, what do you plan on doing, and how does this fit into the group's film goals.
- Outside of class, share your status reports with your group members—use this material to plan.
- In class, as individual members of the group, explain what you have done so far in your roles—where have you been successful, where have you met with difficulties, and what are your next steps forward?
- In class, as a group, ask for feedback and commentary.

Assignment:
- As a group, please design and write up a documentary outline. Please make this as complete as possible. It needs to include the following information:
- Please upload your research, images, and footage to the online group folder. This material will let your professor look at your work in progress and create a shared space where your group can access it. It also serves as a digital backup.
- As individual members of the group, please write up a status report based on your group role. It needs to include the following information:
  - What work/research have you done?
  - What do you plan on doing with this work/research?
  - What work/research do you plan on doing?
  - What work/research do you have left?

Final Documentary Template

(These requirements are closely tailored to what the documentary project looked like in the context of a historical methods course. Please note, for example, the primary source and secondary source requirements to see an example of what this means. However, as emphasized earlier, this project is adaptable to other fields and disciplines. For example, let's say, in the context of a Philosophy course, the professor tasks their students to create short documentaries about critical thinking in everyday life. They might have to explore cognitive biases or logical fallacies; they might have to film or find examples of five of each. The documentary project serves only as a vehicle that carries the goals of the course, and, in doing so, helps students take ownership over their learning and develop transferable skills in the process.)

Activity:
- Turn in your final short documentary project.

Objectives:
- Construct a well-developed, filmed, edited historical narrative based on an object.
- Appraise what you learned about the craft of history by completing your documentary.

Assignment:
- As a group, your film needs to include the following material:
  - Your object must be 25 years old or older.
  - Your documentary must tell a story about the past through your object.
  - Your documentary must be no shorter than 10 minutes but no longer than 20 minutes.
  - It must include at least five relevant secondary historical sources.
  - It must consist of at least five relevant historical primary sources.
  - It must have at least one interview with an appropriate expert.
  - It must include pertinent footage, settings, images, and music.

- It must be well-filmed, well-edited, and well-made.
  - Please upload your documentary to our course folder.
- As an individual, write a short essay, at least two pages, that addresses the following questions (please note: these questions can be changed and modified):
  - Do you think making a historical documentary helped you better understand "what is history"?
  - Did filming and engaging with a historical artifact help you better understand "what is history"? Why or why not?
  - Do you see yourself using the various skills learned through this project outside of this class? If so, how? If not, why?

Release Form Template

Project name: _____

Date: _____

Interviewer: _____

Name of person(s) interviewed: _____

Description of how the interview will be used in the film:

Please list any restrictions you have regarding the use of this footage:

By signing the form below, you give your permission for any tapes and photographs made during this project to be used by researchers and the public for educational purposes, including publications, exhibitions, World Wide Web, and presentations.

By giving your permission, you do not give up any copyright or performance rights you may hold. I agree to the uses of these materials described above, except for any restrictions noted below.

Name (please print):

Signature:

Researcher's Name (please print):

Researcher's signature:

Skill Assessment for Film Project

(This is a new aspect of the project that I created after the first iteration of the course as a method of sorting students by skills and interests. This will ensure a fairer distribution of talent and labor. However, I also plan on using this as a post-project assessment. I would like to use it at the end of the semester to see if students believe they made progress in developing their skills. I would encourage courses to develop and modify this assessment as applicable to their classes and courses. It creates moments of individual reflection for students and provides valuable feedback for the professor.)

Documentary and filmmaking require a variety of skill sets to be successful. As such, please fill out this skill assessment so that we can ensure a fair and equitable distribution of talents and interests when we put groups together. These assessments work best when you are honest and forthright in your responses.

Research

An excellent short documentary requires strong research skills; you will need to dig deep into your subject in terms of primary and secondary sources. Please initial the option that best describes you and circle and answer the associated question:

Experienced and Fluent
Some Experience and Fluency
Needs Development

On a scale from 1 through 5, how would you rate your interest in this position?

Writing

An excellent short documentary requires strong writing and storytelling skills in scriptwriting; you will need to tell an exciting and coherent story based on research. Please initial the option that best describes you and circle and answer the associated question:

Experienced and Fluent
Some Experience and Fluency
Needs Development

On a scale from 1 through 5, how would you rate your interest in this position?

Filming

An excellent short documentary requires visual storytelling, good shots, composition, and imagery. You will need to work with the director, writer, and researcher to bring their work to life. Please initial the option that best describes you and circle and answer the associated question:

Experienced and Fluent
Some Experience and Fluency
Needs Development

On a scale from 1 through 5, how would you rate your interest in this position?

Communication

An excellent short documentary requires excellent communication and coordination of all the various members of the crew, the interviewees, and the professor. You will need to work with everybody in the group to bring the short documentary to life. Please initial the option that best describes you and circle and answer the associated question:

Experienced and Fluent
Some Experience and Fluency
Needs Development

On a scale from 1 through 5, how would you rate your interest in this position?

Editing

An excellent short documentary requires amazing footage, montage, pacing, and sound. You will need to take the work done by the director, cameraperson, and screenwriter and assemble it into a completed short documentary.

Experienced and Fluent

Some Experience and Fluency

Needs Development

On a scale from 1 through 5, how would you rate your interest in this position?

Assignment Rubric Templates

Group Object Reflection Paper Rubric

Criteria (or Standard)	1	2	3	4	Feedback
The group clearly defines and lists what sources of information they will need to tell the story of their object by detailing key concepts, backgrounds, peoples, places, things, and ideas.					
The group clearly defines and lists what resources they have at their disposal for their short documentaries; for example, family, community, university resources, landscapes, buildings, other objects, etc.					
The group clearly defines and lists the kinds of imagery they might require for creating their short documentaries; for example, maps, paintings, photographs, footage, etc.					

1 = standard not met; 2 = standard partially met; 3 = standard met; 4 = exceeds expectations

Group Short Documentary Pitch, Contract, and Responsibility Details Rubric

Criteria (or Standard)	1	2	3	4	Feedback
Your documentary pitch is clear, concise, and tells the reader what your film will be about and what it will try to argue.					
The various roles required to make the short documentary are clearly spelled out, and who will fulfill those roles is established.					
The group's arbitration process is clearly defined and actionable; it details in clear steps how the group will resolve issues.					

1 = standard not met; **2** = standard partially met; **3** = standard met; **4** = exceeds expectations

Individual Status Report Rubric

Criteria (or Standard)	1	2	3	4	Feedback
A clear statement with concrete examples of the work you completed on your project.					
A clear statement of how your work fits into the larger short documentary project.					
A clear statement of your work plan and the work you plan on achieving over the next few weeks.					
A clear statement of what work you have left to complete in terms of your role in the short documentary project.					
Did your group complete the required group work aspect of this assignment?					

1 = standard not met; **2** = standard partially met; **3** = standard met; **4** = exceeds expectation

Final-Cut or Rough-Cut Short Documentary Rubric

Criteria (or Standard)	1	2	3	4	Feedback
Your short documentary focuses on an object 25 years old or older.					
Your short documentary tells a story about the past through your object.					
Your short documentary uses your object and other related research to make an argument about the past.					
Your short documentary is no shorter than 10 minutes, but no longer than 20 minutes.					
Your short documentary includes at least five relevant and scholarly secondary historical sources.					
Your short documentary includes at least five relevant historical primary sources.					
Your short documentary includes at least one interview from an appropriate expert.					
Your short documentary uses well-shot, steady, well-framed footage.					
Your short documentary's audio is clear, understandable, and relevant.					
Your short documentary's editing is smooth, unintrusive, and helps you tell your history/story through effective use of shots.					

1 = standard not met; **2** = standard partially met; **3** = standard met; **4** = exceeds expectations

Defining and Embedding Service-Learning as a Fundamental Course Component

James Barbre

The presence of service-learning across secondary and post-secondary education is not new and has been increasing. The value of these experiences is regarded as received wisdom, as service-learning experiences have been adopted across a range of educational institutions, from middle school through postsecondary. Embracing service-learning in terms of one's own academic specialty and/or teaching load presents several benefits to new faculty members.

In higher education, refining and structuring service-learning as an embedded course component and function brings about unique course-based contribution to the overall mission of the university or academic unit. Additionally, the promotion and tenure guidelines of most colleges and universities have teaching, research, and service components that are often complementary with service-learning and may be focused in a manner that provides value to the mission of the particular university or college and to the developing expertise of the individual(s). These professional requirements may enable the faculty member to "think outside the box" in an academically entrepreneurial manner as it relates to the development of experiential student learning:

Faculty who use service-learning discover that it brings new life to the classroom, enhances performance on traditional measures of learning, increases student interest in the subject, teaches new problem solving skills, and makes teaching more enjoyable. In addition, service-learning expands course objectives to include civic education.[1]

In this chapter, I will discuss how the definitions and understanding of service-learning have evolved over time and offer general suggestions for effectively embedding the service-learning in one's own teaching load, regardless of the subject or discipline. A means of structuring and assessing these experiences in terms of program outcomes and objectives must be central to the enterprise. Individual faculty are the experts in their fields and so will be the best judge for how this enterprise connects to their teaching and course design, research, or service.

My career has been in teacher education. My own approach toward the development of a professional educator rests on providing and developing experiences that add value beyond the immediate course and to provide the opportunity to develop skills and understanding in the field. In developing and applying these skills, students connect their own learning with both important and banal elements of society beyond the walls of classrooms. This ongoing process is essential to the mind and experiences of an educated person. Service-learning experiences occur in a range of forms. Some are field experiences, internships, service-based service-learning, research-based service-learning, or advocacy-based service-learning.

Regardless of the academic discipline, a generalized framework for service-learning is an essential starting point and may be readily adapted from one field to another. Tenure-track and non-tenure track faculty may find this a daunting addition to take on or develop, but the rewards of doing so have the potential to enrich the student's experience(s) in the course and help shape the resulting perspective that academic study seeks to impart. For those who choose to teach in post-secondary settings, an aspiration walking through the door is to make a difference in student learning and the world. Boyer, Bringle, and Hatcher argue that the university should do more than simply prepare students for a career. They should be working to prepare them for responsible citizenship and an engagement to their communities.[2]

---

1   Bringle, Robert G., and Julie A. Hatcher. "Implementing Service-learning in Higher Education." *The Journal of Higher Education* 67, no. 2 (1996): 221–39. p. 222.

2   Ibid.

The Evolution and Significance of Service-Learning

Modern service-learning is a historical reflection of a grass roots form of civic engagement. Through the years, service-learning has been promoted by several prominent activists and scholars. These occur sometimes in general terms but often through particular contexts of social struggle at a given point in history. Early progressive social thinkers included Jane Addams, John Dewey, Mahatma Gandhi, Paulo Freire, and many others. Each espoused the value of these experiences in cultivating the necessary mindsets and commitment required for positive social change.[3] As emphasized by the quote below, a deeply held belief lies in the empowerment provided through education and must intersect with service. These are crucial components in the development of a forward-looking sense of self-efficacy. The Civil Rights Era was fertile ground for actions such as these.

> During the American civil rights movement, many activists implemented a form of education as service. In 1964, the Student Non-Violent Coordinating Committee (SNCC) and the Congress of Racial Equality Sponsored the Mississippi Freedom Summer. As part of the Freedom Summer, Freedom Schools were set up as alternative educational institutions that featured courses on African history, culture, and basic academic skills. The primary reason for these schools was to impart empowerment through education, both for the students in Mississippi as well as the college volunteers that staffed many of the schools.[4]

In the broader field of education, John Dewey is a seminal figure, and his advocacy for experiential education is well known. He saw student learning and the kinds of outcomes that experiential education brought about as a fundamentally progressive series of actions: "It thus becomes the office of the educator to select those things within the range of existing experience that have the promise and potentiality of presenting new problems which by stimulating new ways of observation and judgment will expand the

---

3   Busch, David. "A Brief History of Service-learning." Social Change 101. https://www. socialchange101.org/history-of-service-learning/.

4   Ibid.

area of further experience."[5] With this kind of semi-open-ended and evolving perspective comes the advantage and necessity of reflection. In this experiential and reflective process, the role of the educator is often to help students unlock the value of service and service-learning. Blouin and Perry argue that service-learning has historically been envisioned as being most compatible with the fields of education and sociology.[6] In these or other disciplines, though, the ability for any student to work with a community-based organization (CBO) offers numerous rewards that include increased civic engagement, enhanced job skills, and greater appreciation for diversity.[7]

Regardless of their degree, a majority of future college graduates will interact in real time with other individuals. Vizenor, Souza, and Ertmer offer an analysis of the perceptual benefits of these kinds of experiences and include business, communications consulting, journalism, and engineering in their study.[8] Respondents to their study indicated that service-learning provided numerous opportunities that benefitted both the students and the community partners they served. Results show that partner organizations benefited from their unique contributions in that "[T]hey used the suggestions for planning and decision making, for improving practice, and for utilizing products."[9] Another community partner indicated their using the student report as part of their strategic planning process. A third stated that they "formulated an entire marketing campaign" based on the data and recommendations provided by students.

They also wrote about focusing their advertising reach, updating training curriculum, improving recruitment and training practices, and increasing their outreach. One community partner reported that the project resulted in continued collaboration between two university entrepreneurial

---

5   Dewey, John. *Experience and Education.* Macmillan; New York (1938) p. 75.

6   Blouin, David D., and Evelyn M. Perry. "WHOM DOES SERVICE-LEARNING REALLY SERVE? COMMUNITY-BASED ORGANIZATIONS' PERSPECTIVES ON SERVICE-LEARNING*." *Teaching Sociology* 37, no. 2 (04, 2009): 120–135. https://proxyeast.uits.iu.edu/login?url=https://www.proquest.com/scholarly-journals/whom-does-service-learning-really-serve-community/docview/223528441/se-2?accountid=11648.

7   Blouin, David D., and Evelyn M. Perry: p. 121.

8   Vizenor, et al. pg. 5.

9   Vizenor, et al. pg. 8.

programs.[10] There is no real limit to the possible value for these kinds of experiences when they occur in a properly structured form.

The placement and partnerships for service-learning also allow students to bring their own life skills to bear and experience the potential rewards for doing so. This relevance represents a valuable mechanism to help any university deliver on its larger mission. The insights gained through service-learning may be reflected in a program's curriculum by exposing students to real-time professional, and other, settings:

> [R]ather, service-learning is a means to empower students and educational institutions to become more aware of the needs of the communities of which they are a part and to become engaged and civically active in mutually beneficial ways. Community-based service that relates to course and curricular content is becoming increasingly embedded in curricula.[11]

Greater numbers of organizations and/or businesses have taken an interest in this feature of post-secondary education. Different academic disciplines have further developed the definitions and components for service-learning; this advance often involves a communicative relationship with external partners—The National Service-Learning Clearinghouse defines "service-learning" as a teaching and learning strategy that integrates meaningful community service with instruction and reflection to enrich the learning experience, teach civic responsibility, and strengthen communities.[12] Service-learning requires several components in order to be high quality: (1) meaningful service, (2) intentional link to curriculum, (3) reflection, (4) diversity among participants, (5) youth and parental engagement and decision making, (6) mutually beneficial partnerships, (7) ongoing progress monitoring, and (8) appropriate duration and intensity to meet community needs and outcomes.[13] A growing body of research clearly shows that

10   Vizenor, et al. pg. 8.

11   Umpleby, Stuart. "Service-Learning as a Method of Instruction." *Journal of the Washington Academy of Sciences* 97, no. 4 (2011): 1–15. http://www.jstor.org/stable/24536459, p. 2.

12   https://www.ecs.org/clearinghouse/01/02/87/10287.pdf.

13   https://www.ecs.org/clearinghouse/01/02/87/10287.pdf.

students engaged in high-quality service-learning learn to collaborate, think critically, and problem solve.[14]

Course Overview

The service-learning course I will describe is EDUC-M300, "Teaching in a Pluralistic Society." In teacher preparation courses, this is a foundational course that serves to broaden the awareness of and appreciation for diverse perspectives and experiences throughout teaching and education. The course description reads as follows:

> This course is designed to examine teaching effectiveness and excellence related to teaching in a pluralistic society. Academic success is increasingly tied to diversity issues; hence, studying the nature of culture, individual differences among students, and issues related to cultural pluralism such as religion, gender and socio-economic status are critical. Understanding what it means to be a culturally competent teacher, knowing how to integrate multicultural education throughout the curriculum, and being able to identify classroom instructional strategies that respond positively to the personal and ethnic diversity of learners are each components of being a reflective scholar, instructional leader, and global citizen.[15]

It is important that the reader note the need for some form of foundations coursework across most academic or professional disciplines. Service-learning design may be generalized and easily applied in any number of settings and contexts. It also serves to reinforce the idea that any profession is not simply "about us" (the student); rather, we accomplish more when we understand and acknowledge each other's differences and work together for something greater than ourselves.

---

14   Yorio, P. L., & Feifei Ye. (2012). A Meta-Analysis on the Effects of Service-Learning on the Social, Personal, and Cognitive Outcomes of Learning. *Academy of Management Learning & Education, 11*(1), 9–27. https://doi-org.proxyeast.uits.iu.edu/10.5465/amle.2010.0072.

15   Indiana University EDUC-M300 course description.

The epistemological basis used to construct this course comes from Christine Bennett's scholarship in multiculturalism.[16] This framework was established to address the development of multicultural perspectives and has six areas of focus that revolve around core values. The following schematic shows the essential components of this framework and the core values that are informed by these overlapping goals. This framework forms the skeletal structure of the course.

A further explanation for each of these goals is listed below:

1. Understanding Multiple Historical Perspectives

Most of us tend to be ahistorical when it comes to knowledge about Third World nations as well as ethnic minorities within our own society. It is

16   Bennett, Christine I. *Comprehensive multicultural education: Theory and practice.* Boston: Allyn and Bacon, 1986.

difficult to be otherwise, given the nature of the traditional curriculum that emphasizes the political development of Anglo-American civilization. An important goal of a multicultural curriculum, therefore, is the development of multiple historical perspectives that will correct this Anglo-Western European bias. Past and current world events must be understood from multiple national perspectives, and both minority and nonminority points of view must be considered in interpreting local and national events.

2. Developing Cultural Consciousness

Cultural consciousness is the recognition or awareness on the part of an individual that she or he has a view of the world that is not universally shared and differs profoundly from that held by many members of different nations and ethnic groups. It includes an awareness of the diversity of ideas and practices found in human societies around the world and some recognition of how one's own thoughts and behaviors might be perceived by members of differing nations and ethnic groups.

3. Developing Intercultural Competence

Intercultural competence is the ability to interpret intentional communications (language, signs, gestures), some unconscious cues (such as body language), and customs in a cultural style different from one's own. Emphasis is on empathy and communication. The goal is to develop self-awareness of the culturally conditioned assumptions people of different cultural backgrounds make about each other's behaviors and cognitions.

4. Combating Racism, Sexism, and All Forms of Prejudice and Discrimination

Combating racism, sexism, prejudice, and discrimination means lessening negative attitudes and behaviors based on gender bias and misconceptions about the inferiority of races and cultures different from one's own. Emphasis is on clearing up myths and stereotypes associated with gender, different races, and ethnic groups. Basic human similarities are stressed. The goal is to develop antiracist, antisexist behavior based on awareness of historical and contemporary evidence of individual, institutional, and cultural racism and sexism in the United States and elsewhere in the world.

5. Raising Awareness of the State of the Planet and Global Dynamics

Awareness of the state of the planet and global dynamics is knowledge about prevailing world conditions, trends, and developments. It is also knowledge of the world as a hugely interrelated ecosystem subject to surprise effects and dramatic ramifications of simple events, such as the introduction of new technologies or of health and nutrition practices into a society.

6. Developing Social Action Skills

Social action skills include the knowledge, attitudes, and behaviors needed to help resolve major problems that threaten the future of the planet and the well-being of humanity. One emphasis is on thinking globally and acting locally; the goal is to develop a sense of personal and political efficacy and global responsibility resulting in a participatory orientation among adult members of society. Another emphasis is enabling minorities and non-minorities to become change agents through democratic processes.[17]

There are numerous foci across this course, but I am able to draw on the legitimate and essential nature of students' own lived experiences as this becomes essential for the service-learning experience. The service-learning course component becomes an important theme in that students are required to complete 25 hours of service-learning in a setting that is not educational in nature.

---

17   Bennett, Christine I. *Comprehensive multicultural education: Theory and practice*. Boston: Allyn and Bacon, 2018.

Evolution of the IU East Approach

Several years ago, IU East's campus Center for Service-Learning was developed and staffed. With this change, a central coordinator worked to significantly expand the reach and impact of the university's previous efforts and coordination. This shift dramatically increased the organizational approach across academic majors. With a dedicated staff and an established set of protocols, several improvements resulted. One of these outcomes included tracking impact hours, but more importantly, it included the development of a comprehensive database of service-learning opportunities from which students worked with the coordinator to choose their own internships. The coordinator works to ensure fidelity toward the original aims of this course component and also acts as a point of contact for community organizations and/or businesses interested in our students. This position has resulted in a substantial increase in awareness of our service-learning activities and greatly expanded IU East's portfolio of partner CBO's and/or businesses. The Center for Service-Learning collects the data and logs contact hours across each service-learning course throughout the semester. They also collect any essays or written works (always anonymized) on the experience and archive them in documenting our institutional journey.

In education, our goal is for students to be familiar with some of the influential community forces that have an impact on schools and student learning. For this reason, service-learning settings are focused outside of education and with community service in mind. The varied service-learning experiences of students are designed to develop complementary perspectives on students' own academic training. While it would be most efficient to focus on areas strictly related to educator preparation, a more productive approach lies in focusing on the development of a broader worldview. For anyone interested in adopting a similar approach, they would best serve their students by working to provide situations that are closely related to the particular academic discipline or course, but not necessarily the strict focus. This is akin to the education of a person to be an "artist," rather than a "technician." The service-learning assignment breaks down as follows below.

Service-Learning Assignment

During EDUC-M300, students will spend a total of 25 hours on an off-campus site as part of the service-learning experience. The location is to be coordinated with the Center for Service-learning on campus within the parameters established by the instructor.

Following initial contact with the service-learning coordinator, and very early in the semester, you must submit a short proposal (1–2 paragraphs) as to where you will be going and what some of your responsibilities might be. This task will serve as a record for the assignment. If something should change, it is your responsibility to communicate that change to the instructor as soon as possible. Your original proposal serves as the approved area.

As a representative of this university, students will be expected to maintain a professional attitude, appearance, and demeanor at all times. **It is not acceptable that you choose a site with which you already have a pre-existing relationship** (e.g., your church, your child's day care, etc.). The point of this assignment is to get students into a part of the community with which they are unfamiliar. The placement may be related to one or more of the following issues:

- **Class (poverty)**- Habitat for humanity, soup kitchens, missions, YMCA, YWCA, Boys/Girls Club, Head Start
- **Age**- nursing homes, hospice centers
- **Ethnicity**- African American, Asian American, Hispanic, Native American
- **Religion**- church, mosque, Jewish temple related activities (volunteering at your church would not be considered an option unless you **have not** done so in the past)
- **Exceptionalities**- assisted living/group home, centers for disabled citizens
- **Gender**- Family planning, women's shelter
- **Sexuality**- Gay/lesbian task force, HIV/AIDS hospice

Reflection Paper

Toward the end of the semester, students will write a 3–6 page reflection paper which addresses your service-learning experience. This paper will be formatted according to existing criteria for written word outlined elsewhere in this syllabus. In this paper, you should reflect on and address the following questions:

1. What did I discover about myself relative to being an instructional leader, global citizen, and reflective scholar?
2. What were my expectations going into this experience? How accurate were they?
3. What were some challenges I encountered?
4. How was the time spent?
5. What were some memorable/surprising experiences?
6. Why are experiences like this important in education (other discipline)?
7. How did these experiences relate to the ideas/information in M300 (course)?
8. In what ways will these experiences make me a better teacher (other)?

Other Required Documentation

5 points: **Documentation Letter:** A letter from the site administrator/site coordinator documenting the time spent and duties performed (must be on OFFICIAL LETTERHEAD).

5 points: **Thank you note:** a copy of the thank you card or letter you sent to both administrators thanking them for the opportunities to serve at the site.

5 points: Record sheet documenting dates and students served.

Student Experiences and the Larger Dialogue

Dissonance refers to the incongruence students often experience when participating in a service-learning activity.[18] For reasons of unfamiliarity and the developing mind, I have found that students internalize most of these experiences and may remember them fondly or as a period of challenge or success. Crossing social or contextual borders is an experience through which students are encouraged to think critically about their current identity, position, and power, and how these factors have an impact on how they experience border crossing, physically, socially, politically, and culturally.

Student reflective essays are meant to address the implicit or explicit assumptions they may have held at the outset of the service-learning experience, but they also leave room for surprises and/or lessons learned along the way. This assignment seeks to help them articulate what their expectations were at the time and better describe what they have learned along the way. In this manner, the reflective essay serves as a contemplative prompt. The further value in this assignment lies in class discussions where students bring their experiences to the larger group. As the class discusses these issues and students share stories of their experiences, themes of discussion are generated which connect across the different experiences of service-learning. With these discussions, students develop a more nuanced understanding of issues, themes of experience, understanding, and the manner of their presence and impact across a wide range of different settings.

Assessing Student Learning Experiences

One challenge in terms of assessing student learning experiences lies in the manner that they translate back to the course objectives, and this is where different courses and disciplines answer in unique ways. Service-learning can be a time filled with the semi-mundane, or it may not. There is no real way for the instructor to know this difference in experiences due to there being too many variables, but this diversity is a good feature. In

---

18   Hullender, Ren, Shelly Hinck, Jeanneane Wood-Nartker, Travus Burton, and Sue Bowlby. "Evidences of Transformative Learning in Service-Learning Reflections." *Journal of the Scholarship of Teaching and Learning* 15, no. 4 (2015): 58–82. https://proxyeast.uits.iu.edu/login?url=https://www.proquest.com/scholarly-journals/evidences-transformative-learning-service/docview/2387856274/se-2.

education, an important point of linkage comes in how one facilitates the dialogue and connects it back to the original framework and intent. Service-learning experiences are often open-ended but benefit from a cohesive and identifiable framework of objectives. Questions or themes to be addressed must be explicit and connect to the particular course. Equally important is a connection to the larger body of knowledge or profession that students are studying. As service-learning is also an inherently social experience, it is useful to approach the reflective components from a qualitative perspective with a focus on emergent themes. These emergent themes take the form of adaptable knowledge to different situations. In this environment, if the student has a service-learning experience that is not what they thought it would be, they will be able to understand the connective tissue between their situation and experiences of others. Below is an example descriptor rubric that instructors may adapt to their own needs or goals.

It is important to note that this rubric is essentially qualitative in nature. While some colleges and universities may be keen for more quantitative metrics, the faculty member can readily utilize those resources and develop a "synthesis" approach. This would enable them to meet their own course needs but also complement the ongoing work of the college or university.

	5	4	3	2	1	0
Reflection Paper (XX pts)						
Clear Introduction for Topic of Paper (XX points)	Strong connection between areas of assignment	Introduction has a general focus and connection	Introduction is vague with a strained connection to assignment components	Introduction is general and non-specific to assignment	Introduction is lacking or missing	
Required Questions Addressed (XX points)	Clear, well-focused topics. Main ideas stand out and are supported by detailed information	Main ideas are clear, but the supporting information is general or vague in nature	Main idea is somewhat clear, but there is need for more supporting information. Some information not connected to main idea	Main idea is not clear. There is a seemingly random collection of information	Main idea is not clear. Information presented is not relevant to assignment	
Detailed Discussion and Analysis (XX points)	Detailed discussion with relevant examples	Some attempt at discussion, but with limited examples and analysis	Discussion is mostly vague with limited analysis of experience	Superficial discussion with no real insights through analysis	Little to no discussion and analysis as required by assignment	
Writing Mechanics and Organization (X points)	No mistakes in grammar, punctuation, paragraphing, or spelling	Writer makes 1–2 mistakes	Writer makes 3–4 errors	Writer makes more than 4 errors	Writing is not acceptable	
Inclusion of Documentation Letter and Thank You Note (X points)	Thank you notes and documentation letter included		Only one of the required is included with assignment			No Correspondence Included

The Evolving Presence of Service-learning in Secondary and Post-Secondary Education

Post-secondary academic settings are increasingly employing service-learning in similar ways but subject to the unique features of each school or academic discipline. Accreditation agencies, such as the Higher Learning Commission, utilize "co-curricular" requirements to the standards by which they evaluate a university's compliance with the accreditation framework and their own program and student learning outcomes. These requirements under the "Higher Learning Commission's (HLC) Criteria for Accreditation" require *"Learning activities, programs and experiences that reinforce the institution's mission and values and complement the formal curriculum. Examples: Study abroad, student-faculty research experiences, service-learning, professional clubs or organization, athletics, honor societies, career services, etc."*[19]

Professional Benefits to the Faculty Member: Teaching

Service-learning, as a course component, is mostly aligned with teaching because it is part of a course, but it has numerous other areas of application. In the area of coursework, faculty can develop service-learning in ways that I have described above but specifically tailored to their particular student or school needs. This tailoring can come through the revision of an existing course or in the creation of one that is new. Whether it is an online or face-to-face course matters little. Faculty can readily build accountability and guidance into the requirements of this assignment.

In education, our program has advanced graduates design their own high school courses (Literature) where service-learning was a substantial component and complemented the curriculum of the classroom. Another important benefit observed is that, as students become aware of a broader sample of their local community, they build relationships which are often long-lasting. Over the course of several years, numerous service-learning students continue to work in areas where they first conducted their service-

---

19   Bringle, Robert G., and Julie A. Hatcher. "Implementing Service-learning in Higher Education." *The Journal of Higher Education* 67, no. 2 (1996): 221–39. https://doi.org/10.2307/2943981., p. 222

learning assignments, and a few have even chosen careers in those particular fields. The benefit to the faculty member may also come in that they amplify the mission of the academic unit. One advantage in this effect lies in the development of relationships with community members. Often, these community members, or organizations, can be called on in the future. Some may even contribute their expertise by joining a Board of Advisors. The creation of stakeholders for any mission is never easy, but relationships ease the difficulty in substantive ways.

Research

Among the most difficult challenges in entering higher education is the development of a scholarly line of inquiry. In many instances, this sets the initial trajectory for the first several years and has a direct impact on job security. The development of a service-learning component can easily result in a research agenda and publications when approached from a collaborative direction. This area may be something the students are interested in; also, it reflects the kind of mentoring that faculty can develop.

A common refrain in seeking promotion and tenure is that one may not "double dip" in the areas of service and research. Faculty are often expected to keep these activities discrete. While I will not dispute the regulations that universities often operate by, I will argue that this expectation represents a myopic perspective on policy and the requirement for a faculty member to contribute towards the greater knowledge base. The concerted effort that a faculty member makes in their teaching which results in research or other forms of dissemination may often be a regular occurrence. This connection may be observed through the presentation of student research under the guidance of a faculty member at an event on campus or a conference. Should faculty be teaching graduate courses, they have the opportunity to mentor students through the process of review by the Institutional Review Board. Students crave this kind of mentoring and connection to the institution, especially when they aspire to be future academics themselves. An additional benefit is that this line of inquiry builds over time. Research projects may be discrete events, but faculty have the opportunity to collect and analyze data sets over time. Were faculty to focus on service-learning, they could collect data through narratives or other data sources over a longer period of time with the ability to observe, analyze trends, and then present or publish the results.

Service

Service to the school or university works to reinforce and extend the overall mission of a value-added experience. The mission of any college or university should be more than turning out graduates to enter places in the workforce.[20] Graduates should emerge from this period of considerable time and resource investment with the ability to think critically, be creative, and connect with others:

> Institutional changes that support the scholarship of engagement include intentionally clarifying mission in a manner that produces increased congruence between mission and practice, examining how the curriculum can better reflect community engagement, investing in infrastructure that supports community engagement, developing new models for assessing successful engagement in the community, and adjusting the roles and rewards of faculty so that faculty work in the community is recognized and supported.[21]

Speaking in still broader terms, service to the community ultimately helps make your little corner of the world a little better. The successful deployment of a service-learning initiative may invite inquiries from other businesses or CBOs in the town or community, which may lead to further ideas for improved approaches or partnerships. The faculty member's unique position in constructing and executing this outcome represents the potential for so many different kinds of contributions.

---

20   Bringle, Robert G., and Julie A. Hatcher. "Implementing Service-learning in Higher Education." *The Journal of Higher Education* 67, no. 2 (1996): 221–39. https://doi.org/10.2307/2943981., p. 222.

21   Bringle, Robert G., Games, R., & Malloy, E. A. (1999). Colleges and universities as citizens. Boston: Allyn & Bacon.

Conclusion

Research and experience clearly show that service-learning experiences present a plethora of benefits for college students. Experience helps people connect to their passions, but those experiences are of greater value when they are structured and guided. Communication and dialogue are the necessary counterparts for experiences such as these. With a clear set of goals, college instructors have opportunities to connect the theoretical with the applied. This process builds value for the investment of time and effort. Done properly, this investment can also build value for the experience and professional development of the instructor themselves.

Designing an Effective Faculty Led Study Abroad Experience:

A Transcontinental Approach to Mediterranean Food Studies

Dianne Burke Moneypenny

This chapter outlines the process of planning a study abroad course and reviews a sample study abroad experience that focuses on the interconnectedness of nations. While the proposed course is based broadly in the humanities, this type of experience can work for multiple disciplines to allow for transferability of methods. Food studies are particularly advantageous for this book as they can adroitly shift between scientific, economic, cultural, linguistic, and other academic perspectives. With the goal of reducing faculty workload for those considering study abroad, the first half of the chapter discusses the value of study abroad in general, the preference for faculty-led experiences, principles of course design, study abroad learning objectives and outcomes, destination selection, duration, and types of programs that can be offered. In the U.S., the clear dominance of more affluent, Caucasian, female students in overseas study demands that special care is also taken to increase the diversity of study abroad students. The remainder of the chapter outlines research-based and classroom-tested techniques for effective study abroad course design. It concludes with a sample course on food studies in the Mediterranean that employs the practice of experiential learning to promote global competencies.

The Value of Study Abroad

The positive effects of study abroad across disciplines are well documented. Scholars recognize that understanding our globalized society and adapting to differing cultural norms is essential to being able to effectively work in different cultural situations.[1] For college students in the U.S., "Education abroad has become an increasingly important educational program (experience) in global learning and development, intercultural competence, intercultural maturity, and intercultural sensitivity of students."[2] Mondschean & Rountree[3] describe this kind of experiential learning as "interdisciplinary and heavily vested in real-world encounters that are filtered through a person's own past, present, and future...a transformative experience that has a foot in self exploration while the other is potentially affected by emotional change." Other research links study abroad to positive academic outcomes, such as degree completion, percentage of credits passed, and higher GPA.[4] Outside the classroom, Zimmerman, et. al[5] even note overseas study's positive impact on student personality development, while others have found increased civic engagement, volunteerism, philanthropy,

---

1   Roy Achinto, Alexander Newman, Tori Ellenberger, and Amanda Pyman, "Outcomes of International Student Mobility Programs: A Systematic Review and Agenda for Future Research," *Studies in Higher Education* 44, no. 2 (2018): 1–15, DOI: 10.1080/03075079.2018.1458222.; Nicolai Netz and Michael Grüttner, "Does the Effect of Studying Abroad on Labour Income Vary by Graduates' Social Origin? Evidence from Germany," *Higher Education* 82, no. 2 (2020): 1195-1217, DOI: 10.1007/s10734-020-00579-2,.; Nicolai Netz and Fine Cordua, "Does Studying Abroad Influence Graduates' Wages? A Literature Review," *Journal of International Students* 11, no. 4 (2021): 768-789, DOI: 10.32674/jis.v11i4.4008.

2   Larry Braskamp, David Braskamp, and Kelly Merrill, "Assessing Progress in Global Learning and Development of Students with Education Abroad Experiences," *Frontiers Journal* 18, no. 1 (2009): p. 101, DOI: 10.36366/frontiers.v18i1.256.

3   Thomas Mondschean and Melissa Rountree, "Experiential Learning through Short-Term Study Abroad: A Business Approach," *Experiential Learning and Teaching in Higher Education* 4, no. 1 (2021): 49–61, DOI:10.46787/elthe.v4i1.3430.

4   Melissa Whatley and Gonzalez Canché, "A Robust Estimation of the Relationship Between Study Abroad and Academic Outcomes among Community College Students," *Research in Higher Education* 63, no. 2 (2021): 271–308, DOI: 10.1007/s11162-021-09647-7.

5   Julia Zimmerman and Franz Neyer, "Do We Become a Different Person When Hitting the Road? Personality Development of Sojourners," *Journal of Personality and Social Psychology* 105, no. 3 (2013): 515–30, DOI:10.1037/a0033019.

and environmental activism in students who studied abroad.[6] Finally, the Association of American Colleges and Universities classifies study abroad as a High Impact Practice, defined as teaching techniques with "evidence of significant educational benefits for students who participate in them— including and especially those from demographic groups historically underserved by higher education."

While these are all goals for students of higher education, regardless of their disciplinary focus, even staff can benefit and respond more nimbly to the needs of the increasingly diverse and global student bodies of today. Hur[7] found that experience abroad even helps campus leadership better understand the challenges of student immigrants, which promotes the creation of more welcoming campus environments and new initiatives based on intercultural understanding. Institutions of higher learning, at every level, must understand and embrace today's interconnected world to function effectively within it.

Faculty Led Study Abroad

When a faculty member accompanies students for all or a portion of an experience abroad, the trip is categorized as a "faculty led study abroad." While it costs much less to send a faculty member with students abroad than it does for an institution to have a whole satellite campus, this setup allows for similar advantages.[8] Faculty led programs increase accessibility because students who are less prepared, either academically or for world travel,

---

6   Jae-Eun Jon and Gerald W. Fry, "Study Abroad and Engagement at the Local and Global Levels: The Stories Behind the Numbers," *The Journal of Studies in International Education* 25, no. 4 (2021): 407–424, DOI: 10.1177/10283153211016276.; Hongping Zhang and Heather Gibson, "Long-Term Impact of Study Abroad on Sustainability-Related Attitudes and Behaviors," *Sustainability* 13, no. 1953 (2021): 1–19, DOI: 10.3390/su13041953.

7   Jung Won Hur, "Development of Culturally Responsive Leadership via Study Abroad: Findings From a Six-Year Case Study," *Journal of School Leadership* 32, no. 5 (2022): 434–455, DOI: 10.1177/10526846211067632.

8   Debra Flanders Cushing, Mark Pennings, Dino Willox, Rafael Gomez, Clare Dyson, and Courtney Coombs, "Measuring Intangible Outcomes Can be Problematic: The Challenge of Assessing Learning During International Short-Term Study Experiences." *Active Learning in Higher Education* 20, no. 3 (2019): 203–217, DOI: 10.1177/1469787417732259.

prefer this model. For example, Goldstein found that students preferring an "exported campus" experience score higher on measures of ethnocentrism and apprehension to intercultural communication while lower on scales of adventurousness, interest in language learning, various forms of cultural intelligence, and tolerance for ambiguity.[9] Shifting that closed world view is critical, and it appears that a faculty led approach could be the only type of study abroad experience these students would consider. Thus, offering these forms of learning targets a less globally aware student population for focused learning with proven benefits.

Faculty led experiences can also allow for a pre-trip curriculum, align with the home campus academic schedule, be tailored to specific learning needs or interests, allow peers to reflect together on their own culture, simplify tuition and fees, and serve as a mechanism for faculty development.[10] In the author's own experience, traveling with a face or an institution they know can also ease anxieties for apprehensive students. This decrease in anxiety aligns with Goldstein's research above. Most students at the author's institution enroll in study abroad courses led by a professor they have had previously in a "standard" course format.

The need for faculty led study abroad is clear. While decades of research attest to the significance of this pedagogical practice, designing experiences outside the classroom (and country) requires significant faculty engagement from the first steps of trip conception to long after travel has ended. This chapter's intent will be to guide faculty through the complex process of planning and executing an impactful learning experience abroad.

Principles

There are various principles of study abroad to consider when deciding to create a course. At its core, study abroad is a form of experiential learning, long valued as an HIP across disciplines. When designing this kind of learning opportunity, the National Society for Experiential

---

9   Susan Goldstein, "Predictors of Preference for the Exported Campus Model of Study Abroad." *Frontiers: The Interdisciplinary Journal of Study Abroad* 26 (2015): 1–16, DOI: 10.36366/frontiers.v26i1.351.

10   Ibid.

Learning (NSSE) recommends that educators consider seven principles. Abbreviated here, the first principle relates to democracy, truth, and the freedom to "engage in critical thinking, and develop habits of reflection and civil discourse" and to listen and learn "from those whose experiences and values differ from their own." The second principle relates to ethics in pedagogical practices and interactions with host communities. Teaching and modeling the "values, skills, and relationships that foster a spirit of inquiry and fairness without discrimination or disempowerment" is the third key practice for experiential educators. Four is a focus on student growth and goals in curriculum design. The fifth principle emphasizes faculty engagement with research and practices in the field of experiential learning, most importantly "reflection, self-authorship, assessment and evaluation, civic engagement, and the development of personal and social responsibility." With this engagement to research and best practices, educators are expected to assess and share results with others in the field. The final principle details that educators should be aware of and act in accordance with "recognized legal, ethical and professional issues"[11] in experiential education.

Objectives & Outcomes

After understanding these principles, one must consider the proposed study abroad course's outcomes. By definition, study abroad is global learning, and the course must have this objective. According to the AAC&U, "Global learning is a critical analysis of and an engagement with complex, interdependent global systems and legacies (such as natural, physical, social, cultural, economic, and political) and their implications for people's lives and the earth's sustainability." By means of global engagement, students will:

1. become informed, open-minded, and responsible people who are attentive to diversity across the spectrum of differences;
2. seek to understand how their actions affect both local and global communities; and

---

11   National Society for Experiential Learning, Principles of Experiential Learning, https://www.nsee.org/8-principles.

3. address the world's most pressing and enduring issues collaboratively and equitably.[12]

In short, students will focus on self-awareness, perspective taking, diversity, personal and social responsibility, the complex and overlapping global systems, and applications of their newly acquired knowledge.

Recognizing that study abroad outcomes are distinct from disciplinary outcomes, the office of Study Abroad at the University of Hawaii has developed an excellent set of outcomes for study abroad courses. First, students will "demonstrate awareness of own cultural values and biases and how these impact their ability to work with others." It may be surprising that the first outcome of study abroad requires inward reflection; however, awareness of how one's background, experiences, and constructed identity influence behaviors and perceptions is key to reflecting on the novel encounters inherent in study away.

The second objective is demonstrating "knowledge of diversity with a focus on the population or topic of interest in the specific study abroad program." Diversity in this sense includes racism, sexism, able-ism, classicism, homophobia, xenophobia, and religion, but it might require that students consider forms of diversity that are less prevalent in the United States. Students may have to consider such forms as caste, regionalism, or even religious sects, for example.

The third outcome moves beyond knowledge of self and knowledge of diversity into interaction. For this outcome, students must "communicate appropriately and effectively with diverse individuals and groups." This requirement could mean demonstrating proficiency in a target language, but it should not be limited to that. Students should be aware of conversational norms, cues, and other forms of nonverbal communication even if they are using English abroad.

The last outcome requires that students "demonstrate an increased capacity to analyze issues with appreciation for disparate viewpoints."[13] It is important to note that in order to demonstrate an "increased capacity," growth must be present. To measure this development, some form of

---

12   Rubric, Global Learning. "Association of American Colleges and Universities."

13   University of Hawaii Office of Study Abroad

assessment should be taken pre and post study abroad. This process could take the form of a qualitative self-reflection exercise, or it could involve employing a well-established quantitative scale or rubric (such as the AAC&U Global Competence Rubric[14]) for use in a pre and post survey or assignment assessment. Then the scores for each assessment can be compared to assess for growth.

Location

Once educators understand the guiding principles and goals of study abroad, they can begin to consider where to conduct the course. According to the 2019 Open Doors[15] report, study abroad programs in the U.S. are highly European-based and most only study in one country (see Table 1). Sadly, combined with this narrowed perspective, the vast majority of study abroad students are white (70%) and female (67%).[16]

Study Abroad Destinations	% Distribution
Europe	54.9
Latin America/Caribbean	14.8
Asia	11.3
Africa	4.2
North Africa/Middle East	2.1
Oceania	4.3
North America	.5
Multiple Destinations	7.9
Single Country Programs	92.1

Other studies also show this trend is not limited to the U.S. Female students are also more likely to study abroad in Australia and Europe. An analysis conducted in the Netherlands, where females also dominate study

14   Rubric, Global Competence. "Association of American Colleges and Universities."

15   Todd M. Davis, "Open Doors: Report on International Educational Exchange" (2019).

16   Allison L. Hurst, "Class and Gender as Predictors of Study Abroad Participation Among US Liberal Arts College Students," *Studies in Higher Education* 44, no. 7 (2019): 1241–1255, DOI: 10.1080/03075079.2018.1428948.

abroad, found that maternal educational attainment directly correlates to the probability that a student will study abroad.[17] Another recent study found that female students in Germany are more likely to study abroad because of gender-specific interests, because they are more humanities focused, and due to their better performance in school overall which facilitates study abroad.[18] China has the largest population of students studying abroad and, despite the higher overall ratio of male students, women travel to western nations to study abroad more often than men; for instance, some studies show that female students opt to leave China in order to pursue study in countries with broader opportunities for women.[19]

Despite the well-documented benefits, only about 10% of undergraduate university students in the U.S. study abroad. On one hand, academia has acknowledged and touted the effectiveness of study abroad. And, on the other, it has reinforced inequities to cater to female Caucasian students visiting a single, highly developed majority "Caucasian country." There has been a long-standing call to diversify general curriculum across the disciplines. Across all courses at all levels, a shift toward less represented perspectives is critical, but, per the chart above, it appears that diversifying study abroad has been neglected. This gap is an unfortunate lapse as diversity is integral for study abroad, and country selection has been shown to affect learning. The duration of study abroad, discussed in an upcoming section, can also directly impact the diversity of the study abroad student body.

Study abroad locations are frequently chosen by their level of development as measured by the United Nations Human Development Index.[20] When adequately framed and supported, travel to a less developed

17   Christof Van Mol, "Exploring Explanations for the Gender Gap in Study Abroad: A Case Study of the Netherlands," *Higher Education* 83, no. 2 (2022): 441–459, DOI: 10.1007/s10734-020-00671-7.

18   Fine Cordua and Nicolai Netz. "Why do Women More Often Intend to Study Abroad than Men?," *Higher Education* 83, no. 5 (2022): 1079–1101, DOI: 10.1007/s10734-021-00731-6.

19   Fran Martin, "The Gender of Mobility: Chinese Women Students' Self-Making Through Transnational Education," *Intersections: Gender and Sexuality in Asia and the Pacific* 35, no. 1 (2014): 1–44, http://intersections.anu.edu.au/issue35/martin.htm.; Fran Martin, "Mobile Self-Fashioning and Gendered Risk: Rethinking Chinese Students' Motivations for Overseas Education," *Globalisation, Societies and Education* 15, no. 5 (2017): 706–720, DOI: 10.1080/14767724.2016.1264291.

20   Aaron S. Horn and Gerald W. Fry, "Promoting Global Citizenship Through Study Abroad: The Influence of Program Destination, Type, and Duration on the Propensity for Development

country can have a larger impact on global learning than travel to a developed nation.[21] Research in this area lends support to the benefit of working in developing areas, though not necessarily dangerous ones, but cautions about seeking out such places in search of a romanticized other.[22] Interacting with communities in low to medium levels of development, as indicated by the UN Human Development Index, where students interact in areas of extreme poverty or other socioeconomic scarcity, has been shown to have a direct impact on creating a consciousness of volunteerism.[23]

However, teachers must realize that, while students who perceive higher professional benefits may be more likely to choose countries with a greater psychic distance (differences in culture, language, religion, education, legislations, politics, economics, markets, and business), students with more professional/academic obstacles avoid study abroad in these kinds of countries.[24] Furthermore, care is advised when planning and conducting shorter-term study abroad programs in developing nations. Given the shorter time and larger discrepancy between lifestyles, students may find it difficult to move beyond feelings of "cultural superiority" due to less contact time in the local community.[25] Pre-travel preparation that exposes students to the history, culture, political climate, and development levels of the study abroad destination is thus essential in assisting participation in overcoming issues of cultural superiority.[26]

Volunteerism," *VOLUNTAS: International Journal of Voluntary and Nonprofit Organizations* 24, no. 4 (2013): 1159-1179, DOI: 10.1007/s11266-012-9304-y.

21   *International Service Learning: Conceptual Frameworks and Research, Vol. 1*, eds. Robert Bringle, Julie A. Hatcher, and Steven G. Jones, (Virginia: Stylus Publishing, LLC., 2012).

22   Raka Shome and Radha Hegde, "Culture, Communication, and the Challenge of Globalization," *Critical Studies in Media Communication* 19, no. 2 (2002): 172–189, DOI: 10.1080/07393180216560.

23   Horn and Fry, "Promoting Global Citizenship."

24   James Reardon, Chip Miller, and Denny McCorkle. "The Effect of Student Perceived Benefits and Obstacles to Determine If and Where to Study Abroad." *Journal of International Education in Business* 15, no. 2 (2022): 351–372, DOI: 10.1108/JIEB-05-2021-0060.

25   Nancy Wessel, "Integrating Service Learning into the Study Abroad Program: US Sociology Students in Mexico," *Journal of Studies in International Education* 11, no. 1 (2007): 73–89, DOI: 10.1177/1028315305283306.

26   Donnelly-Smith, Laura. "Global Learning Through Short-Term Study Abroad," *Peer*

After considering information on a country's development, overall safety perspectives are found on the U.S. Department of State's website.[27] When planning, educators should be aware of the institution's regulations for study abroad. For example, most institutions may not offer or support study abroad in countries that are under a State Department Level 3 Travel Advisory. If the country of choice is in the acceptable travel advisory range, it is important to also check on recommended vaccines through the CDC site.[28]

Time Abroad

Time abroad can directly impact the diversity of students who enroll. The increased prevalence of shorter-term study abroad options has democratized this educational practice by increasing enrollment of underrepresented groups.[29] As stated previously, female students are most likely to study abroad. However, affluence also affects a female student's likelihood of participation.[30] The expectation for career interruption causes female students of a lower economic status to opt out of study abroad; it does not have the same effect on males.[31] Short term options decrease barriers to studying abroad for many students.[32] Shorter trips are more affordable overall, require less time to ask off work, are less disruptive to other courses, and can ease the time away from family obligations, make

Review 11, no. 4 (2009): 12–16, https://link.gale.com/apps/doc/A214547673/AONE?u=anon-b1f6 588&sid=googleScholar&xid=35980cd3.

27   https://travel.state.gov

28   www.cdc.gov/travel

29   Elizabeth Niehaus and Ashley Wegener, "What Are We Teaching Abroad? Faculty Goals for Short-Term Study Abroad Courses," *Innovative Higher Education* 44, no. 2 (2019): 103–117, DOI: 10.1007/s10755-018-9450-2.

30   Nicolai Netz, Daniel Klasik, Steve R. Entrich, and Michelle Barker. "Socio-Demographics: a Global Overview of Inequalities in Education Abroad Participation," *Education Abroad: Bridging Scholarship and Practice*, eds. Anthony C. Ogden, Bernhard Streitwieser, Christof Van Mol. (London: Routledge, 2020): 28–42.

31   Cordua and Netz, "Why do Women," 1079–1101.

32   Matthew G. Interis, Jon Rezek, Kristen Bloom, and Annika Campbell, "Assessing the Value of Short-Term Study Abroad Programmes to Students," *Applied Economics* 50, no. 17 (2018): 1919–1933, DOI: 10.1080/00036846.2017.1380292.

program choice less overwhelming, and smooth out anxieties about the unknown destination.[33] Historically underrepresented student perspectives indicate that shorter term, affordable courses designed for diverse students were the study abroad course models they most favored.[34]

Defining short term study abroad is an interesting undertaking as definitions vary across organizations. Traditionally, short term is considered less than a year, or a semester, abroad. However, for students who work or have children or other obligations, the idea of a six week session over summer, for example, is less feasible. More time abroad also raises the cost of the course for students. In the author's experience, increased time abroad is inversely proportionate to student enrollment overall and specifically for those of underrepresented groups. Programs from one to three weeks are recommended.

Experience Type

Once the location is selected, the professor will want to consider what type of program to offer. Options include international service learning, internships, language learning programs, on-site research programs, traditional group travel programs with hotel stays or homestays, or a combination of any of the above. Each type of program has different best practices that must be considered. For more information, see "Internships Abroad" and "Language Learning" referenced below.[35]

---

33   Melissa Whatley and Rosalind Latiner Raby, "Understanding Inclusion and Equity in Community College Education Abroad," *Frontiers: The Interdisciplinary Journal of Study Abroad* 32, no. 1 (2020): 80–103, DOI: 10.36366/frontiers.v32i1.435.

34   Ecker-Lyster, Meghan, and Nadzeya Kardash, "Study abroad: Perspectives from Historically Underrepresented Student Populations," *Journal of College Access* 7, no. 1 (2022): 99–115, https://scholarworks.wmich.edu/jca/vol7/iss1/8.

35   Internships abroad: https://www.cas.edu/standards.
Language Learning: https://forumea.org/resources/guidelines/language-learning/
Student research abroad.

Sample Study Abroad Program

This section gives an overview of a sample study abroad program that addresses the necessary outcomes of study abroad. The course is a Mediterranean food studies course that involves travel to Europe and North Africa with a topic of broad appeal. As mentioned in the introduction to this chapter, food studies is an ideal theme when it comes to transferability across disciplines. This topic should appeal to a wide base of students and faculty.

Furthermore, travel to Africa was an essential component of the course development to address the limited number (approximately 2%) of study abroad courses that visit this region and to emphasize diversity across disciplines. The course planners recognized that students might be less intimidated by a course that bundles a less unfamiliar North African destination with more familiar European destinations. A significant portion of coursework furthers the mission of diversity by purposefully flipping the stereotype of a dominant Europe to recognize Africa's footprint in the region. Significant built-in reflection via a travel journal and an ethnographic research project also ensures that this program is more effective in meeting outcomes.

The sample study abroad program underscores national/intercontinental interconnectedness. The Mediterranean Sea functions as a historical center. Food products and practices as well as ways of thinking and living traversed the water. Trade crisscrossed the sea long before the formation of Greek, Roman, and Egyptian Empires, and it also played a central part in their histories. The food culture resultant of this exchange has led to a UNESCO denomination in 2013 as an Intangible Cultural Heritage of Humanity. UNESCO defines this title as:

> A set of skills, knowledge, rituals, symbols and traditions concerning crops, harvesting, fishing, animal husbandry, conservation, processing, cooking, and particularly the sharing and consumption of food. Eating together is the foundation of the cultural identity and continuity of communities throughout the Mediterranean basin. It is a moment of social exchange and communication, an affirmation and renewal of family, group or community identity. The Mediterranean diet

emphasizes values of hospitality, neighborliness, intercultural dialogue and creativity, and a way of life guided by respect for diversity. It plays a vital role in cultural spaces, festivals and celebrations, bringing together people of all ages, conditions and social classes. It includes the craftsmanship and production of traditional receptacles for the transport, preservation and consumption of food, including ceramic plates and glasses. Women play an important role in transmitting knowledge of the Mediterranean diet: they safeguard its techniques, respect seasonal rhythms and festive events, and transmit the values of the element to new generations. Markets also play a key role as spaces for cultivating and transmitting the Mediterranean diet during the daily practice of exchange, agreement and mutual respect. [36]

The routes of Mediterranean exchange have left an indelible mark on its cultures. The purpose of the proposed study abroad program is to investigate how food cultures based on Mediterranean systems have propagated and grown to serve as cultural identifiers in the unique lands that form this region.

When people (or students) refer to the Mediterranean region, they may most commonly think of Italy and perhaps southern France and neglect the contributions of many nations. At the very least, the interpretation is likely to be Eurocentric. A quick Google search of "Mediterranean travel" confirms this European bias (and is an interesting in-class activity as well). However, UNESCO includes Cyprus, Croatia, Spain, Greece, Italy, Morocco, and Portugal as places benefitting from the heritage of humanity related to the Mediterranean diet. Students must understand that this was a two-way exchange between Africa and Europe and much of the flow of goods and knowledge occurred FROM Africa INTO Europe.

To emphasize Africa's influence, students travel to Morocco. Its proximity to Spain and the Atlantic Ocean made it a significant exit point from Africa to European entry and vice versa. Other travel is to Puglia, Italy—Italy as a center of the movement and foundation of the Roman Empire and Puglia specifically due to its history of being conquered by Greece and

---

36   Decision of the Intergovernmental Committee: 8.COM 8.10. UNESCO Intangible Cultural Heritage. https://ich.unesco.org/en/decisions/8.COM/8.10.

Spain. Finally, students study in Spain, a key player in Mediterranean and Atlantic culture. Italy and Spain are high demand destinations for students; so, coupling those with other less popular regions helps promote the trip and further emphasize that these popular destinations rarely (i.e., never!) functioned alone. Other destinations can, of course, benefit this course topic as well. Professor expertise or connections may favor the selection of different Mediterranean countries.

The pre-trip course that is integral to the study abroad experience provides students with opportunities to directly familiarize themselves with the Mediterranean peoples, cultures, histories, and foods. This course includes both hands-on experiences in fields, tastings, preparing meals in kitchens; conversations with cultivators, fishermen, scientists, producers, and members of distinct cultural groups; and visits to cultural sites from museums to markets to cathedrals, from urban metropolises to small towns. The course provides the opportunity for students to engage in academic discussions of diet and culture through the lenses of history and identity but also via engaging with current topics related to globalization, food industrialization, the role of government in food, global climate change, population growth, and more. Other disciplines could emphasize nutrition, agricultural techniques, representations of food in art, or trade economies, just to name a few. However, designing a way for students to grapple with all of these new experiences is essential.

Study abroad practices with the highest impact emphasize reflection on what learners have seen, heard, or experienced. The Experimental Learning Model[37] helps educators and learners visualize the learning process that can occur on study abroad. Designing activities that include reflection and experimentation are therefore key to a successful learning experience abroad.

The proposed course incorporates these theories from pre travel, during travel, to post travel assignments. It is a semester long course with two weeks of travel occurring after the semester. The outcomes include exhibiting increased intercultural sensitivity via course material and study abroad;

---

37   Angela M. Passarelli and David A. Kolb, "Using Experiential Learning Theory to Promote Student Learning and Development in Programs of Education Abroad." *Student Learning Abroad: What Our Students are Learning, What They're Not, and What We Can Do About It*, eds., Michal Vande Berg, R. Michael Paige, and Kris Hemming Lou, (Virginia: Stylus, 2012), 137–161.

creating dishes based on cultural customs in diverse Mediterranean locations; explaining the principles of the Mediterranean diet and its impact on the histories, economies, environments, and cultures of Western Europe, Eastern Europe, and Northern Africa; and conducting ethnographic research projects that require them to devise a research plan, collect data, assess the data, and assimilate it into a final research product. The main course text/required reading is "Food: A Culinary History," edited by Jean-Louis Flandrin and Massimo Montanari and translated by Albert Sonnenfeld. See syllabus below for more information.

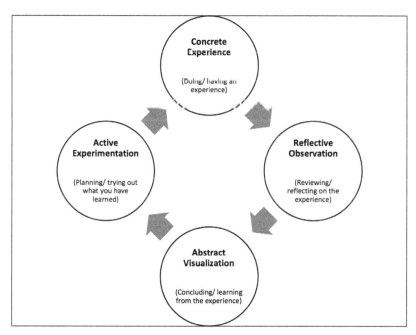

Two key assignments for the course are the travel journal and ethnographic research project. The travel journal is 10% of the overall course grade. For language learning students, instructors can decide whether to require that all or some portion of the journal be written in the target language. There are clear benefits to requiring use of the target language for purposes of proficiency; however, having to use a second language can limit a student's ability to express themselves. The instructor must weigh these variables before deciding which language allows students to best meet course outcomes.

The University of Kentucky has developed an Education Abroad Toolkit[38] containing many model assignments, including Journaling Across Cultures based on Morais and Ogden.[39] The toolkit describes this assignment's value as "help[ing] students record their learning experiences, document[ing] learning and growth, and help[ing] students cope with intercultural adjustment. The journal is structured to encourage students to record thoughts and events experienced in the course, and also to reflect on them in the context of global citizenship and academic development." Recommendations for professors are to include the journal assignment in the syllabus, with structure requirements, writing frequency demands, and other criteria for grading. The journal should also count toward a course grade, as it will require a significant time investment for students. Evaluation should occur before, during, and after traveling and should include a quantitative grade and written feedback. Periodic check-ins or scaffolded due dates (see syllabus below) are key to prevent students from procrastinating on the writing requirement. Faculty may elect to allow electronic journaling at their discretion. This technique may more easily allow students to turn in the journal at predetermined points using the internet; also, physical journals can be cumbersome for faculty to collect and carry while traveling.

This Morais, Ogden, and Buzinde[40] journal assignment defines and encourages students to always consider five themes when writing: (1) social responsibility, (2) global competence, (3) civic engagement, (4) self-concept, and (5) self-efficiency. Each entry should also include three parts: expressives, impressions, and narratives. "Expressives" are for reflections on the five themes, thoughts, and feelings about an event and how they influence academic learning and global citizenship. "Impressions" include chronological details (who, what, when, where, and why) and the five senses (smell, taste, sound, sight, touch). "Narratives" require storytelling and using descriptive writing.

---

38   uky.edu/toolkit.

39   Duarte Morais, Anthony C. Ogden, and C. Buzinde, *Embedded Education Abroad Faculty Toolkit: Developing and Implementing Course-Embedded Faculty-Led International Programs*, (University Park: The Pennsylvania State University Schreyer Institute for Teaching Excellence and University Office of Global Programs, 2009).

40   Ibid.

The sample course described here further deepens the expectations above by requiring specific cultural reflections to increase understanding and promote global learning. Students must select from eleven prompts, developed by the instructor, to encourage deep reflection on cultural beliefs. Students elect when to use one of the prompts, but they must use each at least once and label them with the selected theme number. If they don't intentionally label the prompt, it can be difficult to decipher which theme students have selected. It also allows students to ensure their having completed all the assigned topics. These are the travel prompts developed for this study abroad experience:

1. What challenged you today? What happened? What did you do/think? How did you feel? Did it change cultural beliefs? (Allowing students a specific place to express challenges can help them process these issues and not over-generalize.)[41]

2. What surprised you today? What happened? What did you do/think? How did you feel? Did it change cultural beliefs? (This prompt allows students to note something they did not expect. In doing so, it may reveal their unconscious biases or expectations and help them process those elements. Self-awareness is an important piece of study abroad.)

3. Describe a memory from today that you will never forget. What happened? What did you do/think? How did you feel? Did it change cultural beliefs? (Allowing students to consider the long-term impact of this experience can help them value it more.)

4. What happened today that changes your perspective on something and why? (Specifically requiring students to reflect on changed perspectives can help highlight how they are growing through this experience.)

5. Describe something emotional that happened today (happy, sad, pleasing, etc.). (Again, this is more of an emotional outlet or even venting post which can be important tools to deal with stress.)[42]

6. What did you experience today that was different from your home state or the U.S.? Did you feel comfortable? Why or why not?

41   Ibid.

42   Ibid.

(Requiring students to note differences, either positive or negative, can help them move toward understanding.)

7. Talk about academics! What are you learning? Has this experience influenced your academic confidence and abilities? How/how has it not? (Emphasizing academic gains abroad can help students see the long-term value of this experience.)

8. Global competence means having an open mind when one tries to understand other cultures. With competence, a person can interact, communicate, and work effectively outside of his/her comfort zone. Have you had any experiences that revealed a lack of global competence so far? How you feel you are improving in your global competence? (This prompt requires self-reflection on growth in the specific area of global competence, an important outcome of study abroad.)

9. Social Responsibility. What experiences have you had that influenced your perceptions of global interdependence and concern for others and the environment? (This prompt requires self-reflection on social responsibility and interconnectedness, important outcomes of study abroad.)

10. Open! Your pick. Say what you want or need to say here. You can be creative. Write a poem. Draw a detailed and labeled picture. It's open for you to express yourself. (This allows students the flexibility to say what they need to say.)

11. Goodbye, _____ (country). What were your 3 most impactful experiences in this country? What will you always carry with you thanks to this experience? (Allowing students to consider the long-term impact of this experience can help them value it more.)

Student research is another HIP; linking it with study abroad, another HIP, can create an even more powerful educational experience for students. The second key assignment for the sample study abroad course is an ethnographic research project (See appendix II). Ethnographic research is an ideal mode for students to gather information from their new surroundings. The name can intimidate students; thus, it is important to explain that ethnography just means on-site research via interview, survey, or observation. The project is 20% of the course grade, and it involves a multi-step, scaffolded approach to research. The course requires an interview component for ethnographic research, but students should also select another one of the methods listed below to bolster their studies. They should be provided this list with the descriptions so students understand what each approach entails. Per Purdue University OWL,[43] ethnographic research can take the form of:

1. Interviews: Interviews are one-on-one or small group question and answer sessions. Interviews will provide a lot of information from a small number of people and are useful when you want to get an expert or knowledgeable opinion on a subject.

2. Surveys: Surveys are a form of questioning that is more rigid than interviews and that involve larger groups of people. Surveys will provide a limited amount of information from a large group of people and are useful when you want to learn what a larger population thinks.

3. Observations: Observations involve taking organized notes about occurrences in the world. Observations provide you with insight about specific people, events, or locales and are useful when you want to learn more about an event without the biased viewpoint of an interview.

4. Analysis: Analysis involves collecting data and organizing it in some fashion based on criteria you develop. They are useful when you want to find some trend or pattern. A type of analysis would be to record commercials on three major television networks and analyze gender roles.

In order to engage in the research practice, traveling students are required before traveling to turn in their research proposal that connects course readings with an idea for on-site research for professor approval. Note, ethnographic research is traditionally associated with the social sciences, but it can be thematically transferred to many disciplines. For example, students can interview locals on their perspectives of certain goods. Once their proposals are approved, students complete a literature

---

43   Stacy Weida and Karl Stolley, "Welcome to the Purdue OWL." *Purdue OWL: Establishing Arguments* (2014), https://owl.purdue.edu/owl/general_writing/academic_writing/establishing_arguments/index.html.

review of existing research on the topic and create the interview questions. These literature reviews require that students read and explain recent studies in the field, thereby exposing them to higher level disciplinary knowledge. Northeastern University developed an excellent resource for students conducting ethnographic research interviews.[44]

During the trip, students complete data collection and analysis, comparing what they studied in their literature review to their actual observations from the study abroad. After the trip, students write a rough draft research paper, complete a presentation, and then turn in a final draft that reflects professor feedback. The papers and presentations should include the following components: an introduction, a literature review (completed pre-departure), the results (collected while abroad), a discussion that connects their own views to the literature review (analysis that can occur while abroad and upon return), why this research matters, limitations of their study, and a conclusion. Note, as the students are completing the project for a course, this research does not require approval from an institutional review board (IRB). However, if a student wishes to publish or present this work publicly, they must obtain IRB approval.

Rubrics for assessing this project are pulled from the AAC&U Value Rubrics on Inquiry and Analysis.[45] For the presentation component, the AAC&U Oral Communication rubric works well (see link in footnotes). Any of these rubrics can be edited to reflect such course criteria as time or page requirements, specific pictures in situ, professional dress, asking questions of other presenters (i.e., being an engaged viewer of other projects), target language use and proficiency, etc.

The last key assignment to discuss here for a study abroad course focuses on diversity and experiential learning is the final onsite reflection. This reflection should occur on the last or penultimate day abroad. For language learning students, this reflection occurs in English. It allows them to blow off steam and reflect deeply using their native tongue, which can help them process their experiences abroad more deeply. This reflection should occur in the form of a reception or celebration of their experience abroad. After

---

44   Mary Kay Gee and Charlotte Ullman, *Teacher/Ethnographer in the Workplace: Approaches to Staff Development*, (Grayslake Illinois: Lake County College, 1998), 1–12.

45   https://www.aacu.org/initiatives/value-initiative/value-rubrics

a time of free conversation and snacking, students and professor(s) should gather and sit in a circle to promote a feeling of equity and to celebrate study abroad as a real educational achievement. Ask for a volunteer and propose one question at a time. While each course will have unique needs, the most common questions employed by the author are:

1. What were your top three experiences abroad?
2. What was one bad experience and how did you overcome it?
3. Tell us about a time you had to check your privilege.
4. How are you changed from this experience? What will you take with you?

Going around the circle, each student (and the professor) answers one question. When all have answered, the professor then presents the next question, which circulates through the group. While these questions may seem benign, they actually require deep reflection on the part of each student and create an interconnected group (and professor) reflection as well. Often, the bare honesty and vulnerability of the students in this group reflection are awe inspiring and lead to tears of empathy and understanding for all involved. This group reflection invariably leads to some of the most profound moments an educator can experience and serves as a reminder as to why these study abroad courses should be offered.

Students have reflected on the happiness of people who seemingly "have nothing" as much greater than that of Americans who "have everything." They have shared very personal reflections on their relationships with their mothers in the U.S. as compared to the healthier dynamics with their host mothers. They have expressed guilt at the economic and military arrogance of the U.S. in relation to poorer nations. They have reflected on the worth or lack of worth found in romantic relationships "back home." They have felt pride in the emphasis on accessibility and safety in the U.S., yet they have expressed rage at the treatment of women in the U.S. and abroad. They reflect on the differences between who they were before the trip and who they are returning home. In short, the geographic and psychological distance provided by study abroad can create a pressure cooker for self-reflection, critical thinking, and analysis.

Repetition of these assignments across years of study abroad courses and varied destinations has demonstrated their effectiveness and allowed for modifications. The impact of study abroad is clear and profound. The call to offer these courses, to actively seek engagement from underrepresented students, to visit underrepresented areas, and to emphasize the world's interconnectedness is loud and persistent in our society. With the resources provided in this chapter, from the beginning stage of how to design a study abroad experience to the final reflection tools for students, instructors will have a guide to becoming experts in highly effective teaching through study abroad.

Appendix I

Mediterranean Food Studies Syllabus

COURSE OUTCOMES	IUE CAMPUS OUTCOMES
1. Students will exhibit increased intercultural sensitivity via course material and study abroad. 2. Students will create dishes based on cultural customs in diverse Mediterranean locations. 3. Students will explain the principles of the Mediterranean diet and its impact on the histories, economies, environments, and cultures of Western Europe, Eastern Europe, and Northern Africa. 4. Students will conduct ethnographic research projects that require them to devise a research plan, collect data, assess the data, and assimilate it into a final research product.	1. Communicate clearly and effectively in written and oral forms (course outcome 3). 2. Access, use, and critically evaluate a variety of relevant information sources (course outcomes 2, 3, 4). 3. Apply principles of inquiry to define and analyze complex problems through reasoning and discovery (course outcomes 3, 4). 4. Demonstrate the ability to relate within a multicultural and digitally connected world (course outcomes 1, 3). 5. Demonstrate a deep understanding of a field of study (course outcome 4).

Text: *"Food: A Culinary History." Edited by Jean-Louis Flandrin and Massimo Montanari. Translated by Albert Sonnenfeld*

Grade Breakdown:

Discussions: 15%

Throughout this course there will be online writing assignments in the Discussions tool. These should always use academic language and address the given prompt, including a question for other students. Students are required to post and respond to 2 other students' questions. These responses should be substantive. Point out similarities and differences between your opinions. Suggest ideas for further research. If the original post focuses on an issue, expand it to a more global approach. On the other hand, if the original post gives an overview, dig down to give a more focused example.

Participation and Professionalism: 15%

Your grade will be based on completing homework in a timely manner, using proper etiquette and professionalism in the classroom space/communications, maintaining a positive attitude, working in a collaborative manner to complete tasks, and demonstrating respect for the professor and peers. This applies to time spent in the course in the U.S. AND abroad. International travel, though a worthwhile and life changing experience, is not necessarily an easy experience. Glitches are to be expected and patience on all our parts can make the experience go much more smoothly. Often, instead of Plan A, we must think through other options and end up on Plan D. This is part of leaving our comfort zones. Patience, a positive attitude, and hard work are key for group dynamics. Students should understand that failure to demonstrate any of these traits will be reflected in grading by the professor for the participation and professionalism portion of the course grade and also, perhaps, by peers in their assessments for group projects.

Chapter Presentation: 5%

Students will individually select one chapter from the list of course readings to present to the class. Only one student may present per week or unit (depending on unit length), and these will be selected on a first come, first served basis. These presentations should be 15 minutes in length. They should include a well-structured and visually appealing PowerPoint, study guide handout, and reading based questions to guide class discussion.

Cooking Demo Project: 15%

In groups of 2–3, students will select a country from the list and prepare an approved dish from that country. The presentation should include information on dish history, ingredients and their history, and cultural information. Students may make an edited video of the dish preparation, prepare the dish live, or a bit of each. If students elect to make a video, they must include live presentation elements as well. If students prepare the dish live, they must be well practiced and finish within the time constraints. Students must provide one small food sample to all course members. Funding is available for ingredients.

Ethnographic Research Project: 20% (See Appendix)
Pre-travel:
    Proposal 5%
    Literature Review 15% (as discussion)
    Survey 10% (as discussion)

During travel:
    Data collection and analysis 5%

Post travel:
    Rough draft 20%
    Presentation 20%
    Final draft 25%

Exams 20%

Travel journal 10% (See handout)

Course Schedule: Hybrid class meets 1 day per week for 3 hours.

Unit 1: FOOD TODAY. (1 week/16)
    Course introduction: The Mediterranean Diet. Food Industrialization.
    Documentary: Food, Inc.
    Theories of food
    Discussion
    Quiz (Small exam grade)

Unit 2: Prehistory and Early Civilizations (week 2/16)

Readings (one chapter presented by student)

Introduction: The Humanization of Eating Behaviors, by Jean-Louis Flandrin

1. Feeding Strategies in Prehistoric Times, by Catherine Perles
2. The Social Function of Banquets in the Earliest Civilizations, by Francis Joannes
3. Food Culture in Ancient Egypt, by Edda Bresciani
4. Biblical Reasons: The Dietary Rules of the Ancient Hebrews, by Jean Soler
5. The Phoenicians and the Carthaginians: The Early Mediterranean Diet, by Antonella Spano Giammellaro

Activities: Bread baking

U2 Exam

Discussions

Unit 3: The Classical World (week 4/16 weeks)

Readings:

Week 1: (one chapter presented by student)

Introduction: Food Systems and Models of Civilization, by Massimo Montanari

6. Urban and Rural Diets in Greece, by Marie-Claire Amouretti
7. Greek Meals: A Civic Ritual, by Pauline Schmitt-Pantel
8. The Culture of the Symposium, by Massimo Vetta
9. The Diet of the Etruscans, by Giuseppe Sassatelli

Activities: Olive oil tasting

Week 2: (one chapter presented by student)

10. The Grammar of Roman Dining, by Florence Dupont
11. The Broad Bean and the Moray: Social Hierarchies and Food in Rome, by Mireille Corbier
12. Diet and Medicine in the Ancient World, by Innocenzo Mazzini
13. The Food of Others, by Oddone Longo

Activities: Pasta making

U3 Exam

Discussions

Unit 4: From the Late Classical Period to the Early Middle Ages (Fifth–Tenth Centuries) (week 5/16)

Readings: (one chapter presented by student)

Introduction: Romans, Barbarians, Christians—The Dawn of European Food Culture, by Massimo Montanari

14. Production Structures and Food Systems in the Early Middle Ages, by Massimo Montanari

15. Peasants, Warriors, Priests: Images of Society and Styles of Diet, by Massimo Montanari

Activities: Guest lecture: Daron Olson, World History and food

Unit 5: Westerners and Others (week 6/16)

Readings: (one chapter presented by student)

Introduction: Food Models and Cultural Identity, by Massimo Montanari

16. Christians of the East: Rules and Realities of the Byzantine Diet, by Ewald Kislinger

17. Arab Cooking and Its Contribution to European Culture, by Bernard Rosenberger

18. Mediterranean Jewish Diet and Traditions in the Middle Ages, by Miguel-Angel Motis Dolader

Activities: Guest lecture on religion: Ange Cooksey

Activities: Chef Santorini, Indianapolis field trip

Unit 6: The Late Middle Ages (Eleventh–Fourteenth Centuries) (week 7/16)

Readings:

Week 1: (one chapter presented by student)

Introduction: Toward a New Dietary Balance, by Massimo Montanari

19. Society, Food, and Feudalism, by Antoni Riera-Melis

20. Self-Sufficiency and the Market: Rural and Urban Diet in the Middle Ages, by Alfio Cortonesi

21. Food Trades, by Francoise Desportes

22. The Origins of Public Hostelries in Europe, by Hans Conrad Peyer

23. Medieval Cooking, by Bruno Laurioux
Activities: Food in Art, Ann Kim

Week 2: (one chapter presented by student)
24. Food and Social Classes in Late Medieval and Renaissance Italy, by Allen J. Grieco
25. Seasoning, Cooking, and Dietetics in the Late Middle Ages, by Jean-Louis Flandrin
26. "Mind Your Manners": Etiquette at the Table, by Daniela Romagnoli
27. From Hearth to Table: Late Medieval Cooking Equipment, by Francoise Piponnier
Activities: Guest lecture Andrea Quenette, Communication through food

Unit 7: The Europe of Nation-States (Fifteenth–Eighteenth Centuries) (week 8/16)
Readings: (one chapter presented by student)
Introduction: The Early Modern Period, by Jean-Louis Flandrin
28. Growing without Knowing Why: Production, Demographics, and Diet, by Michel Morineau
29. Colonial Beverages and the Consumption of Sugar, by Alain Huetz de Lemps
30. Printing the Kitchen: French Cookbooks, 1480–1800, by Philip Hyman and Mary Hyman
31. Dietary Choices and Culinary Technique, 1500–1800, by Jean-Louis Flandrin
32. From Dietetics to Gastronomy: The Liberation of the Gourmet, by Jean-Louis Flandrin
Activities: Guest lecture Justin Carroll (Colombian Exchange)

Unit 8: The Contemporary Period (Nineteenth and Twentieth Centuries) (week 10/16)
Readings:
Week 1: (one chapter presented by student)
Introduction: From Industrial Revolution to Industrial Food, by Jean-

Louis Flandrin

33. The Transformation of the European Diet, by Hans Jurgen Teuteberg and Jean-Louis Flandrin

34. The Invasion of Foreign Foods, by Yves Pehaut

35. The Rise of the Restaurant, by Jean-Robert Pitte

36. The Food Industry and New Preservation Techniques, by Giorgio Pedrocco

Activity: Documentary-Cooked 2016

Week 2: (one chapter presented by student)

37. The Taste for Canned and Preserved Food, by Alberto Capatti

38. The Emergence of Regional Cuisines, by Julia Csergo

39. The Perils of Abundance: Food, Health, and Morality in American History, by Harry A. Levenstein

40. The "McDonaldization" of Culture, by Claude Fischler

Activity: Documentary-Fed Up (2014)

Unit 9: Today and Tomorrow, by Jean-Louis Flandrin and Massimo Montanari (weeks 11–14)

Topics: Climate Change, Food Security, Globalization

Interviews with Cinzia Rascarro (Italy), and Greece contact

Readings: Minestrone as Secret Weapon

Activities: Organic chemistry guest lecture and test

Ethnographic Research Proposal Due

Cooking Classes & Demonstrations:

- Greek Food-group 1
- Italian Food-group 2
- Spanish Food-group 3
- Moroccan Food-group 4

WEEK 15: PRE-TRAVEL
Orientation
Ethnographic Research Literature Review and Questions Due

Time Abroad:
Tentative Travel Schedule:
Day 1 Travel
Day 2 Half day in Lecce, (cooking/dinner with Stile Mediterraneo) 3 hours
Day 3 Lecce Gourmet tour, local business and producers, 4 hours, Jewish culture museum, 1 hour
Day 4 Lecce cooking class and Italian culture, 4 hours
Day 5 Lecce area mozzarella demonstration, tasting, and olive oil tour, 6 hours
Day 6 Gallipoli-Seafood market, interview fisherman and markets, 5 hours
Day 7 Travel and half day in Athens, Phyllo and cultural interviews, 4 hours
Day 8 Bike tour and architecture museum, 3 hours and 3 hours
Day 9 Acropolis, vegan tour, 2 hours and 3 hours
Day 10 Islands/capital, 5 hours
Day 11 Travel and Valencia tapas tour, 3 hours
Day 12 Market tour and paella class, 4 hours
Day 13 Market and farm tour, 5 hours
Day 14 Sevilla Alcázar, Hammam, 5 hours
Day 15 Travel day and Morocco Fes tour, 2 hours
Day 16 Jewelry class and art school tour, 4 hours
Day 17 Market tour, cooking class, dinner, and hammam, 6 hours
Day 18 Blue City, 5 hours
Day 19 Depart

Upon Return:
Presentation of Research Findings

Appendix II

Mediterranean Ethnographic Research Project

PURPOSE:

Skills: For this project students will conduct research in Puerto Rico on a topic of their choosing. In doing so they will learn to assimilate research from texts and other sources, including ethnographic study. Students will learn to conduct research in English and Spanish, analyze data, write about their findings, and present their work at IUE Student Research Day. I have broken this down into stages. This part (Part I) of the project involves preliminary research and development of a research plan.

KNOWLEDGE:

While completing this assignment, students will critically analyze sources, develop a research topic, and develop research questions. In the next part of the project, students will culturally immerse themselves, interview/survey respondents, record the results, analyze the results, compile data in a written report, and present the report to peers and faculty.

Thinking critically, using a second language, interacting in another culture using course orientation, developing an instrument to collect, analyze, and present data in written form are valuable skills post-graduation. According to the 2017 NACE Survey (http://www.naceweb. org/talent-acquisition/candidate-selection/the-attributes-employers-seek-on-a-candidates-resume/) employers want employees with expertise in problem solving (77.3%), written communication skills (75%), verbal communication skills (72%), and analytical skills (64.4%). This assignment will help you to hone those skills.

TASK:

1. In our last unit, you proposed 2 research projects. With feedback from your professor, you should now have selected one.
2. Finish reading your 2 texts.
3. Write a discussion post about how you can use the texts, including what you just read in finishing each, in your research. Cite the

texts or audios. Use direct quotes and in-text citations (MLA style: https://owl.english.purdue.edu/owl/resource/747/01/)

Trust me when I say there are connections in BOTH texts to every project proposal I read of yours.

For example, if you are discussing food, you will need to know ethnic groups and immigration and who lived where, when. These factors seriously influence food because people bring their food traditions with them. Where did they eat? What did they eat? How did they eat? With whom did they eat? When did they eat? It's in there. Also, don't forget, the absence of a theme is VERY VIABLE for research.

If you need ideas, just let me know.

4. In another discussion post, you will begin your ethnographic research. Don't be overwhelmed by the fancy word! Ethnography just means on-site research via interview, survey, or observation (http://classroom.synonym.com/put-together-ethnographic-research-paper-4166.html links to an external site).

5. Think about how you want to conduct your research. You can select one method and go very in-depth or you can select a mix of methods (note: everyone will have at least one interview component because of the interview assignment). (Info below from Purdue OWL)

Interviews: Interviews are one-on-one or small group question and answer sessions. Interviews will provide a lot of information from a small number of people and are useful when you want to get an expert or knowledgeable opinion on a subject.

Surveys: Surveys are a form of questioning that is more rigid than interviews and involve larger groups of people. Surveys will provide a limited amount of information from a large group of people and are useful when you want to learn what a larger population thinks.

Observations: Observations involve taking organized notes about occurrences in the world. Observations provide you insight about specific people, events, or locales and are useful when you want to learn more about an event without the biased viewpoint of an interview.

Analysis: Analysis involves collecting data and organizing it in some fashion based on criteria you develop. They are useful when you want to find some trend or pattern. A type of analysis would be to record commercials on three major television networks and analyze gender roles.

6. Consider the following questions when beginning to think about conducting primary research:
    - What do I want to discover?
    - How do I plan on discovering it? (This is called your research methods or methodology)
    - Who am I going to talk to/observe/survey? (These people are called your subjects or participants)
    - How am I going to be able to gain access to these groups or individuals?
    - What are my biases about this topic?
    - How can I make sure my biases are not reflected in my research methods?
    - What do I expect to discover?

    (Purdue OWL)

7. Develop your interview/survey questions. Here is a great resource for how to think this part: https://course.ccs.neu.edu/is4800sp12/resources/ethinterview.pdf

8. Complete the discussion.

CRITERIA:

Rubric for Inquiry and Analysis: Scientific Reasoning by the AAC&U. This will be used for BOTH discussion posts. The percentage will be calculated out of 20 possible points.

	Capstone	Milestones		Benchmark
	4	3	2	1
Assignment Completion (Discussion 1, Discussion 2 with required parts)	All parts thoroughly completed.	Most to all parts completed.	Some parts completed.	Few parts completed.
Topic Selection	Identifies a creative, focused, and manageable topic that addresses potentially significant yet previously less-explored aspects of the topic.	Identifies a focused and manageable/doable topic that appropriately addresses relevant aspects of the topic.	Identifies a topic that while manageable/doable, is too narrowly focused and leaves out relevant aspects of the topic.	Identifies a topic that is far too general and wide-ranging as to be manageable and doable.
Existing Knowledge, Research, and/or Views	Synthesizes in-depth information from relevant sources representing various points of view/approaches.	Presents in-depth information from relevant sources representing various points of view/approaches.	Presents information from relevant sources representing limited points of view/approaches.	Presents information from irrelevant sources representing limited points of view/approaches.
Design Process	All elements of the methodology or theoretical framework are skillfully developed. Appropriate methodology or theoretical frameworks may be synthesized from across disciplines or from relevant subdisciplines.	Critical elements of the methodology or theoretical framework are appropriately developed; however, more subtle elements are ignored or unaccounted for.	Critical elements of the methodology or theoretical framework are missing, incorrectly developed, or unfocused.	Inquiry design demonstrates a misunderstanding of the methodology or theoretical framework.
Language Use	Careful drafting and editing evident. Language reflects near native written ability.	Editing is apparent, but some mistakes are still present.	Some editing is apparent. Many mistakes still present.	Writing reflects little to no editing. Basic grammar errors of agreement, accents, and gender are present.

Experiencing Colonialism in the Dominican Republic:

Hands-on History through International Service-Learning

Christine C. Nemcik

When considering leading a short-term study abroad experience for university students, most history educators are naturally drawn toward offering traditional history study tours. These history tours can be designed to fit naturally into the course content and are a fantastic means of allowing students to experience first-hand the historical sites they are learning about in class. At the same time, many research studies show a rising interest among students and faculty alike in incorporating service projects and service-learning into campus life and university classes, including in study abroad experiences.[1] As a Latin American historian specializing in Central America, I have spent my academic life traveling, living in, and researching regions that are vastly different than the world in which I permanently live. The opportunities for immersion with people from different histories, cultures, languages, socio-economic statuses, educational opportunities, access to fundamental rights, and more have had profound impacts on my views on global issues, including social justice and human rights. Because I live in the United States, a country where basic rights and freedoms are protected under the law—even if not always equally applied—I am privileged with rights

---

1 See for example: Robbin D. Crabtree, "Theoretical foundations for international service learning," Michigan Journal of Community Service Learning, 15(1), (2008): 18–36. http://hdl.handle.net/2027/spo.3239521.0015.102, and Nancy Wessel, "Integrating service learning into the study abroad program: U.S. Sociology Students in Mexico," Journal of Studies in International Education, 11(1), (2007): 73–89. https://doi.org/10.1177/1028315305283306.

and freedoms not afforded to many people living outside the US. Though I teach about differences in history and culture in my on-campus classes, this in-class learning lacks the same impact as an immersion experience in another culture abroad.

A deeper understanding of other peoples and cultures can be gained during any international travel experience, including more traditional study abroad tours. Nonetheless, it can be both tempting and easier to keep oneself apart from the culture in which you are traveling when on an academic study tour. More traditional study abroad trips generally lack an immersive component; instead, students interact almost exclusively with their fellow students and instructors, and interaction with the local culture can tend towards being more observational than immersive. Well-planned international service-learning study abroad experiences, on the other hand, are generally more inherently immersive in nature and have more profound, lasting impacts on students.[2]

Yet historians I know—myself included—may find it difficult to formulate ideas for integrating meaningful service-learning connected to class content in a history course. This difficulty is particularly daunting when creating history-related, international service-learning (ISL) study abroad experiences. When brainstorming with history colleagues on ideas for using service-learning in history courses, most discussions in which I have partaken center around ideas of working on projects with historical societies, museums, and the like. Such service is attractive, valid, and most definitely connected to the discipline of history and provides a service to the community. Nonetheless, there are ways to tie more hands-on service projects into the context of a history class. Hands-on service learning is a means for students to not only engage in service but also do so while working directly with members of the community they are serving. Working side-by-side with and learning from local communities helps to remove the feeling of "otherness" in the relationship, which leads to a deeper appreciation of the local culture.[3] At the same time, this type of service-learning experience

2   Crabtree, "Theoretical Foundations," 2008.

3   Sharon Y. Nickols, Nancy J. Rothenberg, Lioba Moshi, and Meredith Tetloff, "International Service-Learning: Students' Personal Challenges and Intercultural Competence," Journal of Higher Education Outreach and Engagement, 17(4), (2013): 97–124.

can be taxing, particularly because ISL may involve participants being confronted with levels of inequity and injustice, some for the first time in their lives.[4] Introductory education on the host country including history, culture, setting, and language becomes essential in preparing students for the challenges of engaging in a study abroad experience that includes international service-learning. This need is particularly significant when engaging in a developing country with living situations so vastly different from the typical US student experience. Pre-travel exposure through not only readings on history and culture but also websites, videos, and more is vital in this preparation as the latter offer glimpses into life in the host country.[5] In this chapter, I discuss my course on the history and culture of the Dominican Republic, which includes an 8-day international service-learning study abroad trip. The ISL was integrated into the course content to help students understand the historical perpetuation of inequality in the country, and the pre-travel portion of the course works to prepare students to confront this reality when engaging with the community abroad.

Course Overview

In the fall of 2015, Indiana University East (IUE) chose Doc Hendley's book *Wine to Water: How One Man Saved Himself While Trying to Save the World* for the university's OneBook reading.[6] The objective of the OneBook reading is to have the university community read an ordinary book (which anyone at the university can receive free of charge), for faculty to incorporate the book into classes when possible, and to have the author visit the campus to give a talk and participate in other events surrounding the book. When I read Hendley's book for that fall semester, I realized the last few chapters focused on a water filter project in the Dominican Republic founded by a long-time friend, Lisa Ballantine. As a result of my connection to Lisa,

---

4   Richard Kiely, "A chameleon with a complex: Searching for transformation in international service-learning," Michigan Journal of Community Service Learning, 10(2), (2004): 5–20.

5   The syllabus included in this chapter provides information on the materials I have used to help students prepare for ISL study-abroad travel.

6   Doc Hendley, *Wine to Water: How One Man Saved Himself While Trying to Save the World* (London: Penguin Books, 2012).

the IUE School of Arts and Sciences invited her for a campus visit, also connected to the OneBook project. During this visit, Lisa talked about her experience living in the Dominican Republic which led her to develop a water filter project in the country. Lisa told stories of visiting and working in rural communities where she heard elderly people talk about not having gone a day in their lives without stomach pain and she saw children with bellies bloated by parasites from the water they drank and people collecting water from polluted sources because that was their only option. After a year of living in the Dominican Republic, she returned home determined to find a way to help improve the situation. As a ceramic artist, she worked with other artists and scientists to create a water filter that could be locally made using sustainable materials in the D.R. During her talk at IUE, Lisa told of how she then returned to implement the project in the D.R. and the subsequent impacts the filters had on the health of Dominicans. After this visit, the World Languages and Cultures (WLC) Program decided to create a study abroad course in the Dominican Republic centered around a service-learning project with Filter Pure, Lisa's venture, which merged into Doc Hendley's Wine to Water organization in 2017.

The first iteration of this course, SPAN-S370 "Service Learning in Spanish," was taught by a faculty member in the WLC program during the fall of 2016. The course focused on Dominican culture and included an ISL study abroad trip to the water filter factory in the D.R. The time abroad was designed as a Spanish language immersion experience. I took over the course in the fall semesters of 2017 and 2018, teaching it in much the same way. For the spring semester of 2020, I decided to restructure the course as a cross-listed class taught in English, combining SPAN-S270 "Service Learning in Hispanic Culture" and HIST-H221 "Studies in African, Asian, or Latin American History." The new title of the class became "History and Culture of the Dominican Republic with International Service Learning in the Dominican Republic." The global COVID-19 pandemic prevented the course from participating in the study abroad component in the spring of 2020; nevertheless, I structured and planned the class in essentially the same format as I previously taught it, with the primary exception of not including the Spanish immersion element with the study abroad experience.[7] Therefore, while it could certainly be interesting to reflect upon the disruptions to the study abroad portion the global health crisis caused, it is more relevant for this chapter to focus on the overall course content and how, in even the previous iterations of the course, I was able to create successful ISL study abroad experiences that were connected to the history of inequity in the D.R.

As mentioned in the introduction, the study abroad portion of the course was an eight-day service trip in the D.R.; the rest of the course was taught online via Canvas. Students engaged with each other and the course content online for approximately 14 weeks and then partook in the study abroad experience at the end of the semester. Students who enrolled in the course came from a broad spectrum of majors: history, biology, psychology, business, political science, and more. The connecting elements for students was their desire to travel and their shared interest in participating in a service-learning experience.

It is significant to note that while the content of my course was quite specific to an ISL experience with Wine to Water in the Dominican Republic, the overall course structure and assignments can be applied to different locations and service-learning opportunities related to history courses or courses in other disciplines. The key component for the success of such a course is tying in the service-learning project to the history, culture, politics, or other topic(s) being studied. The water crisis lends itself well to this element, as it is a global crisis. Doc Hendley's *Wine to Water* book is relatable to any country or region faced with issues of lack of water, unequal access to potable water, water-borne diseases, water gathering distances, and more. Though the autobiography centers explicitly around Hendley's work in Africa and the D.R., it is easy to see how history, culture, and politics—specifically, histories of war, social and economic inequity, and political instability in the form of dictatorships, fraudulent elections, and more—are tied to the world water crisis. Additionally, while I specifically connected the class to the Wine to Water project, the idea of linking a service component to the study of a region would work with water projects other than Wine to Water as well as other types of service projects. For the

---

7   SPAN-S270 is a Hispanic culture class taught in English, unlike the SPAN-S370 course that is specifically service-learning in Spanish.

IUE course, we did the legwork to plan all the travel and arrangements for in-country needs, but this part can be handled by others, as a simple online search will yield a plethora of "ready-made options" for ISL experiences, including thoroughly planned tours through such educational study abroad companies as EF Educational Tours. Another option is to seek out local organizations or small NGOs that can assist in creating a collaboration with the local community as well as preparing students for the experience. Small NGOS like Wine to Water can assist in connecting faculty and students to communities in developing countries and in "facilitating cross-cultural relationship building and project participation, and providing needed perspectives on development and politics."[8]

The key to connecting the ISL component to course content was the pre-travel preparation through course readings and assignments on international travel, international service, the global water crisis, and Dominican history. Introductory education on the host country, including history, culture, setting, and language, is essential in preparing students for the challenges of engaging in any study abroad experience. In this course, students were engaged with readings, discussions, and other assignments on all these elements from the start of the semester. As mentioned in the introduction, this preparation of students (and even faculty) before the trip is particularly essential when it comes to an ISL experience,   especially when the ISL involves working in communities with levels of poverty, inequality, and injustice previously unfamiliar to participants.[9] Consequently, this course was set up for students to study the history and culture of the country before traveling to gain an understanding of the historical roots of inequality and injustice in the D.R.

The course was laid out in modules of two to three weeks, except for one-week long modules for the introduction, completion of research projects, and the week of travel. I have found that modules of two to three weeks in online classes work better for students than single-week content modules, as they afford students flexibility for completing required work. From the start of the semester, in the class's introduction module, students

---

8   Crabtree, "Theoretical foundations," 23.

9   Kiley, 2004.

read articles on international travel, potential benefits and pitfalls of international service projects, and an introduction to the D.R. Beginning the course in this way immediately sets the stage for tying the service-learning component with the history and culture course content. In Module 2, students began reading Doc Hendley's book, and we delved into the nation's history, starting with readings on the pre-Columbian Amerindian peoples, the conquest, and the colonial period. Subsequent modules were similarly structured, with students reading chapters from Hendley's book alongside readings on Dominican history and others on international travel or study abroad. Learning about the water crisis through Hendley's story, while also learning the history and culture of the D.R., pushed students to begin making the connection between the inequality and injustice that leads to a lack of fundamental human rights—such as the lack of access to clean water—and the historical roots of these inequities. Additionally, reading *Wine to Water* with those sections on international travel further allowed students to see some potential difficulties of traveling abroad and working on a service project through the struggles that Hendley himself went through. This exercise often had a profound impact on students as they read about Hendley working through issues they might face, such as culture shock, reverse culture shock, and the profound impact that such travel can have on a person's global and cultural awareness and desire to be involved in impactful change. As part of these content modules, students engaged with one another in discussions and completed knowledge check assignments (described below) on the readings.

Besides online discussions and knowledge check assignments, two significant assignments for the class helped tie together the course content's components. One task was a project culminating in a PowerPoint research presentation, and the other was the travel journals students kept during the trip. I chose to have students do research projects with a final presentation rather than a research paper since these assignments would then serve as further means for students to learn from one another about specific aspects of the content we were studying as a class. For the research project, I encouraged students to choose a topic not only related to Dominican history or the water crisis but also connected to their major or minor field of study. Having students choose topics in this way had multiple benefits.

One was that they would ideally be working on something that would be of interest to them as it was related to their field of study and thus could also potentially benefit them beyond the class. For example, a biology major in the class with plans to be a doctor did a comparative study of health care in the D.R. and the U.S. This student talked about how the project opened her eyes to how she could be more understanding when working with patients who come from other countries. Another benefit of this type of project is that it is easily transferable to courses in other fields and disciplines. As I was teaching courses in both history and Spanish, I recognized the benefit of creating assignments that I could utilize in multiple different classes. This setup also serves this book well, as this type of project can be useful for other courses in which there are students from diverse major fields of study. Perhaps the most significant benefit of this assignment was that it led to a variety of topics for presentations and broadened the learning of all students in the class.

I did not have a formal assignment to choose research topics. Instead, I used the assignment as an opportunity to interact individually with each student in online meetings to discuss their potential topic choice. In online, asynchronous classes, students can quickly feel disconnected from the professor since there are no regular face-to-face meetings to foster interaction. These one-on-one research topic discussions allowed me to help students figure out a feasible topic (not too broad or narrow and with adequate potential sources) and helped create better connections with each student. After meeting with me to discuss their topics, students were required to submit their topic choice in the assignment on Canvas. Having them submit the topic online after our discussion kept them accountable for their choice. The topic submission assignment also came with the requirement that if they wished to change their focus, they would need to schedule another discussion with me. This guideline was not a punitive measure but meant to keep students on track with their research.

The middle stage of the research project was a check-in assignment on how the research was going. Rather than having this task as an individually submitted assignment, I created a class discussion forum for the check-in. Each student was required to describe their research topic and why the topic interested them, discuss the sources they had accessed thus far, and post any questions or requests for assistance from other students; these inquiries could be related to finding sources, formulating an argument, tying their topic to Dominican history, and more. Students had already been accustomed to interacting with one another in discussions of the course content, but this took those interactions a step further. Opening up with one another to discuss their projects, including successes and frustrations they were encountering in their research, served as a lead-in to collaborations that were more closely related to the upcoming study abroad. It has been my experience that on any study abroad trip, some of the closest connections come through students sharing their successes and frustrations with the faculty leading the trip. This dynamic is prevalent in an ISL study abroad, where students face challenges unique to the service experience. I have experienced students feeling ashamed that they had gone into the study abroad with the assumption that they were smarter than the people they were working with simply because they were more educated, but then discovering they were learning extensively from the Dominicans. Creating a pre-travel opportunity for students to begin to feel comfortable discussing their challenges and frustrations before traveling together opens the doors for their being able to reflect upon these feelings with the group while studying abroad.

The final stage of the project was for students to record themselves giving their presentation and to submit the PowerPoint and recorded presentation in a discussion for all class members to view. Research topics chosen by the students covered a broad spectrum of interests, but almost all were tied to historical inequities in the country. Some of the PowerPoint projects for the class included Historical Roots of Differentiated Access to Health Care (by a biology major), Hurricanes Katrina and Maria: Impacts on the Access to Clean Water in Developed vs. Developing Nations (by a business major), The Effect of Political Corruption on the Water Crisis in the Dominican Republic (by a political science major), and Historic Roots of Current Hostilities between the Dominican Republic and Haiti (by a history major), among others. The diversity of project topics exposed the students to a broader array of information than could be covered in the assigned content of a one-semester class. Students' reflections noted their appreciating more in-depth exposure to a facet of the D. R. or the water crisis before traveling, as they felt more prepared for what they would encounter. Additionally, besides the biology student who connected her project to her future plans, other students talked about the impact these projects, together with service abroad, had on them, particularly in broadening their cultural and global awareness and commitment to being more aware of world issues. Finally, I found that having students present their projects for the entire class—a group of students with whom they would be traveling and living closely for eight days—led to an overall higher project quality. Knowing they would be interacting with those who had viewed and commented upon their projects and that they could be called upon as relative experts on their topics seemed to influence the quality of research and depth of information that went into the final products.

The other significant assignment for the course was the daily journal that students kept during the study abroad portion of the course. Research studies have documented that the incorporation of reflection through journaling is a critical component of ISL.[10] In my experience, students reflecting upon ISL work through journaling while abroad helps them to process their days and deal with culture shock as well as foster continued interest in cultural learning and volunteerism into the future. For these journal entries, students had daily prompts (see the course schedule below) related to activities from the day. Providing questions for daily journaling helps students who may not be accustomed to or comfortable with journaling and allows them to process what may have been challenging experiences. Although vital to the ISL experience, this assignment is much more difficult to assess. Our accommodations in the D.R. were dorms in the Wine to Water ceramic filter "factory" that had unreliable Wi-Fi at best. Students, therefore, tended to record their reflections in handwritten journals or notes on their phones in airplane mode, which they then submitted as screenshots or photos when we returned home. There could be no expectation that the journal entries were professionally or cleanly written. In fact, I encouraged students to "speak in their true voice" and to feel utterly open in saying what they needed to say in the way they felt comfortable saying it. I did not have a rubric for grading journals but based the grades upon students responding

10   See, for example, Humphrey Tonkin, *Service Learning Across Cultures: promise and achievement* (New York: International Partnership for Service-Learning and Leadership, 2004).

to the questions about their day. Including the journaling assignment as the final part of the course allowed students to tie their journals into all other aspects of the class, which helped them to reflect upon how the water crisis is tied to Dominican history and culture and thus how participating in the service-learning experience tied into these topics as well.

Sample Syllabus

The people collecting water from polluted sources because that was their only option in the syllabus below is the topic I used for my class. It is therefore specific to a history course with an ISL component in the Dominican Republic. I have made notes throughout the syllabus on how it can be applied for use in courses with other topics or in other disciplines.

General Course Description

This course studies Dominican history, culture, and the world water crisis. As part of the course students will participate in a study abroad experience, which will further develop their understanding of Dominican culture and the connection between the water crisis and the nation's history. This experience will be completed by working with Wine to Water in the Dominican Republic and engaging with local communities.

Course Learning Objectives

1. Understand the people and history of the Dominican Republic in the Caribbean and global context.
2. Connect current issues in the D.R. to historical roots dating back to the colonial period.
3. Learn to function effectively in another culture.
4. Develop skills in experiential learning and service-learning.
5. Achieve new learning about self and U.S. culture through a process of "defamiliarization."
6. Develop a sense of global citizenship and service.

The first two objectives are course-topic specific. If teaching a course on history or culture, these could be easily modified. For other courses, it would be a matter of what you plan to use as course content to prepare students to partake in an ISL study abroad.

Objectives four through six are significant components of an ISL experience and can be easily adopted into any similar course.

Suggested Course Materials
1. Doc Hendley, *Wine to Water: How One Man Saved Himself While Trying to Save the World* (London: Penguin Books, 2012).
2. Online readings on Dominican History OR Eric Paul Roorda Lauren Derby, and Raymundo González eds. *The Dominican Republic Reader* (Durham: Duke University Press, 2014).
    a. I used *The Dominican Republic Reader* the first time teaching the course but learned that many students did not read it, as the content presentation is extremely dry. It is a readily available option for those who prefer to assign a book for students to read.
    b. The last time I taught the course, I used online articles and websites to cover the content. I have listed all those still active websites and videos in the schedule below.
3. Online readings on international travel and international service-learning

The readings on international travel and international service-learning are included to assist students with preparing for an international experience. Even if students have previously traveled abroad, a study-abroad experience, particularly one that includes service, often presents new challenges, and it is important to have students interact with each other and with you on thoughts and feelings around upcoming travel.

The general readings, videos, and podcasts in the syllabus are adaptable to any study abroad course, and I have used them multiple times in different study abroad experiences to different destinations. The other readings are specific to Dominican culture, history, and the world water crisis. For a course traveling to the Dominican Republic, the sources on the history and culture of the island can be easily adapted. Doc Hendley's book can be used in an ISL course on the water crisis anywhere in the world. It is also a great resource on some challenges of working in service abroad and, as such, could be used for other ISL experiences.

Course Assignments

The two extensive assessments for the course were a research project related to Dominican history or the Dominican water crisis and a service journal kept during the travel portion of the course. Other work for the class included online discussions (including some centered around D.R. history and international travel) and knowledge check assignments. I have included the discussion topics and knowledge check assignments within the "Suggested Course Schedule." Directions for the assignments and their rubrics follow the class schedule. Prompts for the travel journals are also in the class schedule. As mentioned above, I do not use rubrics for grading the journal prompts, as I have found it impossible to grade them for the correctness of writing, since students are encouraged to do them handwritten and submit photos of the pages. They can also be deeply personal and therefore subjective to grade. Instead, I grade on completion, and use them as a way to interact with students on the experience after returning home.

Suggested Course Schedule

I have included the course schedule related to the content covered before studying abroad and the journal assignments for the study-abroad days in the D.R. Each week's content modules and assignments combined elements of Dominican history and the global water crisis.

Early modules also included information and discussions about travel, service and service-learning, and necessary travel-related logistical assignments (applying for a passport, paying for study abroad fees, arranging for meeting at the airport, etc.). I have not included these assignments as they are unique to each study-abroad trip. It is important to note that I have found including these logistical requirements as assignments in the class ensures students are taking care of what they need to in order to travel and makes the trip less stressful for all.

Module 1, Week 1: Course Introduction — this week is primarily an introduction to course structure, course content, and one another.

1. Students post video introductions and get to know one another. This segment is significant for an online course, particularly for when students gather in person at the end of the semester to live and work together abroad.

2. Online Content:

    a. Lauren Kascak with Sayantani DasGupta MD MPH, "#instagrammingAfrica: The Narcissism of Global Travel," *The Society Pages*, December 29, 2014. https://thesocietypages.org/socimages/2014/12/29/instragrammingafrica-the-narcissism-of-global-voluntourism/.

    b. Podcast: "Civics Lessons Beyond the Classroom: Volunteering May not Teach Students About Problems' Roots," NPR Morning Edition, January 7, 2003. https://www.npr.org/2003/01/07/905341/civics-lessons-beyond-the-classroom.

    c. "Dominicans," *Countries and their Cultures*. https://www.everyculture.com/wc/Costa-Rica-to-Georgia/Dominicans.html.

3. Assignments:

    a. Discussion: "#instagrammingAfrica" — "On these trips, we hide behind the lens, consuming the world around us with our powerful gazes and the clicking of camera shutters. When I directed this photo opportunity and starred in it, I used my privilege to capture a photograph that made me feel like I was engaging with the community. Only now do I realize that what I was doing was making myself the hero/star in a story about 'suffering Africa.'" Did reading this article alter your perspective on engaging in service in the Dominican Republic?

Module 2, Weeks 2 and 3: Conquest and Colonialism and Introduction to the World Water Crisis

1. This unit covered chapters 1–4 of Doc Hendley's book as well as the following online resources on Dominican history and studying abroad:

a. "Pre-Columbian Hispaniola — Arawak/Taino Indians," http://www.hartford-hwp.com/archives/43a/100.html.

b. "Dominican Republic: The First Colony," from Richard A. Haggerty, ed. *Dominican Republic: A Country Study.* Washington: GPO for the Library of Congress, 1989. http://countrystudies.us/dominican-republic/3.htm.

c. "The 11 Types of People You Meet Studying Abroad," *Bustle,* August 14, 2014. https://www.bustle.com/articles/33065-the-11-types-of-people-you-meet-studying-abroad-you-obnoxious-american-you.

d. "Studying Abroad: is it really worth it?" NPR Talk of the Nation, August 9, 2012. https://www.npr.org/2012/08/09/158501278/weighing-the-benefits-of-studying-abroad.

2. Assignments

a. Knowledge Check: Explain what you consider were the most significant aspects of the pre-Columbian cultures of the island of Hispaniola.

b. Knowledge Check: What most interested or intrigued you about Doc Hendley's story of becoming involved with the world water crisis and why?

c. Discussion on the purpose of studying abroad: "It used to be about learning a foreign language and learning some content knowledge, the sort of parlance of higher education. And now it's supposed to be about one of those being cross-cultural communication skills. Well, the only way you do that is through experiential learning and getting out and meeting people."
This program in the Dominican Republic was designed with these ideas in mind, but what can individual students do to ensure a profound learning experience?

d. Research project proposal: students received total points for meeting with me to discuss a research topic and then submitting the agreed-upon topic in the assignment on Canvas.

<u>Module 3, Weeks 4 and 5: Early Nationhood</u>

1. This unit covers chapters 5–8 of Doc Hendley's book as well as the following online resources on Dominican history and studying abroad:

   a. "Dominican Republic Declares Independence as a Sovereign State," The History Channel — This Day in History. https://www.history.com/this-day-in-history/dominican-republic-declares-independence.

   b. "Dominican Republic History, 1821–1916," dr1. https://dr1.com/articles/history_1.shtml.

   c. "U.S. Occupation of the Dominican Republic," ThoughtCo., February 13, 2019. https://www.thoughtco.com/us-occupation-of-the-dominican-republic-2136380.

   d. Video: "Banana Wars: The American Invasion of the Dominican Republic," July 13, 2019. https://www.youtube.com/watch?v=_LjM7enC16Y.

   e. Suzy Strutner, "The 5 Types of Travelers You Don't Want to Be… Or Be With," *Huffpost*, September 28, 2013. https://www.huffpost.com/entry/types-of-traveler_n_3998506.

2. Assignments:

   a. Discussion: From the web reading and video: What difficulties did the Dominican Republic experience in becoming an independent nation? What impact do you think this environment would have on the political, economic, and cultural climate of the newly independent country?

   b. Discussion: At the end of this section, Doc takes an R&R, returns to North Carolina after his latest trip to Darfur, and experiences some significant reverse culture shock.
   Why do you think this return was so difficult for Doc? Have you ever experienced culture shock (when traveling) or reverse culture shock (on your return)? What would you say are methods for dealing with culture shock/reverse culture shock?

Module 4, Weeks 6, 7, and 8: Instability and Trujillo

1. This unit covers chapters 9–12 of Doc Hendley's book as well as the following online resources on Dominican history and studying abroad:

   a. Murray Illson, "Trujillo Regime: Cruel, Ruthless" *The New York Times*, June 13, 1975. https://www.nytimes.com/1975/06/13/archives/trujillo-regime-cruel-ruthless-dominican-dictator-ruled-30-years.html.

   b. Marlon Bishop and Tatiana Fernandez, "80 Years On, Dominicans and Haitians Revisit Painful Memories of Parsley Massacre," NPR Parallels, October 7, 2017. https://www.npr.org/sections/parallels/2017/10/07/555871670/80-years-on-dominicans-and-haitians-revisit-painful-memories-of-parsley-massacre.

   c. "The Mirabal Sisters (1924/27/35-1960): The Sisters Who Toppled A Dictatorship" Rejected Princesses. https://www.rejectedprincesses.com/princesses/the-mirabal-sisters.

   d. Watch the film: *In the Time of the Butterflies*

2. Assignments:

   a. Discussion: How does the film's portrayal of the Trujillo regime compare to the web readings for this unit? What do you think was the overall significance of "the butterflies"?

   b. Knowledge Check: From the chapters in *Wine to Water*: What do you think about Doc's determination and optimism? How do you think you would feel or react under similar circumstances?

   c. Discussion: The purpose of this discussion is to keep you focused on your PowerPoint project. What you need to do:

      i. Talk about how you are going about your research, including sources you're looking at and obstacles you've encountered.

      ii. Ask questions of your classmates on areas you could use assistance.

      iii. Respond to your classmates & offer ideas and help.

<u>Module 5, Weeks 9, 10, and 11: Transition to Democracy</u>

1. This unit covers chapters 13–16 of Doc Hendley's book as well as the following online resources on Dominican history and studying abroad (the list here looks like a lot, but they are short readings):

    a. From Richard A. Haggerty, ed. *Dominican Republic: A Country Study*. Washington: GPO for the Library of Congress, 1989:

        i.   "Transition to Elected Government," http://countrystudies.us/dominican-republic/12.htm.

        ii. "Civil War and United States Intervention," http://countrystudies.us/dominican-republic/13.htm.

        iii. Joaquín Balaguer, 1966–78.

        iv. "Antonio Guzmán, 1978–82," http://countrystudies.us/dominican-republic/15.htm.

        v.   "Political Developments Since 1978," http://countrystudies.us/dominican-republic/64.htm.

    b. Sarah Tilotta, "Who's a Citizen? The Question Dividing the Island of Hispanola" NPR Parallels, August 16, 2014. https://www.npr.org/sections/parallels/2014/08/16/340412191/whos-a-citizen-the-question-dividing-the-island-of-hispaniola.

    c. Jasmine Garsd, "Cradle of Black Pride: Haiti, Dominican Republic and the Music in Between," NPR Alt.Latino, February 13, 2014. https://www.npr.org/sections/altlatino/2014/02/13/271594220/cradle-of-black-pride-haiti-dominican-republic-and-the-music-in-between.

2. Assignments:

    a. Knowledge Check: Briefly describe the transitions that Dominican politics went through in the post-Trujillo period and explain whether you would consider the country to have a stable democracy or not.

    b. Discussion: In the early nationhood unit, we examined how the D.R. was tied to Haiti in the immediate post-independence period and how it eventually became its own nation. In the instability and Trujillo unit, we read about the Parsley Massacre perpetrated by the dictatorship. In the current unit, we have articles and a brief video on relations and tensions between the DR and Haiti.

For this discussion, please discuss the issues between the two cultures and countries and how they relate to the tensions that go back to the early national period.

c. Discussion: In the chapters for this unit, Doc goes through some of the most violent experiences of his time in Darfur, and as his time is coming to an end, he shares this thought: "So what's the point? . . . What have I truly accomplished here?" (p. 220).

For this discussion, you should evaluate: 1) what were Doc's accomplishments in Darfur? 2) how did the experiences of this time in Darfur, combined with changes he made upon coming home (including meeting and marrying his wife Amber), lead to him making Wine to Water his full-time life pursuit?

Module 6, Weeks 12 and 13: Present Day Dominican Republic

1. This unit covers chapters 17–20 of Doc Hendley's book; these chapters deal with the water crisis on the island of Hispaniola following the devasting earthquake of 2010.

2. Students additionally used the following online resources:

a. Video: "The Life and Culture of the Dominican Republic People — North Coast DR," June 7, 2016. https://www.youtube.com/watch?v=XUQt3BCRBAA.

b. Video: "The Origin of Caribbean Spanish Accents," November 30, 2011. https://www.youtube.com/watch?v=U-wqPc8lFh4.

3. Assignments:

a. Knowledge Check: After finishing Doc's book, reflect upon your biggest takeaway(s) from Doc's story/journey. What is something you think everyone can or should learn from Doc?

b. Discussion: How do the situation(s) Doc faced in the Dominican Republic and Haiti relate to the history we have studied this semester?

Module 7, Week 14: PowerPoint Research Project
1. Students use this week to complete and submit their research PowerPoint project.

Module 8, Week 15: Service-Learning in the Dominican Republic
Providing the study abroad schedule and travel reflection questions in the syllabus is important. This inclusion helps students begin to think about the experience from the very start of the semester. I would also refer to the journal questions in online discussions and meetings before travel, as this task helps students flesh-out anxieties they may be feeling before the trip.
1. Spend eight days (two days of travel and six days in-country) in the Dominican Republic.
   a. Work in the Wine to Water factory learning from the Dominican workers about the process of creating water filters and making them with instruction from the Dominican workers.
   b. Visit schools with local Wine to Water employees to present water hygiene programs.
   c. Help to conduct educational sessions with families receiving water filters.
   d. Conduct follow-up surveys with families in communities using filters for three to six months.
   e. Cultural activities include visits to a local Dominican church, the Mirabal Museum, and a local artisan market.
2. Assignments:
   a. Study abroad reflective journaling (grading is based on answering the questions and relation of the response to your experience of the day):
      i. Day 1: What challenged you today? About travel, the Wine to Water facility, the dorms, etc.
      ii. Day 2: What surprised you today? This is our first full day in the DR—think about what you observed about people, the town, foods, or other things that impacted you.

     iii. Day 3: Describe an indelible memory you experienced today.

     iv. Day 4: What have you observed from the trip that relates to the history we studied before traveling?

     v. Day 5: What is something you have experienced since you arrived that changed your perspective on Dominican culture, society, or history?

     vi. Day 6: What challenged you today (good or bad) when working for and alongside Dominican Wine to Water employees?

     vii. Day 7: This is our free day spent at the beach. Reflect on the differences between working in the Wine to Water factory, local communities, and being in a more touristy area of the D.R. How does this variety relate to what we learned about the culture and history before our travels?

   b. Nightly group reflection meetings—each night after our family-style dinner, we will discuss the day's activities. The Wine to Water representative working with our group co-leads this discussion.

The journal prompts and the nightly group reflection meetings are some of the most rewarding parts of the experience, for students and instructors alike. The prompts are general enough that they can be adapted to any study abroad experience, whether it includes ISL or not. This setup is intentional as ISL can be an emotionally challenging experience, and the general nature of the questions allows students to decide their comfort level with disclosing thoughts and feelings in the journals. I have found that encouraging students to work on journal prompts after the nightly group reflections leads them to be more thoughtful in their journal writing.

Assignments and Rubrics

The assignments and rubrics below have been created in such a way so that they are easily adapted to other course topics and disciplines with minimal language changes.

Discussion Assignment

Discussion Guidelines:

- Things to note:
  - The prompts I used for the discussion assignments are incorporated into the "Class Schedule" above.
  - The rubric for the discussion assignment can also be used to evaluate the PowerPoint research project check-in discussion. However, in the case of that discussion, it is also important to leave comments on any student questions or requests for assistance with their research.
- Directions for the Discussion (note: these stay the same for all discussions):
  - Start a new conversation thread on the discussion topic.
  - Show that you have read the chapters in the book and watched the relevant online resources for the unit by using information from them when responding to the discussion prompt and your classmate(s).
  - Demonstrate that you have thought about the question(s)— or the comments of fellow students—and respond with information AND analysis.
  - Post at least THREE times (3x)—once starting a new conversation thread and at least twice in response to a classmate's post.
    - Please make your introductory post by the Thursday before the discussion is due to allow time to interact with classmates.
    - All posts must be completed by the Sunday due date.
  - Ensure that your responses do not just politely agree but work to further the discussion's information and analysis.
  - Feel free to agree OR disagree with others, but always be respectful and supportive of others in your comments, even when you disagree with, or correct, information presented by others.
  - NOTE: You will not necessarily find direct answers to the discussion prompts in the readings and other resources for the

unit. Instead, you should discuss your ideas on the prompts and support your thoughts with information from the reading, film, and PowerPoint.

Discussion Rubric:

Criteria	1	2	3	4	Feedback
Created new thread and had at least 2 responses: easy points—simply do all you are supposed to do in the discussion.					
Proper support of classmates: worked to support your classmates and when disagreeing did so in a polite manner.					
Prepared for discussion & posting on time					
Clearly expressed views supported by evidence: your primary post responds to all parts of the discussion prompt and contains information and analysis from the work for the unit. This demonstrates that you have done the unit's work and thought about how to engage on the prompt with your classmates.					
Responses to classmates' work: adds information or analysis not already seen in the thread you are responding to.					

1 = unsatisfactory; 2 = partially meets expectations; 3 = meets expectation; 4 = exceeds expectations

Knowledge Check Assignment

Knowledge Check Guidelines:

- The prompts I used for the knowledge check assignments are incorporated into the "Class Schedule" above.
- Directions for the Knowledge Check Assignments:
  - These are expected to be your personal reflections on the information in the unit.
  - The primary expectations are:
    - The assignment is cleanly written with an academic tone, free of grammatical and spelling errors.
    - Responses contain content from the readings and other resources from the module.
    - Responses contain analysis that takes the information beyond simply restating what was in the readings and other resources from the module.

Knowledge Check Rubric:

Expectation	1	2	3	4	Feedback
Academic tone: assignment is cleanly written, free of grammatical and spelling errors.					
Content: response clearly connects to information from readings, videos, and podcasts assigned in the module.					
Analysis: response relates what was in the readings and other resources to a broader evaluation of the topic.					

1 = unsatisfactory; 2 = partially meets expectations; 3 = meets expectation; 4 = exceeds expectations

PowerPoint Research Project

The objectives and directions for this project are taken directly from my course, and are therefore related to Dominican history and the water crisis.

These guidelines are created to be generic enough so that they can be easily adapted to other course topics and disciplines with minimal changes to the language.

Activity:
- Create a PowerPoint research project based upon an aspect of Dominican history/culture or the Dominican water crisis.

Objectives:
- Students will research a topic on Dominican history, culture, or a topic related to the water crisis in the Dominican Republic.
  - You are encouraged to choose a topic related to your major or minor field of study.
- Stages of the research project:
  - Submit a research topic proposal for approval
    - Schedule an online meeting with me to discuss your research topic choice and submit the topic in the online assignment.
  - Research check-in discussion
    - Post the following in the Research Check-in Discussion:
      - Topic of your research and why the topic interests you
      - Sources you have consulted thus far
      - Any questions or requests for assistance around finding sources, formulating your argument, tying your topic into Dominican history, and more
      - Grading is based on the rubric used for online discussions in the class
  - Final Research project
    - Created in PowerPoint and posted in our online discussion to be viewed and discussed with classmates
  - Students submit a one-page written abstract and a bibliography of their project

<u>Final Research Project:</u>
- PowerPoint requirements:
  - Ten slides minimum
  - Use at least eight academic scholarly sources (books, journal articles) and at least two primary source documents
  - Citations must be included throughout the PowerPoint when necessary and in the Chicago Manual of Style format
  - Using sources assigned for the course is acceptable, but only one of them may count within the source number requirement
  - PowerPoint should be engaging with images, tables/charts, videos, etc.
  - The project needs to include a combination of information from your research and your analysis of the findings
  - The project should tie your research to the history we studied during the semester
- Presentation Requirements:
  - Students must record their presentations and post the recording and PowerPoint for classmates to watch and discuss
  - Recordings may be done via Zoom, Google Meets, YouTube, etc. (make sure you have allowed access to anyone with the link)
  - The presentation should expand upon the information on the PowerPoint slides, not simply read from what is contained therein

PowerPoint Project Grading:

Expectation	1	2	3	4	Comments on rating.
Organization and Grammar: PowerPoint is clearly organized and does not contain issues with organization, grammar, spelling, and other technical issues.					
Content and Analysis: Presentation contains a combination of information and analysis that is clear, does a thorough job of explaining the topic, and demonstrates that the presenters found and analyzed sufficient research sources to cover the topic. Presentation meets the time and length requirements.					
Creativity: PowerPoint contains images, tables, quotes, music, and/or other supplements that support the information in the presentation and that make the presentation more creatively appealing to the audience. The creative nature of the materials is clearly connected and lends to the presentation topic.					
Citations: Citations are provided when needed to support quotes, factual information that is not common knowledge, or for copyright images and are properly formatted in Chicago Manual of Style formatting.					

Expectation	1	2	3	4	Comments on rating.
Bibliography: Bibliography contains at minimum all required primary and secondary sources. The bibliography is in Chicago Manual of Style formatting and in proper alphabetical order by author's last name or website title if no author is named.					
Presentation: Presenter clearly expands upon the information on the slides with explanations of bullet points, data, photos, and other graphics, either through audio explanation or through PowerPoint notes.					

1 = unsatisfactory; 2 = partially meets expectations; 3 = meets expectation; 4 = exceeds expectations

Immersive Assignments and Learning Experiences in the Classroom

Acting out History:

Using Student Plays to Engage Historical Content

Daron W. Olson

In recent years, innovative approaches to teaching have emphasized the importance of making students an integral part of the learning process and ensuring they are not merely the professor's passive observers. One of the more successful approaches has been active learning, a technique in which students are in control of the learning process. Two noteworthy active learning approaches have been simulation and role playing. The use of plays—scripted performances done before a live audience—offer another avenue, and they employ elements of both simulation and role play. I have found plays to be especially useful in helping students to understand course themes and thus have employed them in upper-division history courses. I have employed two of these plays, "Her Final Hour" and "Ragnarok and Roll," to enhance the learning experience in my upper-division history courses. The use of plays would also work for classes in other disciplines.

My experience in using plays in the college classroom indicates that they help students to develop additional skills they would not learn in a class based on lecture and more traditional methods. In a 2014 article from the *American Journal of Play*, the journal interviewed three professionals who deal with early childhood education. The article addresses how storytelling, which is the purpose of a play, helps young students to increase their vocabulary, develop essential narrative abilities, and gain literacy subskills such as print awareness and phonemic awareness.[1] Because these skills are

1   "Storytelling, Story Acting, and Literacy in the Boston Public Schools." An Interview with Jason

transferable across academic disciplines, the play format can be adapted to non-history courses as well.

I have also noted that students who perform in plays for my upper-division history courses need to learn their roles much like a professional actor would. A study by Amy Steiger dealing with theatre students notes that students need to research their roles and "read history constantly, aggressively" to perform well. The play as a genre has a transformative effect that engages the student in learning and thinking critically.[2] These benefits have made me endorse the use of plays in the history classroom. Plays have provided a way for students to communicate their love of history in a non-traditional environment and helps them develop points of view they might not have considered in more traditional classrooms.

Overview of the Two Courses

Before turning to the pedagogical importance of plays in the classroom, I will briefly describe the story of each play. I should note that both plays are fictional, though plausible and designed to allow students the creative space necessary to explore course themes.

The play "Her Final Hour" was performed by students in my European Nationalism class.[3] The play, a historical fiction, revolves around a young Norwegian woman named Sigrid who is imprisoned by the German Gestapo for her activities in the Norwegian underground. At her Berlin prison cell, the audience witnesses a series of scenes involving Sigrid. In the initial scene, her chief adversary, the German officer Major Krieger, informs her she has one hour to live unless she gives him the names of the Norwegian resistance's leaders. If she relents, he will free her. He also tells her that during her final hour, she will be visited by friends, family, and acquaintances from Norway.

In the culminating prison scene, the major once again confronts Sigrid as he has done after each of her previous visitors. He tells her she will not be killed because her knowledge makes her too valuable. However, he

Sachs, Ben Mardell, and Marina Boni. *American Journal of Play*, Vol. 6 No. 2 (Winter 2014): 176.

2   Amy Steiger, "Re-Membering Our Selves: Acting, Critical Pedagogy, and the Plays of Naomi Wallace." *Theatre Topics* Vol. 21 Iss 1 (March 2011): 28–29.

3   The course is HIST-B408, European Nationalism and Identity.

relates that his superiors demand blood and he has negotiated for her life. In exchange, she must write down one of her guests' names, who will be executed. After much torment, Sigrid writes on a piece of paper and hands it to him. At this moment the formal play ends and a question-and-answer session with the audience ensues. The audience members are asked whose name they think Sigrid wrote down.

Through her interactions with visitors, Sigrid is confronted with various motivations for either giving up the resistance leaders' names or refusing to do so. By performing in the play, students are provided with a realistic scenario in which issues of national loyalty can be addressed. Rather than viewing patriotism in abstract terms, the students see that making a simple decision becomes much more complicated. For example, the professor argues in a philosophical vein that the future of Norway depends on Sigrid remaining strong and being willing to die to protect the leaders of the Home Front, something he admits he would not have the courage to do. Meanwhile, sister Maren, out of love for Sigrid, wants her to give up the names without regard for larger causes.

"Ragnarok and Roll" was performed by the students in my Scandinavian history course.[4] A comedy noir and historical fiction, the play presents a behind-the-scenes view of a bungling Swedish film company and its attempt to produce a post-apocalyptic play about Vikings and Zombies. Although set in contemporary Sweden, the play aims to explore several historical themes. Among these are (1) the Viking legacy; (2) the role of the state, especially the welfare state; (3) who is truly Swedish and how one must look and act; (4) how non-Scandinavians view Scandinavians; and (5) showing that Scandinavia has traditionally interacted with the outside world.

In comical fashion, "Ragnarok and Roll" details a series of circumstances that threaten the completion of the film. The first obstacle occurs when the producer is unable to obtain additional funding for the film from a local bank. In another scene, the audience learns that the lead actor and actress, despite looking very Nordic, are in fact immigrants—the male lead is Polish, and the female lead is Irish. Further complicating this scenario is the fact that the male lead has difficulty reading the script in Swedish. The producer

4   The course is HIST-B444, The Scandinavian Model.

hired the two immigrants to save costs since unionized Swedish actors cost too much. However, the female lead has an ally in a government official from the labor ministry and any time the two lead actors are harassed, the official shows up to confront the producer and director. These actions are particularly irritating to the American director, who resorts to snide comments about the Swedish welfare state's oppressive socialist hand.

In subsequent scenes, the audience learns the two immigrant actors have a different perception of Scandinavia than do native Swedes. For example, the male lead has a Swedish understudy, who despite his Shakespearean training, failed to land the role because he is short in stature, has dark hair and beard, and dark eyes. The understudy constantly mocks the Polish actor for not being a "true Viking." In a costuming scene, the two immigrant actors insist on wearing horned Viking helmets, a choice that brings derision from the Swedish production crew. The scene is complicated, however, when a Finnish musician from the Viking metal band Val Halen shows up with his guitar, wearing a horned Viking helmet. He has arrived to help produce the film's musical score. The tension in the scene between the immigrant actors and native Swedes highlights the mythical status the Viking age has taken on as a historical symbol for Scandinavia, yet one that perhaps has more significance to non-Swedes.

In the culminating scene, the production team learns that live ammunition was accidentally introduced to the set, resulting in a leg wound to the lead actress. A few minutes later, the film appears completely doomed when the studio owner arrives and declares the studio closed unless the money owed can be produced. The production is saved at the final minute when a video call from the People's Film Commission of North Korea announces it will fund the the film's production. The short video call ends with the Korean spokesperson donning a horned Viking helmet and saying, "Go Vikings!" The two immigrant actors then ask if they will be wearing horned helmets in the movie, the producer reluctantly agrees, and the play ends.

In five short scenes, this modern-day comedy noir permitted the performing students to address the five historical themes in a challenging approach: the Viking legacy; the role of the state; Swedish identity; how non-Scandinavians view Scandinavians; and the larger influence of the outside world. By deconstructing commonly held assumptions about

Scandinavia, the play allowed the students to evaluate these ideas in a more relatable fashion than provided by readings alone. In effect, it presented them with the ability to "step inside" Sweden and view Scandinavia from a unique perspective.

As might be expected, the process of implementing a play in conjunction with a history course requires several steps. It should first be noted that putting on a play works best in an upper-division course with a smaller group of students. Around ten to twelve students seems ideal for this setup. In terms of the two plays described, the original ideas usually came from me as the professor, though I often benefited from talks with colleagues or students who would be taking the course. As part of the course requirement, students were informed at the first class meeting that they would be performing in a play related to the course as their culminating group project. The play is performed in front of a live audience on campus and takes place late in the semester. I would then introduce the basic idea for the play, albeit in very rough form. The students are then informed they should be thinking about the kinds of characters that should be in the play, including the type of character they would like to play. I should mention that during the course, students are also doing more traditional course readings and working on research papers. During the successive weeks, usually the first half of the semester, the students and I work out which characters each of them will play and hone the plot. The students identify four to five themes from the course they want the play to examine. Giving the students control over their characters' development allows them to have ownership in the play, and enhances the active learning component of the play.

Once the cast and plot have been determined, rehearsals commence. The plays employ situational acting. For each scene, the students involved know what they are basically going to say, but they do not have lines to memorize. Since none of the students are professional actors, this method seems to work best, and makes the plays seem realistic to the audience. Normally, a play is rehearsed at least five or six times, and the students will often make suggestions to each other on how to make a scene better, such as suggesting a change to the scene or having another actor say a different line. Again, this process encourages the students to take ownership of the play. In effect, it becomes their production.

On the night of the play, they perform in front of a live audience. A colleague of mine tapes the play so the students can view it later on. As the instructor, I introduce the play to the audience and describe the scenes, if necessary. Because the students have rehearsed the play using situational acting, they are not pressured to reproduce exact lines of dialogue; instead, they only have to approximate the dialogue. Again, this factor makes the plays realistic, and allows the students to improvise their parts, which often creates wonderful moments. Once the performance is concluded, the students assemble as a group and face the audience, taking questions. This important part of the experience allows the students to inform the audience about the motivations behind the play and reinforce its themes. These exchanges often permit the students to reflect on philosophical or ethical questions raised by the audience. In effect, the audience members offer an almost-instant assessment and critique of the play.

The use of plays in teaching Scandinavian history (or other history courses) is highly satisfying because they meet several pedagogical criteria. Most importantly, the play is the culminating group experience for the students in the class. It allows them to take the themes learned in the course and apply them to a focused and directed effort. Both plays utilize the four key components of the culminating experience: (1) synthesis (creating a play on nationalism or historical legacy); (2) integration (making it part of the course); (3) critical thinking (in how the students develop their roles plus audience questions); and (4) analysis, which comes from discussions after the play and questionnaire. Moreover, the plays meet three additional keys identified in successful culminating experiences: (1) an assignment that challenges the student; (2) audience presentation, which allows for performance feedback; and (3) a visible group project that the students must produce and present.[5] Both "Her Final Hour" and "Ragnarok and Roll" met these criteria for a culminating group experience.

The use of plays falls under the pedagogical rubric of performance-based, aka drama-based, instruction. As such its approach should

5   Douglas Eder, "Assessment for Senior Assignments, Capstones, and Culminating Experiences—Done Frugally and Joyfully." 31ˢᵗ Annual International Lilly Conference on College Teaching, Miami University, Oxford, OH, November 18, 2011. I attended this session and took notes. The above observations are based on Dr. Eder's talk.

incorporate three main ideas: (1) the performance must be instructional; (2) performance-based strategies must target the subject contexts of the course; and (3) students engage critical thinking through an active-learning environment. Furthermore, performance-based instruction such as plays are highly successful because they meet the following outcomes: (1) they engage the student through individual expression; (2) they provide immediate feedback; (3) they provide visual demonstration or evidence of course learning objectives; and (4) they allow the individual student to connect with the learning community.[6] My experience with using plays in history courses suggests they indeed meet these standards.

As noted earlier, the play resembles role playing because, as Linda B. Nilson observes, it assigns "student roles in a true-to-life, problematic social or interpersonal situation that they act out, improvising the script" and in which the role play incorporates conflict between roles. Likewise, the play resembles simulation because it is "a human enactment of a hypothetical social situation that, while not necessarily realistic, does abstract key elements from reality." Furthermore, they allow "students to 'live out' the hypothesis and implications of theories, giving them intense emotional, cognitive, and behavioral experiences that they will otherwise never have."[7]

I would also like to add my own observations to the analysis of this process. I have found four criteria to be essential. They are as follows:

1. Give each student ownership of their character. Allow them to create and define the character as much as possible.

2. Allow students to make suggestions regarding the plot of the play, including how other characters behave, etc. For example, in "Her Final Hour," one student proposed the idea of a humorous, feuding married couple who disagree on whether the main character should give up the resistance leaders' names. Another example came from the play "Ragnarok and Roll"—the lead

---

6   Bridget K. Lee, "Engaging Students and Creating Authentic Learning Environments Through Drama-Based Instructional and Learning Strategies." 31st Annual International Lilly Conference on Teaching, Miami University, Oxford, OH, November 18, 2011. I attended this session and took notes. The above observations are based on Dr. Lee's talk.

7   Linda B. Nilson, *Teaching at Its Best: A Research-Based Resource for College Instructors*, 2nd ed (Boston: Anker Publishing, 2003), 121–123.

actress came up with the idea of wanting to wear a horned-helmet to provide the centerpiece of the play's Viking legacy theme.

3. The play should make "history come alive," allowing students to engage in the theoretical or historiographical issues in a realistic fashion.

4. Have an assessment mechanism. I employ four forms of assessment, which are:

   a. The audience—after the play, the audience was invited to ask the cast questions. It is important to place the students in front of the audience and expect them to answer these questions. The students should also be expected to offer their own commentary and insights. In this regard the students have done admirably.

   b. After the play, the professor should not only congratulate the students but also give positive feedback, plus any constructive criticism. The professor should also write down any observations while they are still fresh.

   c. As a requirement for the course, the students must fill out a questionnaire that asks them more detailed questions, including how well the play enhanced the learning experience (see the end of the chapter).

   d. I use a rubric to assess how well the students did in achieving key outcomes (see the end of the chapter).

Conclusion

For the conclusion, I would like to provide selected student comments from the Questionnaires:[8]

- "Rehearsing and performing actually did assist me with understanding nationalism because it put me in another's shoes and I had to make important choices using her per nationalism. I would personally state that this is a great way to learn how to empathize with another individual, more importantly to assist in

---

8   "Her Final Hour" Student Questionnaire. December, 2011.

empathizing with how the so-called 'enemy' thinks and perceives things."

- "This has been one of the best learning tools in my career as a student. The play allows the actor/student to experience in depth what people of history have experienced. Playing the role of a historical figure or in this case a fictional figure allows the students to experience history in a more realistic scenario. Listening to a lecture or other students talk does not compare to acting it out."

- "I would recommend this method, especially when it involves concepts that many people may have difficulty grasping if they spend their time just reading about the subject matter. I think the play allows students to study more of the WHY and HOW aspects of the subject, while the reading teaches us WHAT and WHEN, so both are important. By being able to incorporate all of these important elements (what, when, why, and how), I think we can grasp a more complete picture of how concepts such as nationalism theories can be applied."

Reflections on the Use of Plays in the History Class

These comments indicate that students who perform in plays get to experience history as in an "immersive environment," not merely one that is abstract. An instructor in a high school Advanced Placement European History course had his students spend a day portraying Enlightenment philosophers such as Tycho Brahe, Rene Descartes, and Voltaire. A newspaper article in the *Spokesman Review* (Spokane, WA) observed that the classroom was "packed wall-to-wall and filled with chatter about astronomy, political theory, and mathematical concepts." One student mentioned his surprise in learning how Galileo struggled to balance science and religion, while another remarked that after playing Johannes Kepler, the German astronomer, he knew the man "backward and forward."[9] As an active-learning strategy, plays allow students to achieve empathy for

9   Rob McDonald, "History comes alive in LC classroom: Advanced Placement class had students assume the roles of history's greatest thinkers in a modern salon." *Spokesman Review* (Spokane, WA) 3 December 2004, B1.

a character as well as a more critical understanding of historical context. A recent study by Freeman, et. al indicates that active learning improves student performance in STEM (Science Technology Engineering and Math) courses compared to lecture-dominated courses.[10] As an active learning strategy, the play format's immersive environment would benefit learning in non-history courses as well.

Empathy for historical subjects becomes especially important when addressing under-represented aspects of history. Often the dominant narratives of history inform students that historical actors have predominately been white males. Although students can read about historical actors who challenge this stereotype, the dynamic aspects of these actors are sometimes lost on students. The use of plays is one way to allow students to realize the complexities of historical actors. One East Bay (California) Elementary school that adopted plays to expand its students' interaction with history had successful outcomes with regard to reversing the dominant paradigm. Students at Tassajara Hills Elementary read biographies and roleplayed such characters as Martin Luther King, Jr. and Rosa Parks. One teacher at the school observed that "Play-acting historic moments makes material come alive for students and helps them identity with 'heroes from their culture and other ones.'"[11]

Studies on the benefits of active learning practices such as acting, or roleplaying, indicate that active learning environments increase motivation among students. Liudmila Mikalayeva has identified five main sources of increased student motivations, which are novelty effect, progressive goal achievement, competitive setting, peer dynamics, and multilayered experience. Two of these sources are relevant to the use of plays in history classrooms. A well designed simulation will build up skills continuously through steadily enlarging the knowledge horizon. In terms of the plays I have used, the class rehearses the play several times before performing it live.

---

10   Scott Freeman, Sarah L. Eddy, Miles McDonough, Michelle K. Smith, Nnadozie Okoroafor, Hannah Jordt, and Mary Pat Wenderoth, "Active learning increases student performance in science, engineering, and mathematics," *Proceedings of the National Academy of Sciences of the United States of America*, Vol. 111, No. 23 (Jume 10, 2014): 8410–8415.

11   Jeanine Benca, "Students see black history in new light; East Bay school highlights books that go beyond what's taught in most history classes." *Oakland Tribune* (Oakland, CA) 24 Feb. 2004: 1.

During this process, I offer feedback but so do the other students, and their collective cooperation enhances the production and gives the respective students a sense of self-efficacy for attaining it.[12]

Peer dynamics likewise play an integral role in the efficacy of a historical play. In such collaborative ventures as roleplaying or acting, peer pressure from others means students strive not to let the team down and perform well in front of peers. Their level of preparation is much more visible in simulations than in lectures, and students feel "the need to make greater individual investment."[13] As a result of this team-centered approach, plays provide students with opportunities to bond together through shared experience. Thus, students take ownership and control of their learning since having choice and control have been shown to positively increase motivation for its own stake.[14]

Students who have acted out history in my classes indicated this form of active learning enhanced their experience with historical material. By acting as characters, students present history in a collaborative framework that tells a story. Moreover, this method allows students to experience the complexity and nuance of a historical situation in ways that would not have been possible in a traditional classroom. The key is shifting from passive observer to active participant. Acting effectively allows students to have that "historical immersion" experience that is often not available in other platforms. Through the active learning offered by acting, students increase their empathy, knowledge, and comprehension of the historical actors and historical situations they are studying.

12   Liudmila Mikalayeva, Motivation, "Ownership, and the Role of the Instructor in Active Learning" *International Studies Perspectives*, Vol. 17 No. 2 (May 2016): 215–217.

13   Ibid, 217. See also Patrick J. McCarthy and Liam Anderson, "Active Learning Techniques versus Traditional Teaching Styles: Two Experiments from History and Political Science" *Innovative Higher Education* 24: 279–294.

14   Mikalayeva, 217.

Sample Syllabus Overview

HIST-B408 European Nationalism and Identity

Generic Course Description:

"This course explores the development of European nationalism and identity by: (1) explaining what nationalism is; (2) summarizing the basic interpretations of nationalism; (3) comparing different types of national identity; and (4) applying nationalism in historical context."

General Course Learning Objectives (CLOs):

Students who pass this course with a C grade or higher will be able to:

1. Explain what nationalism is
2. Summarize the basic interpretations of nationalism
3. Compare different types of national identity
4. Apply nationalism in historical context
5. Interpret nationalism through the class play

Suggested Course Reading Materials:

1. *Nations and Nationalism: A Reader*. Edited by Philip Spencer and Howard Wollman. New Brunswick, NJ: Rutgers University Press, 2005.
2. Anthony D. Smith, *Myths and Memories of the Nation*. (Oxford and New York: Oxford UP, 1999).
3. Anthony D. Smith, *Nationalism and Modernism: A Critical Survey of Recent Theories of Nations and Nationalism*. (London and New York: Routledge, 1998).

Suggested Course Assignments:

1. Individual and Group Reflection Papers
2. Group Discussions over Key Topics
3. Quizzes for Subject Assessments
4. Student Character Creation

5. Class Play
6. Research Paper

Suggested Course Schedule:

In this upper-division undergraduate course, which is 15 weeks long, I approached the teaching of nationalism as one involving a certain level of subject mastery with the application of nationalism using the class play. As the class worked on the play while still doing readings and other activities, I used their feedback to help them prepare for the play while also seeking their feedback on how to improve the play.

Week #1: Introduction, What is Nationalism, and Why are We Doing a Play on Nationalism?
1. On the first day we go over the syllabus and I inform the students about the play. I ask them why I would think having them do a play is a good idea in a course on European nationalism and identity.
2. We start with the background of nationalism by studying the French Revolution

Week #2: Theories of Nationalism, Part I.
1. Assign Spencer and Wollman, Introduction and Chapters 1–5; Smith, *Nationalism and Modernism,* pp. 8–24, 27–44; 117–142.
2. Group Discussions on theories of nationalism
3. Assign individual and/or group Reflection Paper

Week #3: Theories of Nationalism, Part II.
1. Assign Spencer and Wollman, various readings; Smith, *Myths and Memories,* pp. 3–55; 97–123; Smith *Nationalism and Modernism,* pp. 170–198.
2. Group Discussions on theories of nationalism
3. Discuss initial idea of class play, "Her Final Hour." Ask students about potential roles they could play in this production.
4. Assign individual and/or group Reflection Paper

<u>Week #4: National Identity, Part I.</u>

1. Assign Anthony D. Smith, *Nationalism: Theory, Ideology, History*, 2nd ed. (Cambridge: Polity Press, 2001, 2010), pp. 9–46 (this is an outside reading I use because it really frames what national identity is about).

2. Assign some examples of myth, memory, and national identity. Here are a couple that I use: *Bo Stråth, "Introduction: Myth, Memory, and History in the Construction of Community" (*Myth and Memory*): 19–46.

3. *Hayden White, "Catastrophe, Communal Memory, and Mythic Discourse: The Uses of Myth in the Reconstruction of Society" (*Myth and Memory*): 49–74.

4. *Lutz Niethammer, "Maurice Halbwachs: Memory and the Feeling of Identity" (*Myth and Memory*): 75–93.

5. Outside of class, using our online course site, I have them watch *Mrs. Miniver*, which is a pro-British WWII film.

6. Group Discussion of why national identity is important and why national memory is different from historical memory.

7. Additional discussion about student roles in the play. For next week, they must submit a basic description and share with class.

8. Assign individual and/or group Reflection Paper.

<u>Week #5: National Identity and Foundation Myths.</u>

1. Assign example readings. Here are some I like to use:
Hugh Trevor-Roper, "The Invention of Tradition: The Highland Tradition of Scotland" in *The Invention of Tradition*, eds Eric Hobsbawm and Terrence Ranger (Cambridge: Cambridge UP, 1983):15–41. Wolfgang Kaschuba, "The Emergence and Transformation of Foundation Myths" (*Myth and Memory*): 217–226. *Arve Thorsen, "Foundation Myths at Work: National Day Celebrations in France, Germany and Norway in a Comparative Perspective" (*Myth and Memory*): 331–350. Markus Kornprobst, "Episteme, Nation-Building and National Identity: the Reconstruction of Irishness," *Nations and Nationalism* 11:3(2005): 403–421.

2. Group Discussion on what foundation myths are and how they inform different national identities.
3. Students share a basic description of their characters and the significance of their roles in the play.
4. Assign individual and/or group Reflection Paper.
5. Take First Quiz over material covered in the first four weeks.

Week #6: The Role of History in National Myths.
1. Assign examples of this approach. Here are three I like to use:
Henry Kamen, "The Myth of the Historical Nation" in his *Imagining Spain*, 1–37;
John Hutchinson, "Archaeology and the Irish Rediscovery of the Celtic Past," *Nations and Nationalism* 7(4) (2001):505–519; Adrian Lyttelton, "Creating a National Past: History, Myth, and Image in the Risorgimento" in *Making and Remaking Italy*, eds Albert Russel Ascoli and Krystyna von Henneberg, 27–74. I also assign YouTube videos as there are several on the subject.
2. Group Discussions on why history is important to national identity.
3. I present the basic outline of the play "Her Final Hour." Students offer feedback and we decide which suggestions to incorporate into the play.
4. Assign individual and/or group Reflection Paper.

Week #7: Class and National Identity.
1. Assign readings on the topic. Here are some I like to use:
Uffe Østergård, "Nation-Building Danish Style" in *Nordic Paths to National Identity*, 37–53; Bo Stråth, "The Swedish Path to National Identity" in *Nordic Paths to National Identity*, 55–63; Patrick O'Mahony and Gerard Delanty, "Nationalist Mobilisation and the Cultural Construction of the Irish Nation" in their *Rethinking Irish History*, 60–93; Sheila Fitzpatrick, "The Bolshevik Invention of Class" in her *Tear Off the Masks!*, 29–50
DVD "Battleship Potempkin" (they watch this on the online course site).

2. Group Discussion on why class would be an important factor in the creation of national identity. We also discuss who in society creates national identity—is it a top-down process or can those of the lower or middle classes be leaders of such movements?

3. Further discussion of the play. First rehearsal (this is a very rudimentary run-through and I make sure someone is taking notes as we will often make changes to the initial script).

4. Assign individual and/or group Reflection Paper.

Week #8: Race and National Identity.

1. Assign readings on the topic. Here are some I like to use:
   Etienne Balibar, "Racism and Nationalism," (Spencer and Wollman): 163–172.
   Krishan Kumar, "The Moment of Englishness" in his *The Making of English National Identity*, 175–225; Péter Apor, "The Creative Fear: Fascism, Anti-Semitism, Democracy and the Foundation of the People's Democracy in Hungary" (*Myth and Memory*): 263–279; Susannah Heschel, "Draining Jesus of Jewishness," *The Aryan Jesus: Christian Theologians and the Bible in Nazi Germany*, 26–66.

2. Group Discussions on how race informs national identity. What happens when racism becomes the core of national identity?

3. Second rehearsal of the class play after students suggest any new ideas.

4. Assign individual and/or group Reflection Paper.

Week #9: National Identity: National Heroes and Monuments.

1. Assign readings. Here are some I like to use:
   Lucy Riall, *Garibaldi: The Invention of a Hero* (New Haven: Yale UP, 2007), 129–163, 185–206; Lars Berggren, "Monuments in the Making of Italy" (*Myth and Memory*): 169–186; Rudy Koshar, "Monuments," *From Monuments to Traces: Artifacts of German Memory, 1870–1990*, 15–79.

2. Discussion on why nations need heroes. In class group exercise: assign them a European nation and have them sketch the outlines of a fictional hero for that nation.

3. Third rehearsal of the class play.
4. Second Quiz for material covered in Weeks 4–8.
5. Hand out prompt for the research paper and discuss requirements with students.
6. Optional: assign individual or group Reflection Paper (students who have turned in all previous Reflection Papers do not need to turn in on this week).

Week #10: Language and National Identity.

1. Assign readings: Here are some I use:
   Charles Blattberg, "Secular Nationhood? The Importance of Language in the Life of Nations," *Nations and Nationalism* 12:4(2006): 597–612; Hubertus F. Jahn, "'Us': Russians and Russianness" in *National Identity in Russian Culture*, eds Simon Franklin and Emma Widdis, 53–73; Pille Petersoo, "Reconsidering Otherness: Constructing Estonian Identity," *Nations and Nationalism* 13:1(2007): 117–133; Risto Alapuro, "Nineteenth-Century Nationalism in Finland" in *Nordic Paths to National Identity*, 55–74.
2. Discussion on how language can be a pillar of national identity and how it can impact ethnic nationalisms within nations.
3. Fourth rehearsal for the play. Students submit a one-page character description they share with the other students. Other students can offer feedback, including suggestions on how to improve the other students' characters in the play.
4. Assign Research Paper Proposal and Five Primary Sources (due next week).
5. Assign individual and/or group Reflection paper.

Week #11: Transnational Identity.

1. Assign readings. Here are some I use:
   H. Arnold Barton, "The Cultural Vision" in his *Sweden and Visions of Norway*, 87–117; Ezequiel Adamovsky, "Russia as a Space of Hope: Nineteenth-Century French Challenges to the Liberal Image of Russia" *European History Quarterly* (2003:3): 411–449;

Bo Stråth, "The Baltic as Image and Illusion: The Construction of a Region between Europe and the Nation" (*Myth and Memory*): 199–214.

2. Group Discussions on why regional identities exist. In-class assignment: make an argument for a new regional identity. Have groups critique each other.
3. Fifth rehearsal for the play. Students discuss costume options for the play.
4. Students submit Research Paper Proposal and Five Primary Sources.
5. Assign Research Paper: Five Secondary Sources (due next week).
6. Assign individual and/or group Reflection Paper.

Week #12: Empires and National Identity.

1. Assign readings. Here are come I like to use:
Catherine Hall, "The Nation Within and Without," in *Defining the Victorian Nation: Class, Race, Gender and the Reform Act of 1867*, Catherine Hall, Keith McClelland, and Jane Rendell, eds (Cambridge: Cambridge UP, 2000), 179–233; Krishan Kumar, "Empire and English Nationalism," *Nations and Nationalism* 12:1(2006):1–13; George V. Strong, *Seedtime for Fascism: the Disintegration of Austrian Political Culture, 1867–1918*(Armonk, NY and London: M.E. Sharpe, 1998), 3–18, 86–106; Gunda Barth-Scalmani, Hermann J.W. Kuprian, and Brigitte Mazohl-Wallnig, "National Identity or Regional Identity: Austria Versus Tyrol/Salzburg" in *Austrian Historical Memory and National Identity*, Günter Bischof and Anton Pelinka, eds (New Brunswick, NJ and London: Transaction Publishers, 1997):32–63.
2. Group Discussions: Why does nationalism work within some empires but not others?
3. Sixth rehearsal for the play.
4. Assign individual and/or group Reflection Paper.

Week #13: Student Presentations on Research Papers.
1. Students present their created nations, including national identity.
2. Seventh and final rehearsal for the play.
3. Third Quiz over material covered in weeks 9–12.

Week #14: Student Presentations on Research Papers and Class Play.
1. Remaining students present their created nations and national identities.
2. Class play performed in front of a live audience on campus.
3. Students take Class Play Questionnaire.

Week #15: Final Examination.
1. Students take the Final Examination.
2. Students turn in questionnaire about the play.
3. During the final weeks of the semester, I have been having individual meetings with students to go over their research papers. They are required to submit early drafts that I critique.
4. Students submit their research papers.

Sample Syllabus Overview

HIST-B444 The Scandinavian Model

Generic Course Description:
"This course explores modern Scandinavia by 1) identifying the key events and people of modern Scandinavia; 2) interpreting transnational forces that shaped the region; 3) assessing the validity of a unique Scandinavian model of historical development; 4) illustrating important themes of modern Scandinavia through the play performance."

General Course Learning Objectives (CLOs):
Students who pass this course with a C grade or higher will be able to:
1. Identify the key events and people of modern Scandinavia
2. Interpret transnational forces that shaped the region

3. Assess the validity of a unique Scandinavian model of historical development
4. Illustrate the important themes of modern Scandinavia through the play performance
5. Summarize Scandinavia's contributions in the modern world

Suggested Course Reading Materials:

1. Byron J. Nordstrom, *Scandinavia since 1500* (Minneapolis and London: University of Minnesota Press, 2000).
2. Mary Hilson, *The Nordic Model* (London: Reaktion Books, 2008).
3. Francis Sejersted, *The Age of Social Democracy: Norway and Sweden in the Twentieth Century* (Princeton, NJ: Princeton University Press, 2011).
4. Veli-Pekka Lehtola, *The Sámi People: Traditions in Transition.* Revised Second Edition (Fairbanks: University of Alaska Press, 2004).

Suggested Course Assignments:

1. Individual and Group Reflection Papers
2. Group Discussions over key topics
3. Quizzes for Subject Assessments
4. Student Character Creation
5. Class Play
6. Research Paper

Suggested Course Schedule:

In my course, which is 15 weeks long, the students need to understand the concept of a special path of historical development known by the German term Sonderweg. First, I have them tackle the concept of the Sonderweg and then, as they explore the history of modern Scandinavia, they can assess whether such a concept is valid for Scandinavia. I have listed the basic readings from the recommended textbooks. Instructors should add outside readings or videos as they see fit. As the class worked on the class play, I used their feedback to help them prepare for the play while also seeking their feedback on how to improve the play.

Week #1: Course Introduction; the Concept of the Scandinavian Model, and Why are We Doing a Play on Modern Scandinavia?
1. On the first day we go over the syllabus and I inform the students about the play. I talk briefly about the concept of the Scandinavian Model and have a short discussion.
2. I ask them why I would think having them do a play is a good idea in a course on European nationalism and identity.
3. At the end of the week I give a short background lecture on Scandinavia prior to 1500.

Week #2: An Introduction to the Sami. Early Modern Scandinavia.
1. Assign Lehtola, pp. 9–33; Nordstrom, Chapters 3 and 4. Mary Elizabeth Ailes, "Wars, Widows, and State Formation in 17th-Century Sweden"; *Kekke Stadin, "The Masculine Image of a Great Power."
2. Group Discussion on the Sami: who are they and what is their relationship to Scandinavian majority?
3. Assign individual and/or group Reflection Paper.

Week #3: Scandinavia and the Age of Enlightenment.
1. Assign Nordstrom, chapters 5–7; Lehtola; 34–35; H.Arnold Barton, *Scandinavia in the Revolutionary Era*, 1760–1815, pp. 359–383.
2. Group Discussion: How did the Enlightenment impact Scandinavia? Was it different from the rest of Europe?
3. Assign individual and/or group Reflection Paper.

Week #4: The Long Nineteenth Century, part I: The Napoleonic Wars and Nationalism
1. Assign Nordstrom, Chapters 8 and 9; Lehtola, pp. 36–41; *Nordic Paths to National Identity*; YouTube: Jean Sibelius, "Finlandia"; YouTube: Edvard Grieg, "Morning Mood."
2. Group Discussion: How did the Napoleonic Wars impact Scandinavia, especially Finland and Norway? Which challenges faced the Sami?

3. Group Assignment due at end of week. Pick one of the four nations in Nordic Paths to National Identity. Which groups in your nation favored nationalism and which ones opposed it? Why? What were the one or two key factors in the creation of your nation's national identity?

Week #5: The Long Nineteenth Century II: Modernization.
1. Assign Nordstrom, Chapters 10 and 11 (pp. 213–253); Lehtola, pp. 42–49.
2. Group Discussion: How was modernization in Scandinavia different, what was it like Europe?
3. Assign individual and/or group Reflection Paper.
4. Take First Quiz on material over weeks 1–4.

Week #6: World War I and the Interwar Years.
1. Assign Nordstrom Chapter 12, pp. 257–290; Lethtola, pp. 50–51; Henning Bro, "Housing: From Night Watchman State to Welfare State: Danish Housing Policy, 1914–1930"; Edelbalk and Olsson, "Poor Relief, Taxes, and the First Universal Pension Reform: The Origin of the Swedish Welfare State Reconsidered."
2. Group Discussion: What was the concept of Scandinavian or Nordic Neutrality? How neutral were the Scandinavian nations during World War I? Origins of the Welfare State.
3. Assign individual and/or group Reflection Paper.

Week #7: World War II.
1. Assign Nordstrom, Chapter 13, pp. 291–320; Lehtola, pp. 52–56; Sejersted, Chapter 2, pp. 50–98; Kathleen Stokker, *Folklore Fights the Nazis(excerpt)*.
2. Lecture on Scandinavia in World War II.
3. Group Discussion on Scandinavia during World War II. Forms of resistance.
4. First Discussion on the play, "Ragnarök and Roll."
5. Assign individual and/or group Reflection Paper.

Week #8: The Contemporary Era, 1945–1970.
1. Assign Nordstrom, Chapter 14, pp. 321–346; Lehtola, pp. 57–75; Sejersted, Chapters 6 and 7, pp. 185–240.
2. Group Discussion on Social Democracy and the Cold War.
3. Assign individual and/or group Reflection Paper.
4. Take Second Quiz on material over weeks 5–7.
5. Students bring rough sketch of their character for the play. First rehearsal of the play.

Week #9: The Contemporary Era: 1970–2010.
1. Assign Nordstrom Chapter 14, pp. 346–357; Lehtola, pp. 76–111; Sejersted Chapters 8, 10, and 14, pp. 241–266; 289–329; 447–456.
2. Group Discussion on the challenges to the Scandinavian Model and challenges to the Sami Life.
3. Assign individual and/or group Reflection Paper.
4. Second rehearsal of the class play after students suggest new ideas.

Week #10: The Scandinavian Model: Consensual Democracy and Economic Life.
1. Assign Hilson Chapters 1 and 2, pp. 25–86.
2. Group Discussion: Is Scandinavian democracy unique? Does Scandinavia have an economic "middle way?"
3. Assign individual and/or group Reflection Paper.
4. Assign Research Paper Proposal and Five Primary Sources (due following week).
5. Fourth rehearsal for the class play. Students submit a one-page description that they share with the other students.

Week #11: The Scandinavian Model: Social Welfare and International Relations.
1. Assign Hilson Chapters 3 and 4, pp. 87–147; Christiansen and Petersen, "The Dynamics of Social Solidarity: The Danish Welfare State, 1900–2000," Pauli Kettunen, "The Nordic Welfare State in Finland."

2. Group Discussion: Is the Scandinavian Welfare State radically different? Which principles guide Scandinavian foreign relations?
3. Take Third Quiz on material from weeks 8–10.
4. Assign individual and/or group Reflection Paper.
5. Assign Research Paper Preliminary Draft and Five Secondary Sources (due the following week).
6. Fifth rehearsal for the class play. Students discuss costume options.

Week #12: The Scandinavian Model: Equality and Ethnicity; Conclusion.
1. Assign Hilson, Chapter 5 and Conclusion, pp. 148–187.
2. Group Discussion: How equal is Scandinavia? Who belongs to the Scandinavian nations and who does not?
3. Assign individual and/or group Reflection Paper.
4. Assign Research Paper First Rough Draft.
5. Sixth rehearsal for the class play.

Week #13: Rehearsal and Research.
1. Students continue to work on their Research Papers.
2. Seventh and final rehearsal for the class play.
3. Take Fourth Quiz on material covered in weeks 11–12.

Week #14: The Class Play.
1. Students continue to work on their Research Papers.
2. Students perform the play "Ragnarök and Roll."

Week #15: Finals Week.
1. Students take Play Questionnaire.
2. Students submit Essay: "Is There a Scandinavian Model of Historical Development?"
3. Students submit Research Paper.

Class Play Actor Rubric

Criteria	1	2	3	4	Feedback
Student acted in historical context					
Student developed their role					
Student's role targeted a key course theme					
Student analyzed the play in post-play discussion					
Student suggestions improved the performance					
Student's communication skills improved during the rehearsals and the play					

1=standard not met; **2**=standard partially met; **3**=standard met; **4**=exceeds expectations

Class Play Questionnaire for "Her Final Hour"

1. Did developing your character give you insight into the themes of nationalism?
2. Did you find that rehearsing and then performing in the play enhanced your understanding of nationalism?
3. Using a play in this manner is an example of an *Active Learning Model.* Do you think active learning creates a better learning environment for you as a student? Given that the discipline of History tends to study dead people, how effective is the use of play in a history course in making the past come alive?
4. Would you recommend this method of active learning to other students? What does the play allow you to do that a more traditional classroom setting does not?
5. What did you enjoy about the play? What do you think could be improved?

"Her Final Hour" Play Outline

<u>Act 1, Scene 1:</u>
*Main character, Sigrid, looking tired, sits alone in her prison cell.

*German officer, Major Krieger, enters. Tells her they have brought her visitors from her hometown. She gets to visit them, but she only has one hour to live, unless she gives up information on the Norwegian Underground to Major Krieger.

<u>Act 1, Scene 2:</u>
*A neighboring farm's son (about 22 years old). He will tell Sigrid that Norwegian morale is good, though food shortages are making it tough on some. He tries to avoid the subject of her impending death. He represents the survivor who is trying to be neutral.

*A local businessman enters her cell. He tells her that the German order is the new reality and that she should admit this fact. She asks him if he is prospering from the war. He doesn't deny it. He represents those who are willing to collaborate.

*One of Sigrid's history professors from the University visits her. He had been very idealistic about Norwegian nationalism in the classroom, but in this situation he admits that Sigrid is braver than he could ever be. She nods and simply says that she took his words to heart even if he cannot act on them. The professor represents the idealism of nationalism.

*A high school friend of Sigrid enters next. He uses humor to tell crazy stories, but in a moment of seriousness he asks her if she has given up the names. She answers no. He nods his approval. He is very much like her and represents those most willing to fight for Norway.

*Sigrid's uncle enters. He is consoling and she asks him what she should do. He tells her a parable about how inside every person are two wolves: the wolf of love and the wolf of hate. He cannot tell her what she should do, but he hopes she will choose the wolf of love. The uncle represents the philosophical side of nationalism.

*Sigrid's sister enters next. She hugs Sigrid and cries. She pleads with Sigrid to give up the names of the Underground so she can get her sister back. The sister represents the innocent side of nationalism.

*Sigrid's mother enters. She holds a crying Sigrid and comforts her. Sigrid asks her what to do and the mother says that what she wants is for her daughter to leave the prison. However, that might not be the best path for Norway. She tells Sigrid that her love of nation might be stronger than that of her mother. Thus, the mother represents the sacrifice that nationalism can require.

Act 1, Scene 3:
*After the guests have concluded their visits, Major Krieger comes in with a swagger. He asks Sigrid if she enjoyed seeing her friends and family. She nods yes. He asks her if she would like to see them again. She nods yes. All she has to do is reveal one name of an underground leader. Sigrid looks weak, tired, and haggard, but she defiantly says no. She expects the major to call in the guards, but instead he looks at her. "Very well. I should have you shot, but you are too valuable. So instead, I will have you pick one of your visitors to take your place. Who do you choose?" She takes a notepad and writes down a name.

Post-Play
*The course instructor has the students come to the front and face the audience. He/she asks the audience questions. The first is who they would have picked to take Sigrid's place. I allow the students to answer as many of the questions as possible. It allows them to share in the experience of creating the performance.

"Ragnarök and Roll" Play Outline

Act 1, Scene 1:

*Two men sit in an office in Stockholm, Sweden. One is from Sweden, and he is telling the other about his studio's latest film project called "Ragnarök and Roll," which is about a post-apocalyptic Sweden populated by Zombies and normal Swedes who resort to being Vikings in order to survive. The producer has brought in an American to help sell the film. Then, the producer gets a phone call. When he answers he says things like "oh no," and "this cannot be true" and "why are you doing this to me?" When he hangs up the phone, he informs the American director that the bank has denied his request for additional funding. The American director is quite concerned, but the Swedish producer says not to worry for they can shoot most of the scenes.

Act 1, Scene 2:

*The director meets the two lead actors. The male lead is tall with red hair and beard and the female lead is tall with long blonde hair and blue eyes. However, the director soon learns the two lead actors are immigrants—the male lead is from Poland and the female lead from Ireland. The director asks the producer why and is told it is a cost-saving move since Swedish actors are unionized. The director has the duo act out a scene, but the Polish actor keeps messing up his lines. One of the production assistants explains he has trouble reading Swedish and therefore learning his lines. The director begins to curse out the Polish actor and threatens to fire him. At this point, another man enters the scene. He is tall with dark skin and hair. However, he is a native Swede and is the union representative for Swedish actors. The female lead has contacted him with a complaint and the union representative threatens to have the production shut down for overworking the two actors. This leads to a confrontational argument between the American director and union representative. The American director resorts to snide remarks about the oppressive socialist hand of the Swedish welfare state. But he must relent to the union representative's demands.

Act 1, Scene 3:

*In this scene we see that the Polish lead continues to have problems. His Swedish understudy continually interjects the correct lines. The Swedish understudy gets irritated and complains that he is a native speaker and has Shakespearean training, but he failed to land the lead role because he is short and has dark features. The understudy constantly mocks the Polish actor for not being a "true Viking."

Act 1, Scene 4:

Next, we see a costuming scene in which the two immigrant actors insist on wearing horned Viking helmets, a choice that brings derision from the Swedish production crew, including the historian who is the technical adviser to the film. The scene is complicated, however, when a Finnish musician from the Viking metal band Val Halen (a spin on Valhalla and Van Halen, suggested by a student) shows up with a guitar, wearing a horned Viking helmet. He has arrived to help produce the musical score for the film. The scene becomes a standoff between the lead actors and the film crew. The American director bangs his head against a wall.

Act 1, Scene 5:

In the culminating scene the producer is talking with the American director, who is threatening to leave the shoot and "never set foot again in this socialist dystopia." The producer assures him that he has a couple promising potential sources of funding. They are interrupted by a member of the film crew who tells them live ammunition was accidentally introduced to the set, resulting in a leg wound to the lead female actor. A few minutes later the film appears completely doomed when the owner of the studio arrives and declares the studio closed unless the money owed can be produced. The producer, director, and owner have a tense conversation. The production is saved at the final minute when a video call from the People's Film Commission of North Korea is seen on screen. The woman spokesperson tells them the commission will fund the film's production. The short video call ends with the spokesperson donning a horned Viking helmet and saying, "Go, Vikings!" The two immigrant actors then ask if they will be wearing horned helmets in the movie and the producer reluctantly agrees as the play ends.

<u>Post-Play:</u>
The instructor and the students stand before the audience and take questions.
I allow the students to answer as many of the questions as possible. It allows
them to share in the experience of creating the performance.

Incorporating Cross-Cultural Learning in Survey-Level History Courses:

Teaching U.S. and World History through Day of the Dead Altar Building Projects

Christine C. Nemcik

Most history educators can relate to the experience of teaching a beginning-level survey class where a portion, perhaps even a majority, of the students admit they enrolled in the course for reasons other than being interested in the topic. These reasons for taking the course may range from "it fits a general education requirement," to "I have to take it for my major," to "my advisor told me it was a good idea," among others. Further discussion with those same students frequently reveals they "don't really like history," or that "history is boring," or "not really relevant" to them. Often these sentiments arise from students having previously encountered history taught as a "dead" subject, so it is understandable that they do not see its relevance to their lives. They have learned to approach history with the attitude that it is something we just need to know, and it is a subject learned through memorization.

I was just such a student when I entered my first college-level history survey course. My experience with history courses in high school was that of classes focused on memorizing names and dates and writing basic book reports. Like many students who have entered my history survey courses with a negative attitude, I determinedly did not like the course and history had no relevance to me. What I quickly discovered, however, was that history is a subject that could come alive and that transformation of history to a living subject happens best when the professor encourages students to engage in innovative ways with the subject matter and with each other. I had previously experienced this concept with courses in other disciplines, but this moment was the first time I found history, a subject I previously disliked, to be engaging. This first experience of being engaged in learning history not only sparked my love of the subject but also served as a guide to which I returned when I began my career teaching college history. I was determined to create engaged classes in which students work with the materials and each other in creative learning experiences. That is what is both unique and most significant about this current book, the sharing of engaged learning assignments transferable across disciplines, allowing other educators to easily bring meaningful experiences to their students.

Admittedly, my students have at times been dismayed at my not simply being a lecturer; some students have, at times, even complained they were not learning anything because they were not being taught through lecture. Although students claim to prefer or learn better from lectures, decades of research dating back to the 1970s show that lecture is one of the least effective forms of student learning.[1] Generally, when reflecting upon different class activities through the semester, my students realize they have gained a greater understanding of the material when working on innovative projects that push them to think about the information in new or different ways.

One method I found particularly successful for keeping students engaged in beginning-level survey courses was incorporating cross-cultural and interdisciplinary learning into classes. Innovative cross-cultural projects encourage students to relate to the course content in new and creative ways. Beyond that, innovative projects of this nature can be utilized across disciplines. This chapter will explain how I have incorporated the building of Day of the Dead altars in my fall semester "Perspectives on the World to 1500" history survey course to foster student interest in research projects by having them dig deeper into less commonly known facets of the civilizations we were studying in class.[2] The idea of using Day of the Dead altars to dig

---

1   For recent studies, see for example: Carnegie Mellon University. "Learning is more effective when active." ScienceDaily. www.sciencedaily.com/releases/2021/09/210930140710.htm., Louis Deslauriers et. al, "Measuring Actual Learning versus Feeling of Learning in Response to Being Actively Engaged in the Classroom," *Proceedings of the National Academy of Sciences* 116, no. 39 (April 2019): pp. 19251–19257, https://doi.org/10.1073/pnas.1821936116., and more.

2   Though this chapter highlights the altar assignment for an ancient world history course, I have used it successfully in a U.S. history survey course and in different Spanish language and Hispanic culture classes.

deeper into aspects of a course topic can be utilized similarly for courses in other areas. For example, students could create altars that highlight the biological advances of a particular culture for a biology class, look for detailed information on the life and works of an artist or writer for an art or English class, and more.

The information below outlines the overall structure of the course and the ways I fit the cultural project into course content. In my experience, this project, and others like it, has been a successful assignment for engaging students in the subject matter of the class and helping them see connections between different countries, regions, and cultures, all while conducting research relevant to the place and time under study. As an appendix, I have included the general course syllabus, the structure of assignment parts, and the rubrics I used to evaluate the project and that the students used as peer reviews for each other.

Course Overview

When I was first slated to teach HIST-H108, "Perspectives on the World to 1500" at Indiana University East (IUE), I was initially overwhelmed by the idea. My doctorate is in Latin American History, and I had minor studies in Western European History and United States History. My primary focus in studies and previous academic appointments was the modern world from 1500 to present. Before that course assignment at IUE, I had primarily taught courses in Latin American history, U.S. since 1865, interdisciplinary, international studies courses, and Spanish language and Hispanic Culture. My initial feeling of trepidation over how to create a course covering this early time period that was not my specialty led me to the idea of creating an interdisciplinary, cross-cultural project that fit into my comfort zone and led to the Day of the Dead altar project. I found this assignment not only fit the interdisciplinary nature of my background and teaching but also was adaptable for other history courses. It could be adopted relatively easily by others as an engaging cultural assignment for history and other disciplines as referenced above and further elaborated upon later in the chapter.

I structured my "Perspectives on the World to 1500" course for the students to learn the early history of the world through an in-depth focus on early civilizations. The textbook I used for the course was Aran MacKinnon and Elaine MacKinnon, eds. *Places of Encounter: Time, Place, and Connectivity in World History,* Volume 1. This title is a non-traditional history textbook, as the chronological history is developed through chapters that each focus on a particular early civilization. The chapters start with pre-history and the development of early civilization: "Hadar: The Legacy of Human Ancestors (4,000,000–100,000 BCE)" and "Makapansgat and Pinnacle Point: Three Million Years of Human Evolution in South Africa (3,000,000–2,000 BCE)," and go through "Potosí: a Motor of Global Change (1545–1600s)" and "Malacca: Cosmopolitan Trading Port of the Early Modern World (1500–1824)."[3] In addition to this textbook reading, students read online articles, primary source documents, and blogs about the early history of the world. We broadened our outlook on this history through discussions analyzing the readings' contents. We took this investigation further with in-class debates on the efficacy of using videos, from documentaries to parts of the "Crash Course World History," and even discussed what can be learned of history from historical fiction films.

The idea to incorporate a project focused on the Day of the Dead came partly from the format of the *Places of Encounter* textbook, which sets a foundation for learning history by concentrating on particular civilizations. While the Mexican Day of the Dead celebration is a way for families to welcome back and connect with the soul of a departed loved one, aspects of the celebration fit well with learning about the history and culture of a historical place and its people. The most recognized part of the Day of the Dead celebration is the *ofrendas*, or the altars that contain common elements of photographs, foods, drinks, and favorite items of the departed loved one. This aspect of the holiday is what students focused on in their cultural assignment. I introduced the Day of the Dead project at the start of the semester, connecting the assignment to discussions of how we learn about other people and cultures, which created a natural tie-in to the class. Additionally, most students have at least heard of the holiday, and many know of and have seen examples of *ofrendas*. This basic understanding of *ofrendas* among students was even more prevalent after the release of the

---

3   Aran MacKinnon and Elaine McClarnand MacKinnon, eds., *Places of Encounter: Time, Place, and Connectivity in World History* (Boulder, CO: Westview Press, 2012).

Disney film *Coco* in 2017, and this familiarity helped create greater buy-in to the project from students.

The Day of the Dead altar research and building was a little more than a half-semester project that took place in stages, leading up to the creation of the Day of the Dead altars in mid-October at the end of Hispanic Heritage Month. What follows are the scaffolded assignments that led to the creation of the altars, assignments that can be modified and adapted to similar projects in other areas of the humanities, social sciences, and other disciplines as well. The project started with initial full-class readings and discussions of the holiday, what is typically included in altars, and how and why the celebration can be tied into early world history. In this early stage, students did readings about the celebration's history, which, though thought by most to be a modern holiday, has its roots 3,000 years ago in the Aztec empire rituals around the dead, combined with Spanish cultural and Catholic religious elements. In the early weeks of the semester, we use parts of class periods to break up the regularly-scheduled content with learning about the history of the holiday: watching short videos about the Day of the Dead, discussing the history, and looking at pictures of altars and the elements they included. After watching an initial video and doing some readings that I provided,[4] I tasked students with finding other articles, blogs, and photos that helped with their understanding of the holiday's background. They then shared these elements on our online course site, and together they determined what they believed to be the most significant elements that must be included in a Day of the Dead *ofrenda*. From the start of the project, and through all the subsequent stages, the students take ownership of their learning process. Following a constructivist learning approach, the focus is on student learning through engagement with the subject matter rather than being simply taught about these materials through instructor lectures or reading a textbook.[5]

4   Regina M. Marchi, *Day of the Dead in the USA: The Migration and Transformation of a Cultural Phenomenon* (New Brunswick: Rutgers University Press, 2009), is a great book to draw portions for some short readings that are easily digestible by students as it relates to, and expands upon, some of their basic understanding.

5   For more information on constructivism, see for example: Kevin S. Krahenbuhl, "Student-Centered Education and Constructivism: Challenges, Concerns, and Clarity for Teachers," The Clearing House: A Journal of Educational Strategies, Issues and Ideas 89, no. 3 (May 3, 2016): 97–105, https://

The project's next stage began with dividing the class into groups and "assigning" each group a civilization that would be their "departed loved one" for whom they would create an altar. The first time doing this assignment was a learning experience on what not to do at this stage. I announced that students could form their own groups and choose the civilization they wanted to research and create an altar for, thinking the work might go more smoothly if the students were already comfortable with their group members and were working on an altar for the civilization in which they were most interested. Having students choose their groups did not work well for two primary reasons: groups tended to be of varying sizes (generally too large or too small), and in a few groups, only a couple of people carried the weight of the project. I have since found that random group assignments, completed through dividing the class alphabetically or having them count off and everyone who was a 1 in the same group, 2 in the same, and so on, worked better. This strategy also kept the groups manageable, which I found to be 4–6 students. As far as choosing their civilization, all the groups the first time wanted to have Ancient Greece or Ancient Rome. To solve this issue, I put those options and others (Egypt and the Aztec Empire) on paper and had each group draw from a hat, which created a sense of fairness amongst groups.

The next project stage was the group research portion to decide what they would include in their *ofrenda*. This process necessitated researching the cultural, political, economic, and other aspects of the civilization, from foods that were most common and those that were special, to clothing and jewelry, currency, professions, and more. The expectation was that groups would learn all they could about what was historically significant to their "lost ancestors;" they would then have to agree on what would be included in the altar to the civilization. Some of this stage was done outside of class, through dividing the students into "sections" of the course set up in our course Canvas site. Thus each group had a dedicated collaborative space to work together on their project, which allowed them to work together outside of class time, without having to gather in person to do so. I also

doi.org/10.1080/00098655.2016.1191311. Michael F. Moscolo, "Beyond Student-Centered and Teacher-Centered Pedagogy: Teaching and Learning as Guided Participation," Pedagogy and the Human Sciences, 1 (1) (2006): 3–27.

devoted half a class period each week for the groups to collaborate in real-time and to pull me in for feedback while working together. One of the most exciting outcomes of this project stage is that it filtered naturally into the overall day-to-day content of the class. As the students were working through the research for their group altar, they naturally started to talk more about the cultural aspects of the other civilizations we were studying in class and how we can still see some of the historical, cultural, political, economic, and other aspects of these societies in our world today. The syllabus and assignments included below explain student engagement throughout the process of the project, from the research through presentation stages, and the ways the assignment and methodology can be transferable to other courses and subject matters.

By mid-October, the groups were expected to be able to assemble their altars. At IUE, the World Languages and Cultures Program traditionally presents Day of the Dead altars, created by the Spanish language and Hispanic culture classes, which are open to the campus and public for viewing and voting as part of Hispanic Heritage Month activities. Class groups present the altars at the end of the Hispanic Heritage Month celebration, around October 15, and the altars remain up through the Day of the Dead on November 2. The altars were displayed in the campus library and promoted in campus and community information about IUE Hispanic Heritage Month programming. Additionally, photos of the altars were put into a voting survey widely distributed by students and faculty via LMS course sites and social media platforms, thus engaging an even broader audience in the projects. The students in my world history class in 2017 were the first groups outside of the WLC program to participate in this event, and other history classes would follow. The creation of the altars dedicated to ancient civilizations took a measure of ingenuity and creativity. They were not gathering items of significance to a personal loved one, and some things of significance were not readily available to them. However, this potential barrier turned into a great avenue for discussion as students worked together within and across groups to problem solve, overcoming any obstacles. Some examples include students who were art majors and made recreations of ancient artifacts, business majors who created replicas of counting and financial systems, and in one case science majors who added diagrams of aqueducts.

As a part of the altar-building section of the project, the groups were required to participate in the presentation of their altar to the greater campus and local community, thereby putting students in the roles of educators as they informed the attendees about the societies they researched. Students stood alongside their creations as WLC faculty briefly explained Hispanic Heritage Month and Day of the Dead, and then each class or group gave a brief presentation of their altar. The guests, including students, faculty, staff, administrators, and community members, then circulated among the groups asking more in-depth questions about the altars. Besides simply including physical artifacts in the altars, groups from my history class had to include in their altars written explanations that detailed their research on the historical significance of artifacts they incorporated. They could do this through note cards put alongside the items or short paragraphs taped onto the backs of the shoeboxes used for their altar builds. This requirement also assisted them in the final stage of the research project.

Before elaborating on the final stage of the assignment, I think it is essential to say a brief word on the projects that were created by the students in the first iteration of this assignment in a history course. Although the division of students into groups and the choosing of civilizations did not initially unfold ideally, the altars created by the students were creative and both culturally and historically relevant. The group that worked on Ancient Egypt created a pyramid surrounded by examples of and information about food, clothing, precious metals, and other items that were significant to the culture. A business major in that group created a document that showed the "accounting" of an emperor's holdings. They also had a mummy created from a stuffed animal wrapped in tissue paper and images and information on socially, culturally, and politically significant figures from Egyptian history. The Aztec Empire group included a few creative art students who drew or painted artistic renderings of Aztec gods and even created pieces of pottery in pre-Columbian Amerindian style. They also cooked foods that were important in the Aztec diet. Significantly, the Ancient Greek and Rome groups did not do as much with their altars, though science majors in the Roman group did create an inventive diagram explaining an early aqueduct. I believe that from the start, these students in the Ancient Greece and Rome groups felt they "had it easy" because the information about their civilizations was easy to find.[6] As the last part of the altar-building and presentation, students had to complete peer evaluations and self-evaluations, assessing their and peers' contributions to the project. Peer evaluations are a best practice in creating effective group-work projects, and self-evaluations are an important aspect of learning in a student-centered constructivist environment.[7] These evaluations were used in the participation and professionalism portion of the student's class grades, furthering student ownership in the assessment of their learning.

After the building and presentation of the altars, the final part of the Day of the Dead altar assignment for groups was to write up their research findings and the significance of what they included in their altar. This process was expected to take the form of a two-to-three-page synopsis rather than a research paper, though they were required to have a bibliography of their research sources in the write-up. This part of the assignment was for students to formally connect the cultural project to historical research. This portion of the project was the most problematic in terms of evaluation. Unfortunately, it fell on the shoulders of only a couple students per group to do this portion of the assignment, as most of the group had moved on to other work after presenting the altars. This dynamic, however, was not a failure in my eyes but rather a learning moment for me as an educator, as I realized the self- and peer evaluations needed to come after the project was completed in its entirety, not simply after the altar presentation, and this adjustment was employed in subsequent assignments.

Although this first iteration of the Day of the Dead altar building project in a history course necessitated some adaptations along the way, overall, I considered it successful enough to use again in subsequent classes. I have adopted it in U.S. history courses—where students pick a historical figure or historical group (for example: feminists, European immigrants, unionists, Civil Rights activists, among others) for their altar. I have also used it in fully online courses, where students create virtual altars through collaboration on Prezi, PowerPoint, or even in Adobe Creative Cloud.

6   This evaluation came from the comments on the project's self- and peer evaluations, and it was something I made a note of needing to address in future iterations of the project.

7   Michael A. Abelson and Judith A. Babcock, "Peer Evaluation Within Group Projects: a Suggested Mechanism and Process," *Organizational Behavior Teaching Review*, 10(4) (2016): 98–100.

This project allows students to view history through a cross-cultural and interdisciplinary lens that carries over into engaged learning in the rest of the course. As mentioned previously, similar methods could be utilized across disciplines in the humanities, social sciences, sciences, and more. The most important aspect of this project is that students are actively engaged in their learning throughout the entire process, using methods (conducting research, creating displays, and presenting findings) that are transferrable to other subjects and courses as well. An added bonus in the case of my class was that students discovered history can be a living subject, in that when you learn in an engaged environment and you teach others (through the altar presentations), the connections to the past are more easily seen all around us in the current world.

Sample Syllabus Overview

The syllabus below is specific to an ancient history course. I have made notes on ways to adapt language when necessary to make the Day of the Dead project transferable to courses in other disciplines.

General Course Description

This course surveys the historical origins of human civilizations from the Neolithic Revolution to the onset of the modern era. Students will gain insight into how cultures developed and diffused as well as how cross-cultural encounters significantly impacted the course of human societies.

Course Learning Objectives

1. To gain a factual and chronological understanding of important events, people, and forces in world civilizations to 1500 C.E.
2. To understand the interplay between political, economic, and cultural forces over time.
3. To learn to think in historical terms, and understand how events and patterns of behavior shaped the world in which we live.

4. To enhance critical thinking skills, including utilizing innovative ways to analyze materials, formulate an argument, and present information.

Suggested Course Materials
1. Aran MacKinnon and Elaine McClarnand MacKinnon, eds., *Places of Encounter: Time, Place, and Connectivity in World History* (Boulder, CO: Westview Press, 2012).
2. Regina M. Marchi, *Day of the Dead in the USA: The Migration and Transformation of a Cultural Phenomenon* (New Brunswick: Rutgers University Press, 2009), select excerpts.
3. Video: "Día de los muertos: a history" https://www.youtube.com/watch?v=lfdWV0QkwH4.

Course Assignments

The Day of the Dead (DoD) project is a major assignment students work on through the first two-thirds of the semester. I would suggest other courses use the assignment in the same way, incorporating it throughout the course schedule up until the Day of the Dead, allowing students to work on the research as a part of the class's weekly flow. Other assignments for the class include chapter quizzes, in class discussions, role playing exercises, debates, and reflection papers. The project takes the place of writing a research paper for the class.

Suggested Course Schedule

Again, it is significant to note that when I have used this assignment, it is a part of the first 9–10 weeks of the semester. I have included here a sketch of the semester, with information on how I incorporated the project in the entire time frame.

Week one: Course Introduction—this week is primarily an introduction to course structure, course content, and one another.
4. Give a basic explanation of the DoD project as part of the discussion of course assignments.
5. Student reflection papers on pre-knowledge—include a question

on what they know about Day of the Dead in the reflection.
Note: this exercise sets the stage for students to begin thinking
about Day of the Dead and allows you to determine how much
material should be included in helping them to understand the
tradition.
Note: for courses in other disciplines, this task could include
asking about a person, topic, or other element that students have
a particular interest in, or pre-knowledge of, and utilizing these
responses when having the students choose the subjects of their
altars.

Weeks 2 and 3: The Birth of Civilization

1. This unit covers the first 3 chapters of *Places of Encounter*.
   Students get a feel for learning history through the in-depth study
   of particular civilizations, including artifacts from the civilizations.
2. Week 2 DoD project—learning the cultural significance of DoD
   altars.
   Note: this stage is important to include in any course or discipline
   using this project, as students need to begin thinking about both
   the tradition and how their current course can be tied to it.
   a. students read selections on the tradition of DoD
   b. in class show video(s) on the history of Day of the Dead and
      on *ofrendas*
   c. discussion of readings and videos and how the DoD altars can
      be connected to and utilized in the current class
3. Week 3 DoD project
   a. divide students into groups
   b. each group chooses a civilization for their project
   c. set up course "sections" for each group in the LMS so that
      students have a space to collaborate outside of class time

Weeks 4 and 5: Ancient East and West

1. This unit covers Chapters 4 through 6 of *Places of Encounter*.
2. Weeks 4 and 5 DoD project
   a. students begin research on their group's civilization

Note: for courses in other topics, the research portion could be similar by focusing on the history of a person or topic in the discipline.

    b. in class, set aside half a class period per week to allow students to collaborate, and check in with each group about getting started

    c. group check-in assignment #1

Weeks 6 and 7: The World of Rome and Moving into Late Antiquity

1. This unit covers outside readings on Ancient Rome (not included in the textbook), and Chapters 7 and 8 of *Places of Encounter*.

2. Weeks 6 and 7 DoD project

    a. groups continue research on their altar subject

    b. groups should be making decisions on what will be included in their altars

    c. in class, set aside half a class period per week to allow students to collaborate

    d. meet with each group during class to make sure they are on track to build and present their altars

    e. group check-in assignment #2

Week 8: Day of the Dead Project Creation

1. Set aside the week of altar building and presentation to focus solely on the projects.

2. Students gather items they need for the creation of their altars. Note: this process may necessarily include students creating or building artifacts that tie into the subject of their altar.

3. Building of the altars in the designated space in class or on campus, or in virtual platforms.

4. Student groups present the altars and explain the significance of included elements. Note: this aspect is a vital component of the project's constructivist nature as it increases engagement by turning students into teachers.

<u>Weeks 9 and 10: Late Antiquity</u>
1. This unit covers Chapters 9 and 10 of *Places of Encounter*.
2. DoD project
   a. groups write up and turn in the synopsis of, and research bibliography for, their project
   b. students fill out self- and peer evaluations

<u>Weeks 11 and 12: Heading West—Europe in the Middle Ages</u>
1. This unit covers Chapter 11 of *Places of Encounter* and assigned online readings.

<u>Weeks 13 and 14: Renaissance and the Shrinking World</u>
1. This unit covers Chapters 12 through 14 of *Places of Encounter*,
2. This is an excellent time to tie back to the DoD project as this unit goes into the explorations in the New World.

<u>Week 15: Final Assessments</u>

Assignments

The assessments and rubrics below are sufficiently generalized in that they can be transferable to other courses and disciplines with minor suggested alterations.

Group Check-in Assignment #1
<u>Group Work:</u>
- Decide how you will organize your project's research.
- Decide the role of each group member in researching elements of your altar.
- Check in regularly with your collaboration group online as to where each person is in their portion of the research.

<u>Assignment:</u>
- In-class—schedule 10 minutes to meet with me as a group to discuss the progress of the group research.

- Outside of class—fill out a group responsibility form documenting each group member's responsibility for the research on your civilization.

Group Check-in Assignment #1

Responsibility: Please document how the group is dividing research of your civilization	Group member(s) working on this portion:	Feedback comments from Professor:

Note: language in the first column should be adapted to the project. For example, "Please document how the group is dividing research on (the topic, person, artistic style, scientific discovery)."

Group Check-in Assignment #2
Group Work:
- Continue to work on research for your altar.
- Check in regularly with your collaboration group online as to where each person is in their portion of the research.
- Decide on the elements you will include in your DoD altar, and which group members are responsible for gathering each item.

Assignment:
- In-class—schedule 10 minutes to meet with me as a group to discuss the progress of the group research.
- Outside of class—fill out a group responsibility form to document what each group member will contribute to the altar building.

Group Check-in Assignment #2

Responsibility: Please document the elements to be included in the DoD altar	Group member(s) working on this portion:	Feedback comments from Professor:

Day of the Dead Altar Building and Presentation

Activity:

- Create a Day of the Dead altar for an Ancient Civilization.
  Note: this would be adapted with the language that was used in the rubric above.

Objectives:

- Gather elements to display, including items of cultural, social, economic, and political significance to the society.
  Note: this could be generalized: Gather elements to display related to the findings of the research on your topic.
- Explain the elements of the altar to include with the display.
- Present your altar to the rest of the class and a broader campus and community audience.

Group Work:

- Decide on what is significant to display on your group's DoD altar.
- Decide on who will contribute which elements of the display.
- Consult with me on any printing or other items you need assistance with.

- Divide the work of creating the written explanations of the elements of your altar.
- Work together to create the group presentation of your altar.

Assignment:
- Design, build, and present your assigned civilization's Day of the Dead altar. The altars need to include the following:
  - Food, drinks, clothing, currency, architecture, and documents significant to your civilization. These can be in the form of photos or actual objects that represent these artifacts.
  - Written explanation of the historical, social, cultural, economic, or political significance of each item distinctive to your civilization.
  - May include other traditional elements to DoD *ofrendas* (candles, flowers).

The final section, or the actual wording of the assignment, is the one portion that may be more disciplinary-specific. Though the first two bullet points in the assignment may be transferable to any subject, it may be necessary to change the language to make it applicable to what the students are being asked to research for the project.

Research Synopsis and Bibliography
Activity:
- Submit a two-to-three-page summary and a bibliography of the research for your altar.

Objectives:
- Explain why you included each of the items in representing your civilization on the altar.
- Verify the validity of your research through the documentation of your resources.

Group Work:
- Decide together on who will put together the project summary.

- Decide together on who will put together the bibliography.
- Work together to read through the summary and bibliography, checking for accuracy of information and proofreading for grammatical errors.

Assignment:
- Write a summary of the elements included in your Day of the Dead altar.
- Write up a bibliography of research conducted in designing your project.
- Conduct self- and peer evaluation of group work.

Rubrics

Check-in Assignments

Expectation	1	2	3	4	Feedback
Group scheduled an in-class meeting with the professor in the allotted time frame.					
Group came prepared to the meeting with questions about the project and any requests for assistance.					
The assignment form outlined the responsibilities of each group member's contribution to the project.					

1 = unsatisfactory; 2 = partially meets expectations; 3 = meets expectations; 4 = exceeds expectations

Self- and Peer-Assessment of Group Work (each student fills out a form for themselves and each of the group members)

Expectation	1	2	3	4	Comments on rating
Group member actively participated in online collaboration for the project.					
Group member carried out the portion of the research they agreed to do.					
Group member contributed agreed upon elements to the DoD altar.					
Group member participated in the live (in-person or virtual) presentation of the altar.					
Group member contributed to the written explanations included with the altar.					
Group member contributed to the writing of the project summary and bibliography.					
Group member contributed to the proofreading of written work for the project.					

1 = unsatisfactory; 2 = partially meets expectations; 3 = meets expectations; 4 = exceeds expectations

Day of the Dead Altar Building and Presentation

Expectation	1	2	3	4	Comments on rating
Altar includes elements of social, cultural, economic, and political significance to the civilization.					
Written explanations of the included elements clearly explain the historical significance of the included items.					
Altar is organized, neat, and cleanly displayed.					
Group members were prepared to present on what they chose to include in the altar and why.					
Group members were prepared to answer questions on their altar, including the research they contributed.					

1 = unsatisfactory; 2 = partially meets expectations; 3 = meets expectations; 4 = exceeds expectations

As noted with the related assignment above, the wording on this assignment rubric is the one portion that may be more disciplinary-specific. Though the first expectations may be transferable to any subject, it may be necessary to change the language to make it applicable to what the students are being asked to research for the project.

Project Summary and Bibliography

Expectation	1	2	3	4	Comments on rating
Project summary is organized and cleanly written, free of grammatical and spelling errors.					
Project summary meets expectations for length.					
Project summary includes a brief, clear explanation of the research that went into the items included in the altar.					
Bibliography is structured in Chicago Manual of Style format.					
Bibliography demonstrates that the group consulted a variety of sources in researching their civilization for the project.					

1 = unsatisfactory; 2 = partially meets expectations; 3 = meets expectations; 4 = exceeds expectations

On the Means of Production:

Open-Source Textbook Projects in Introductory History Courses and Beyond

Justin M. Carroll

When I was a new faculty member teaching introductory courses at Indiana University East, my students—often non-majors and mostly captive to university and system-wide general education requirements—found the historical narratives offered in my classes intimidating. When I dug deeper and asked why, I discovered many of these students lacked explicit knowledge about how historical narratives develop. In fact, throughout their educational experiences, my students had only encountered finished scholarly products. They only witnessed the final form of years of intensive research, writing, and revision in terms of lectures, articles, monographs, and textbooks. Many students struggled to understand how scholars and publishers produced historical narratives or presented knowledge. Given my course might be the only history course they would take over their careers, I found these insights both concerning and compelling.

Simultaneously during this period, I also noticed a consistent trend from semester to semester regarding course texts and textbooks. As a young man, I went to an undergraduate university where buying course textbooks was not a worry; my parents would buy them for me, which was true for most of my university friends. Later, as a graduate student at Michigan State University and the primary interface between course, professor, and students in lecture courses, I never had issues with students not having their textbooks. However, at IUE, I met and encountered a different student body. I learned quickly that many of my students worked full time, and a sizeable cohort could not afford to pay for textbooks; they had to wait a week or two and sometimes three to gather the funds. I found this challenge frustrating and worrisome in equal measure. I wanted to get into the course material as soon as possible, but I also never wanted my course to burden an already expensive education.[1]

To address these concerns, in late 2018, I latched upon the idea of using an open-source textbook in my introductory HIST-H105: American History course, which explores North American history through the American Civil War and Reconstruction.[2] In this project, each student would develop a chapter around a primary source chosen from a list I compiled. At the end of the semester, the class would publish their work online via Pressbooks with their names firmly attached and under a Creative Commons license.[3] I developed this project as an iterative process; students in subsequent semesters would add new material for our course text while revising, editing, and reworking chapters from prior classes. I hoped to achieve two things: first, create a permanent open-source textbook for my course that students can take ownership over, and second, help students better understand how knowledge gets produced, disseminated, and revised. This assignment offers an adaptable and remarkably vibrant learning experience for most

---

1   For data related to textbooks, costs, and student struggles, see: Melanie Hanson, "Average Cost of College Textbooks" EducationData.org, August 12, 2021, https://educationdata.org/average-cost-of-college-textbooks (Accessed April 3, 2022).

2   Open Pedagogy deeply influenced the development of this project. Soon after Indiana University East hired me as an assistant professor, I began to orient my courses towards the incorporation of increasingly high-quality, accessible, digital, and, often, free resources. Open pedagogy privileges openness, creativity, reflection, community, and student-centered development, often in collaborative, critical, and participatory digital/online contexts. For a discussion of these attributes, see Bronwyn Hegarty, "Attributes of Open Pedagogy: A Model for Using Open Education Resources." *Educational Technology*, July/August 2015, 3–13. For an overview and discussion of how to self-assess and incorporate open pedagogy in the classroom, see: Eric Werth, Katherine Williams, "The Why of Open Pedagogy: A Value-First Conceptualization for Enhancing Instructor Praxis." *Smart Learning Environment*, vol. 9, 2022, 1–22. For a useful guide I consulted in the development of this assignment, see: *A Guide to Making Open Textbooks with Students*, Elizabeth Mays, editor. (Montreal: The Rebus Community for Open Textbook Creation). https://press.rebus.community/ (Accessed September 22, 2022).

3   At the beginning of the course, before COVID-19, we planned on using Pressbooks to build this project. However, this plan proved futile set against a global pandemic. However, in subsequent iterations of the course, this platform will be a larger part of the process.

humanities and non-humanities-based classrooms, particularly in contexts where writing and textually communicating are core course components. Moreover, it provides a space where students can practice the types of soft skills jobs that careers increasingly require and expect, for example, critical thinking, excellent communication, and real-time adaptability.

In this chapter, I will demonstrate how richly rewarding and pedagogically valuable this project turned out to be by highlighting how students became more critical of primary and secondary sources and how they developed a greater sense of how scholars produce knowledge and revise it over time. Likewise, I will give an overview of this course and how the open sourcebook project operated over IUE's 15-week semester. I will also discuss the significant missteps, pitfalls, mistakes, and global catastrophes the students and I encountered and how we collectively addressed them. By way of an appendix, I have included a shell syllabus, course handouts, and course readings, which I will refer to throughout the chapter.

Overview

Before I implemented this project in the Spring of 2019, I first had to confront what no textbook meant for my courses. At IUE, the History faculty used shared textbooks in our United States and World History (HIST-H105, HIST-H106, HIST-H108, and HIST-H109) surveys to ensure every student had a similar content background. In my sections, I often used my lectures and discussion questions to offer a competing narrative to the textbook. I use these divergences to create a sense of intellectual tension and disruption. I work to develop a learning environment centered around helping students develop critiques, observations, and questions about competing accounts of historical events or processes. I create moments of debate and disjuncture and prod my students to look for themselves as they read the course material and listen to my lectures. For the most part, this approach worked well. However, with this new project in mind, I had to give up a well-developed and nuanced course structure for something uncertain.

I spent the summer and fall before the class started looking at ways to diversify the number of historical and intellectual voices encountered in my HIST-H105 course. First, I spent hours looking for scholarly articles on which to build a narrative of U.S. history and subvert students' prior expectations and certainties. For example, under the State of Indiana Social Studies Guidelines and Standards, most Indiana students learn about colonial North America in 4th grade.[4] How complex could this material be? Moreover, much of what my students learn outside the classroom is often tinged with heritage, nostalgia, and the superficiality of popular culture reproductions.[5] So, I could assume they knew about the Puritan world and the Salem Witch Trials. Still, I could not imagine they would have a nuanced understanding of either. This calculus led me, for example, to pick Elaine Breslaw's "Tituba's Confession: The Multicultural Dimensions of the 1692 Salem Witch-Hunt," which challenged the idea that Tituba was an enslaved African woman who participated in witchcraft but instead explored how the multicultural world of the early English Empire in North America shaped the contours and content of her confession.[6] By employing a diverse array of secondary sources that challenged pervasive notions of United States History, I wanted to highlight the contested and evolving nature of historical discourse and create a weekly space to discuss issues related to argumentation, research questions, historiography, and primary source usage. These concepts, central to the field of History, connect to the central concept of the textbook project.

Since I increased the diversity and scope of my course readings, I wanted my course to feature an equally diverse array of lecture voices. I slowly lined up a series of content experts from different historical fields and academic disciplines to guest lecture in my class. In this new course structure, I stepped into a more curatorial place and worked to montage different perspectives into a holistic and multi-focal portrayal of the American past. For example, through Canvas, IUE's learning management system, I often link, employ,

---

4   For these standards, consult: Indiana Academic Social Studies Standards, Indiana Department of Education. https://www.in.gov/doe/students/indiana-academic-standards/social-studies/ (Accessed April 5, 2022).

5   For classic explorations of this idea, see: James W. Loewen, *Lies My Teacher Told Me: Everything Your American History Textbook Got Wrong.* (New York: Atria Books, 2007); James W. Loewen, *Lies Across America: What Our Historic Sites Get Wrong.* (New York: The New Press, 2019).

6   Elaine G. Breslaw, "Tituba's Confession: The Multicultural Dimensions of the 1692 Salem Witch-Hunt," *Ethnohistory* vol. 44, no. 3 (Summer 1997), pp. 535–556.

and offer a wide array of easily accessible online content such as pre-recorded academic lectures, popular podcasts, interactive maps, sequential art, and other digital media to extend and complicate the narratives I offer in my physical classroom. During this semester, I asked my colleague Dr. Daron Olson, an associate professor of World History, to come into my classroom early in the semester to place U.S. history into a larger global context for my students. Moreover, IUE has a vibrant Spanish language program. Dr. Dianne Moneypenny, an associate professor of Spanish Language who works on Medieval and Early Modern Spain, came to my course and provided my students with an excellent overview of the Spanish Empire in the 16th and 17th centuries. In doing so, I realized the joy of creating a class that decentered my voice as the professor. Together, we all worked toward presenting History as a complex array of competing perspectives and vistas for my students. Complimentarily, since the project puts the students in a position to be some of these competing perspectives through the creation of their chapters, these practices, both inside and outside the classroom, model how academic debates and intellectual discourses operate and function in a microcosm. This experience fostered students with the ability to modify, adapt, and weave varying strands of knowledge into new and unique tapestries. In the context of the job market, this is a vital and lucrative skill.

As my preparation ended, I shifted focus away from secondary readings and lectures toward the heart of the textbook project. Over several weeks, I developed a list of 40 primary sources my students would interpret for their chapters. Because of the complexity of the course, I wanted something manageable, so I only chose textual primary source examples to begin with, which later turned out to be a misstep. Regardless, I wanted students to have a complete range of primary sources reflecting historical topics generally appearing in a standard U.S. history survey. This stage of planning took a considerable amount of time and care. As the students would ultimately devote a significant amount of time working to contextualize, interpret, research, and explain their sources, poorly chosen primary sources would be a source of frustration, anxiety, and disruption for weeks on end.

With this material in place, I constructed and scaffolded the assignments across IUE's 15-week academic semester. To ensure week-to-week engagement with the readings, I created a standard "reading notes" assignment that asked students to locate the thesis of the article, explain why the argument matters, provide two aspects of the article they found intriguing/confusing and a question they would like to ask the author. These short writings proved useful and valuable during class discussions and served the larger purpose of the textbook project. This assignment helped students identify essential aspects of historical argumentation, narrative construction, and historiographical debates.

Next, I broke the textbook project into six individual assignments. I tried to have each assignment crescendo and build directly into the next. As a professor, I like when students can see and appreciate their progress over time in safe and measured ways. I created a close reading assignment related to their primary source, which evolved into a primary source annotation assignment. Next, they would engage in a light research assignment and write an introduction to their primary source. Finally, they would develop their primary source chapter's visual and illustrative aspects and create a series of discussion questions related to their work. This material would culminate in a fully formed chapter for the textbook.

With a clear structure in place, I started the spring semester of 2020 with optimism. I walked into class and told my new students, "We will create a book this semester." This pronouncement met awkward silences, concerned looks, and nervous laughs. "For many of you," I explained, "this will be the first and only history course you'll take as university students, and I would love for you to leave this course with two things: (1) a clear, albeit contested, narrative of United States history, and (2) a clear sense of how historians produce and present knowledge about the past." I wanted these students to see the interplay between how we narrate the past and how these narratives exist. When they left the course, I hoped they would leave with new skills and techniques to treat the past and debate about the past in a more nuanced manner. They would become more sophisticated consumers of history and knowledge by experiencing the productive nature of historical accounts through experience.[7]

---

7   My overall pedagogical approach across my courses is constructivist in orientation. As such, I try to foster learning environments where students can take active ownership and responsibility for their learning and create space to practice preexisting skills or develop transferable new ones. In the context of this project, student initiative, creativity, passion, and interest guide the development of their chapters

I spent the first week of the course helping my students understand and practice reading and dissecting primary and secondary sources. We spent time in small and large groups discussing how to find arguments, understand the structure, explore their evidence, and read footnotes—basic skills of history but applicable to other majors as well. From there, we talked about how primary sources build narratives. We explored what primary sources can tell modern readers about the past and how historians employ them to craft arguments as evidence. Though I introduced these ideas during the first week, given the nature of the course, we revisited these ideas in different ways across the semester as core elements of their book projects.

During this week, the students and I also worked through the list of primary sources they would explore in their book chapters, and I asked them to skim them. I encouraged them to pick a source that resonated most closely with their interests and passions. They had until the end of the second week to finalize their primary source. From the start, they impressed me with the diversity of their options. Students picked, for example, a sermon by Jonathan Edwards, an account of the Pueblo Revolt, writings by Harriet Beecher Stowe, a list of Connecticut Blue Laws, and numerous others. I was worried, initially, my students would pick "familiar" sources, sources they might have prior knowledge of, but most pushed beyond and leaned toward newer choices.

One of the initial drawbacks of the structure I created manifested at this point in the semester. Namely, some students had to engage their primary sources before encountering the course content related to their chapters. For example, a student who picked a source related to the Civil War would have to wait weeks for the associated readings and lectures. I tried to ameliorate this tension by asking students to conduct light research once they narrowed down their primary sources. For example, if they showed interest in slavery

and the textbook. As a result, through hands-on experience, they develop a wide array of skills and practices that can be applied in other academic and intellectual contexts. For a discussion and overview of constructivism and the works I consulted when I started teaching at Indiana University East, see: *Constructivism: Theory, Perspectives, and Practice*, Catherine Twomey Fosnot, editor. (New York: Teacher College Press, 2005); James Pelech, *The Comprehensive Handbook of Constructivist Teaching: From Theory to Practice*, Gail Pieper, editor. (Charlotte: Information Age Publishing, 2010); Yvon Cano-Fullido, "Constructivism Learning Theory: A Paradigm for Teaching and Learning," *IOSR Journal of Research and Method in Education*, vol. 5, No. 6 (November–December 2015), 66–70.

in 17th-century Virginia, I suggested books, articles, and places to look for material to help. I told them about JSTOR, HathiTrust, and Archive.org and even encouraged them to look at Wikipedia overall. During this stage, I tried to provide students with enough knowledge to avoid major missteps, but I also left space for them to grow, discover, and negotiate other hurdles. I wanted to create as much security for the students as possible in this project.

Between weeks three and four, I turned my students' attention toward the "close reading" of their primary sources. This assignment asked students to read their primary source multiple times. For their first reading, I asked them to read for the "big picture" and, once finished, write a paragraph highlighting the "who," "what," "where," and "when" of their sources. This step gave them little to no trouble and created the conditions to help them skim below the surface.

Next, after a day or so, I asked them to re-read their source from a different perspective. They considered what the author wanted to express with their writing and why the author communicated this information. I explained that being a historian often required creative reconstruction of the past, and this practice required empathy and intuitive leaps guided by evidence. Once finished, they wrote a paragraph explaining what the author wanted to achieve with their source.

During the third read-through, I asked my students to look for potential biases, limitations, and problematic aspects. Students in my introductory courses often take primary sources at face value, discussing the creator's perspective as if it represented all people of that time and place. I hoped this assignment would address this tendency, and again, they had to write a paragraph about their observations.

Finally, and I am sure the students were sick of their sources by this point, I had them do one final reading from the perspective of History as a discipline and explore what the source could tell historians about the past and why it matters. Through this iterative process, I hoped to simulate, in a microcosm, the historical processes scholars perform when they labor, and to create space for my students to practice reading for a purpose, a crucial transposable skill.

Once finished, I had my students compile these four paragraphs into a short paper that guided the later construction of their chapters. This early work allowed me, during the grading, to monitor any issues students might be having with their source. For example, if a student misinterpreted an aspect of their primary source, I could quickly clarify the meaning and direct them toward solid ground early in the process.

Between weeks five through eight, the students, armed with their close readings and my feedback, started the research-oriented process related to annotating their primary sources. In this assignment, I asked them to explore the essential people, places, things, and ideas in their primary source that might require more information and explanation from the perspective of future readers. For example, in a source about slavery, a student might annotate the word "chattel" as a concept. Or, perhaps, the document refers to the Bight of Benin, and the students can flesh out what this locality means for the source. I asked my students to develop a list of the eight-to-twelve most essential annotations and to consult nine different sources to create and write their short explanations. By week eight, they turned in their selected annotations and the works cited page. Students offered solid annotations that helped make the primary source more legible.

At the halfway point of the semester, my students traversed from pre-contact North America to the global violence and empire-building of the Seven Years' War (1754–1763). In class, they received lectures from colleagues and read numerous articles. Once a week, we engaged with course material through small group and class discussions.

Between weeks nine and eleven, which at IUE includes our Spring Break, I wanted a mid-way assignment that mirrored the actual research paper writing process, where secondary and primary source research resulted in a narrative about the past and why it matters. I also wanted a self-contained writing assignment that did not require additional research beyond their already completed work. It felt important to create a space where my students could feel like experts over a small aspect of the past.

In this assignment, I required the students to write a short introduction to the primary source, at least three complete paragraphs long. This introduction had to achieve three goals—it needed to:

1. provide the necessary contextual information to understand the source and how it fits into the larger patterns of US history;

2. provide the reader with a sense of the value and limitations of the source; and

3. explain why the reader should know and consider the source important.

At this stage of the textbook project, the students had numerous opportunities to reflect, develop, and receive feedback for their work. They had all the material required to answer these questions when they put pen to paper.

Moreover, in the context of pedagogy, this assignment provided the course space to discuss historical and academic writing best practices. For example, in my lower-level courses, the opaqueness of academic writing often daunts my students, so I work to demystify it. In this space, I stress the importance of clear and jargon-free prose, the need to write for a broad, non-academic audience, the value of editing and revision, and writing in a manner that ensures the historical subjects we study have the agency humans merit.[8] In other words, this project fostered the ability to communicate widely and convincingly to diverse audiences and constituencies. This introduction assignment also proved short enough to provide ample commentary that could be applied later in my students' more extensive writing projects. For example, my students often need help writing in the past tense, appreciate the need for active sentence structures, or understand the purposes and values of footnotes. This assignment established a knowledge base that students, majors and non-majors alike, could take into their respective fields.

I enjoyed this stage of the project the most because it felt like a real test of concept. By week twelve, I could look at the annotated primary sources and the introductions my students crafted side-by-side and consider their overall quality and efficacy. Their work, far from perfect, illuminated the primary source and placed it in a larger interconnected historical context. Over time, I could imagine how their work would culminate into something special—a textbook that could offer an engaging student-driven narrative of the past.

Moreover, this moment also allowed me to critique my project design and assignment structure. For example, I quickly learned that I needed to ask the students to explicitly connect their sources to themes we discussed in the course. I asked for these connections obliquely, and I made the poor

---

8   Beyond personal experience, I draw my writing advice for these discussions from: Ann Curthoys, Ann McGrath, *How to Write History that People Want to Read.* (New York: Palgrave Macmillan, 2011).

assumption they would naturally connect this material on their own. The individualized aspect of the project made these introductions more diffuse than I expected.

At IUE, like most universities, professors assign final exams, papers, or other larger projects students must complete or turn in at the end of the semester. I tried to scaffold the textbook project so most of the assignment's work occurred in the first two-thirds of the course. I created a series of "soft landing" assignments to create space for students to destress and focus their attention elsewhere. As such, in the final weeks, I assigned a short project that required students to find open-source images, maps, timelines, and other visual elements to flesh out and illustrate their chapters and primary sources. For example, if their chapter focused on a primary source related to the internal slave trade of early 19th-century America, I encouraged the students to find maps highlighting the broad movements and patterns of this horrible endeavor across time and place or to look for period newspaper illustrations of slave pens or runaway advertisements. Because historians can only access the past indirectly and so much of it requires creative reconstruction, these visual sources, included in most history textbooks, help the reader connect to long-departed people, places, things, and ideas. In essence, I wanted them to practice their visual communication skills.

However, the assignment created some uneven results regarding the overall quality of images and illustrations. For example, I saw poorly designed maps, low-resolution paintings, or historically inaccurate portrayals of the past. It became apparent that, in the development of this project, I focused too heavily on writing and textual criticism/communication and neglected the importance of visual criticism/communication in the process.

In the future, I will include visual primary sources as actual chapters alongside other textual sources to help illustrate the book. This addition will create space in the class to discuss visual literacy, criticism, and communication more directly. I plan on asking the Fine Arts and Graphic Design faculty of IUE to give introductory lectures related to the skills and practices of visual analysis—for example, what is line quality, color theory, or the purpose of scale and composition—so my students can develop a more nuanced way of seeing, understanding, and explaining the world both past and present. Given, for example, the modern reconvergence of text and imagery in the context of the internet, social media, and cell phones, developing assignments, readings, and discussions around these visual interpretive skills in the context of this project would be helpful in an era of memes and misinformation regardless of major or discipline. With these modifications, this project can help students become more critical consumers of information in an increasingly visually-oriented world and can bring these considerations to bear at a future time in their respective careers.

In our final assignment, I wanted my students to think about the value of questions. When discussing our course readings, I often explored how our course readings began as questions about the past that their authors just wanted to answer. I explained the thesis statements my students worked to locate were the answers to these very questions. After a semester exploring on these issues the students developed review questions for their sources. I showed them examples from other textbooks and asked them to reflect on their experience with these questions. I asked them to consider how good questions could help readers summarize, dig deeper, and connect to the material better.

As the semester ended, my students had everything required to structure their textbook chapters. Earlier in the semester, we discussed the need to make their chapter clear, useable, and engaging; the reader had to enjoy the total experience. Our conversation evolved into a fruitful dialogue about what my students wanted, expected, or needed from their textbooks. They expressed many opinions about how the textbook and chapters should look. They had strong views after a lifetime of experience with these objects, good and bad. We began working through the different perspectives and coming to a consensus about how the chapters should look when, in late March, the global COVID-19 pandemic dispersed my students back to their homes, and the campus closed. We switched to an online learning environment. My students, especially first years, struggled due to this change, and the learning environment we built collapsed in the face of a genuine crisis.

With my students adjusting to the upheavals caused by COVID-19, I told them to compile their information in a PDF instead of a finalized book chapter. Instead of adding extra work to their beleaguered shoulders, I told them about my new plans for their work. In subsequent semesters, new students would take their chapter material and use it to develop a template for the book in terms of look and style. This experience would allow the next cohort of students to play a more significant editorial role in the book-creating process; they would also get to see the work they would be expected to create earlier in the semester. Moreover, this new editorial process could help identify primary source chapters from prior courses that needed to be reworked, replaced, or removed from the course textbook. These last-minute changes created more space for the collaborative potential across disciplines. For example, I imagined a shared assignment between a History and Graphic Design course where the History class produces the material for their chapters. At the same time, Graphic Design students develop the look, typography, layout, etc. In developing the project along these lines, students would communicate ideas and concepts across disciplines and negotiate potential disciplinary gulfs and chasms. Ultimately, my students agreed to these changes, and by the end of week fifteen, they turned in their work, and our first COVID semester ended at IUE.

Exhausted and anxious, I found my students' responses to the project uplifting. For example, one student wrote,

> Honestly, first hearing about this project I was very frustrated. I took this class to fill a requirement for my degree, I'm a business major and have no interest in history. But after diving into the project further, I did enjoy it and found it to be fun. It was a non-traditional way of learning history, and it turned out to be successful in motivating me to learn.[9]

Meanwhile, another student claimed, "The primary source project helped me better understand how professional historians interpret primary sources. In the research I did, I discovered many different viewpoints and details that I wouldn't have thought of. The project showed me how different people approach sources and the information surrounding them."[10] Finally, another student noted, "[W]hen I was doing each assignment I was a

9   This quote comes from an assignment built into the course that asks students to self-reflect on the project and offer suggestions.

10   This quote comes from an assignment built into the course that asks students to self-reflect on the project and offer suggestions.

historian . . . and at the end of the semester when I finally put everything together . . . it made me realize that historians put in a lot of work behind each article . . . But now that I have, I can say I know a lot . . . and I'm glad I chose the one I did."[11] It became clear, reading through the comments, that beyond History, the project created outcomes that mirrored what professors often demand or seek from high impact practices; over the course of the semester, students spent considerable time and effort thinking critically about their primary sources, they applied their self-directed learning in a real-world context, and worked closely with their professor to achieve a unique and compelling result.

Generally, in my experience, my missteps create conditions where students struggle. Even if this is not true, it is best to operate from this vantage because it empowers me to dig deeper into the aspects of my teaching I have control over. Despite the glowing reviews, I know there were rough patches in the assignment and project. As summer came and I was stuck inside with free time, I began developing ways to improve the textbook for the next cohort of students.

First, I planned to diversify the primary sources for the project. In the future, I plan on developing a list of paintings, cartoons, maps, and other visual primary sources for the students to interpret. This change will help illustrate the textbook project and teach visual criticism. Looking back, the exclusion of visual elements hindered the potential of this project, and I want to rectify this limitation.

Secondly, I want to develop a series of editorial boards, for example, a committee tasked with editing, a panel tasked with fact-checking, or another group focused on finalizing the chapters. I want to give students more ownership over the final project in this new structure. Given the diversity of majors in my introductory courses, this change would allow students to pick activities that better reflect their career goals and create space to work with other students who share their interests. For example, an English major might focus on editing, a design major might want to focus on the book's aesthetics, and a history major might be interested in fact-checking. I imagine a workflow with staggered group assignments across the semester.

---

11   This quote comes from an assignment built into the course that asks students to self-reflect on the project and offer suggestions.

Finally, I want to create a system where students can suggest primary sources they think might fit into the textbook. After the initial primary sources I picked become chapters, this process will help my students invest in the project's future by giving them greater control over how the text grows and evolves. Our use of the past is often contingent on the needs and desires of the present, and I would be curious to see what subsequent cohorts of students request regarding historical sources and topics.

All told, despite the disruptions wrought by COVID-19, my students performed amazingly well on their chapters, and the textbook project proved successful. In their work, my students engaged history, historiography, secondary and primary sources, and the basic skills of the historical field in an engaged and productive way. They learned these skills by constructing a primary source textbook mirroring how historians produce knowledge and craft narratives about the past.

In this introductory history course on United States history, my students, mostly taking the course as a general education credit, received a coherent narrative about American history and a clearer sense of what historians do and why that work matters. For history majors, it introduced core concepts and prepared them for method courses and upper-level seminars. In developing an ambitious course-length project, my students and I created a unique learning environment that asked us to do remarkable and compelling work. Projects like this can arm students with the valuable skills required of good democratic citizens and help them find proper moorings in a world set adrift from the truth.

Sample Syllabus Overview

Generic Course Description:
(This course was a Freshman lecture/discussion course designed to teach the rudiments of the historical method and offer a straightforward and nuanced narrative of United States history. Given the number of students who enrolled in the course for its general education credit, I wanted to develop a learning experience highlighting how History as an

academic discipline produces and sustains knowledge. This textbook project incorporated hard and soft skills—critical thinking, problem-solving, management, negotiation, researching, and writing—highly transferable to other academic disciplines and intimately connected to the demands of the broader job market. Hypothetically, any field that relies on journals, monographs, or other forms of writing could easily modify this project to fit their unique course needs. For example, an introductory Sociology course that introduces students to theories or theoretical concepts could develop a course reader centered around writings related to people like Marcel Maus, Karl Marx, Max Weber, W.E.B. Dubois, and others, in which the students develop material conceptualizing or explaining these ideas in a student-friendly manner. In doing so, the students could extend their insights, learning from hands-on experience, into other contexts.)

"This course examines North America's social, political, economic, and cultural developments, from European, African, and Indigenous encounters in the sixteenth century to the turmoil and bloodshed of the American Civil War in the 1860s."

General Course Learning Objectives (CLO):
Students who pass this course with a C grade or higher will be able to:
1. Analyze primary material with an eye toward historiography, historical context, and historical argumentation.
2. Create secondary source materials from a broad range of historical/historiographical evidence into a coherent and well-supported argument or narrative.
3. Express a deep understanding of U.S. history from the pre-contact period to the U.S. Civil War and its major themes, trends, debates, and developments.

Suggested Course Reading Materials:
(Here is a list of articles the students read during their course. I spent time considering these articles in terms of their arguments and how they could be used to frame discussions in the course. In subsequent iterations of the course, I will change and adapt these based on student feedback.)

1. Nathan Nunn, Nancy Qian, "The Columbian Exchange: A History of Disease, Food, and Ideas." *Journal of Economic Perspectives*, vol. 24, no. 2, Spring 2010, pg. 163–188.

2. Inga Clendinnen, "'Fierce and Unnatural Cruelty': Cortes and the Conquest of Mexico." *Representations*, Winter, 1991, pg. 65–100.

3. Cornelius J. Jaenen, "French Expansion in North America." *The History Teacher*, vol. 34, No. 2 (Feb. 2001), pg. 155–164.

4. Elaine G. Breslaw, "Tituba's Confession: The Multicultural Dimensions of the 1692 Salem Witch-Hunt." *Ethnohistory*, vol. 44, no. 3, (Summer, 1997), pg. 535–556.

5. T. H. Breen, "An Empire of Goods: The Anglicization of Colonial America, 1690–1776." *Journal of British Studies*, vol. 25, no. 4, (Oct. 1986), pg. 467–499.

6. Fred Anderson, "A People's Army: Provincial Military Service in Massachusetts during the Seven Years' War." *The William and Mary Quarterly*, vol. 40, no. 4, (Oct. 1983), pg. 499–527.

7. Gregory Evans Dowd, "The French King Wakes Up in Detroit: 'Pontiac's War' in Rumor and History." *Ethnohistory*, vol. 37, no. 3, (Summer, 1990), pg. 254–278.

8. Maya Jasanoff, "The Other Side of Revolution: Loyalists in the British Empire." *The William and Mary Quarterly*, vol. 65, no. 2, (April 2008), pg. 205–232.

9. Lacy Ford, "Making the 'White Man's Country' White: Race, Slavery, and State-Building in the Jacksonian South." *Journal of the Early Republic*, vol. 19, no. 4, (Winter 1999), pg. 713–737.

10. Ray Suarez, "The Convergence Begins." *Latino-Americans: The 500-Year Legacy that Shaped a Nation*. (New York: Celebra Press, 2013).

11. James McPherson, "Who Freed the Slaves?" *Proceedings of the American Philosophical Society*, vol. 139, no. 1, (March 1995), pg. 1–10.

Suggested Course Assignments:

(These assignments relate only to the textbook project and serve to scaffold the overall experience. Over the course of the semester, I used other traditional history assignments, such as primary source analyses, book reviews, and other short writings, to create a holistic learning experience.)

1. Close Reading Primary Source Assignment
2. Primary Source Annotation Assignment
3. Primary Source Introduction Assignment
4. Primary Source Illustration Assignment
5. Primary Source Discussion Question Assignment
6. A finalized Pressbook Chapter

Suggested Course Schedule:

(In my course, which is fifteen weeks long, I organized the textbook project along the following lines. Please note I tried to cut out ideas or readings not directly connected to the project. Moreover, I explained what I did each week and included new ideas from student feedback or my teaching observations. On average, I spent about 20–30 minutes a week on their projects.)

Week #1: Course Introduction and Textbook Project Discussion
1. Explain the textbook project and field any questions the students might have about the project.
2. Discuss primary and secondary sources and how to read and critique them; introduce the students to the sources for the project.

Week #2: The Pre-Contact Worlds and Primary Source Selection
1. By the end of this week, students pick out the primary source for their chapter and receive feedback and suggestions.

Week #3–Week #4: The Columbian Exchange, the Spanish World in America, and Close Reading Assignment
1. During these two weeks of the course, students read their sources multiple times as they develop their interpretations of the source and gain a deeper appreciation of its nuances. I offered individual

meetings to all students to provide additional feedback during these weeks.

2. Provide feedback, readings, and sources to help them clarify their thoughts and shore up any interpretative errors they might have had.

Week #5–Week #8: The French World in North America, The British World in America, Part #1, The British World in America, Part #2, Imperial Development and Crises, Part #1, and the Primary Source Annotation Assignment

1. Students begin annotating their primary sources and starting the research process for their various annotations during these weeks. I offered individual meetings to all students to provide additional feedback during these weeks.

2. As they work on this aspect of their project, highlight examples of annotations in texts and explain why they matter. For example, I showed them an example of an annotated play by Shakespeare.

3. Show the students where to research physically and digitally; for example, I walked them through archive.org and showed them how to search for specific topics.

Week #9–Week #11: Imperial Development and Crisis, Part #2, Spring Break, Revolutionary America, and the Primary Source Introduction Assignment.

1. Students begin writing the introductions for their primary source chapters; they have access to their original readings, annotations, research material, and numerous levels of feedback. I offered individual meetings to all students to provide additional feedback during these weeks.

Week #12–Week #14: The Early Republic, Antebellum America, Part #1, Antebellum America, Part #2

1. By this point in the semester, the students have completed the significantly demanding aspects of their chapters. Students

develop discussion review questions for their chapters and find material to illustrate them during these weeks.

2. Allow students to go back and revise anything about the chapters they would like to improve on; student works grow and evolve. Many students requested this option, which I found helpful to the project's overall quality.

Week #15: Civil War, Course Conclusion, and Finalized Projects

1. During the course's final week, the students compile, revise, and turn all their material into a finalized chapter. We would upload them as a class and organize the material into a digital book in the original project plan. However, COVID-19 disrupted this idea, and instead, we opted to allow the next course to review, edit, and upload the material as a class project.

Assignment and Project Templates

(For this semester, I wanted to focus on primary source analysis as a skill, but the project could have just as easily explored historiography or secondary literature in terms of scholarly debates. To me, primary source analysis requires repetitive engagement from various perspectives. In this assignment, I wanted students to consider how multiple readings provide a big-picture perspective that would eventually allow them to see the finer gradations that appear within their sources.)

Primary Source Close Reading Assignment Template

Overview:

- Read your primary source from multiple perspectives and write down your reflections and the evidence you gathered after each subsequent reading.

Objectives:

- Develop a clearer understanding of your source and what it can tell readers about the past;

- Generate insight and written material that can be used to construct your chapter annotations and introductions.

<u>Assignment Activities:</u>
You will read your primary source four times:
1. In your first reading, you will read your source for the critical information contained within the course;
2. In your second reading, you will read your source for the larger purpose of the primary source—what did the author or creator of the source want to convey to their audience;
3. In your third reading, you will read for argument or bias; what limits or constrains the author's view and source;
4. In your fourth and final reading, you will read your primary source with history in mind; what can this primary source tell us about the past? What value does it contain for the reader?

You will write a paragraph after each reading of the primary source:
1. After your first reading, please write a paragraph describing the important whos, whats, wheres, whens, whys, and hows of your primary source. Cite concrete examples from the source (at least two).
2. After your second reading, write a paragraph describing the larger purpose of the Primary Source, explaining what the author or source tries to convey. Cite concrete examples from the source (at least two).
3. After your third reading, write a paragraph describing the potential limitations of the source and its author. Cite concrete examples from the source (at least two).
4. After your fourth and final reading, write a paragraph describing the potential historical value of the source you just read. Cite concrete examples from the source (at least two).

<u>Assignment Requirements:</u>
- Compile these four paragraphs into a short, well-written paper, with citations for your examples, of no less than 400 words

in length. Format in Times New Roman, 12-point font, and proofread.

Primary Source Annotation Assignment Template

(For this semester, I wanted students to explore primary sources and the connections between the people who created them and the societies in which they lived. To me, this meant exploring the context and providing my students a strategy of historicizing the world. I latched upon annotating as a form of helping them dig deeper in the various people, places, things, and ideas that appeared in their sources. They would locate their own confusions and then clarify them on their own, and through this process, generate materials that would help others. The students became active in the learning process. This dynamic proved interesting; it allowed me to assess what gave them the most confusion about their sources, what they still might be missing in terms of content, and a clear sense of what additional material I could use or engage with in my course in subsequent semesters.)

Overview:
- Annotate your primary source to clarify any issues that might confuse, confound, and might not be readily apparent to the average reader.

Objectives:
- Locate the essential people, places, things, ideas, etc., and write short annotations explaining and contextualizing their importance and value.

Assignment Activities:
1. Read your primary source, underline or highlight the significant people, places, things, ideas, etc., mentioned in the source.
   a. For example, "George Washington" or places like "Mackinaw Island," or even unfamiliar or archaic words like "approbation."
2. Compile a list of underlined or highlighted people, places, things, and ideas, and narrow your list down to 8–12 key annotations.

3. Write a short two- or three-sentence explanation for each of your annotations concerning the source. For example, let's say you are annotating the Declaration of Independence. You might annotate Thomas Jefferson, but think about who Jefferson was when he created the source and not whom he would become. He will become a president, but that's not relevant to who he was in 1776.

4. Your annotation needs to be informative and concise, and directly related to your primary source;

5. You must consult **at least** three scholarly books, journal articles, and encyclopedias to prepare your annotations.

Assignment Requirements:

- Upload your narrowed list of 8 to 12 annotations, your short, written annotations, and your works cited page for the books, articles, and encyclopedias you consulted. Format in Times New Roman, 12-point font, and ensure your annotations are proofread and well written.

Primary Source Introduction Assignment Template

(After weeks of considering, analyzing, and researching their primary sources, I felt it was important to create an assignment that asked students to provide a big-picture assessment of their source and how it fits into the larger processes and developments of United States history. Being able to manage details, connect them to larger patterns, and communicate their importance is a vital skill of historical thinking, but also a valuable skill, in general, that easily translates to a variety of disciplines.)

Overview:

- Write a short historical and contextual introduction to your primary source to connect it to more extensive processes and developments in United States history.

Objectives:

- Practice analyzing, contextualizing, and explaining the purpose of primary sources to an educated and curious audience.

<u>Assignment Activities:</u>

1. Before you start this project, re-read your close reading paragraphs, your annotations, and any other materials related to your primary source.

2. As you write this, you need to keep the reader in mind—they will not know much about your source, so help them understand.

3. Write a short three-paragraph introduction for your primary source focusing on three key aspects:

    a. Provide the necessary information readers will need to understand the source; the who, what, where, and when of the primary source and its creation;

    b. Give the readers a clear sense of how the primary source fits into the more significant processes and themes of United States history;

    c. Explain why the reader should appreciate the source and why the source matters.

<u>Assignment Requirements:</u>

- Upload a primary source introduction of at least 400 to 600 words in length. Format in Times New Roman, 12-point font. Proofread carefully.

Primary Source Illustration Assignment Template

(In subsequent iterations of the course, I plan on replacing this assignment with visual primary sources such as illustrations, paintings, artifacts, buildings, maps, etc. In treating visual literacy as an afterthought to the textbook, I created uneven results and set my students up to struggle more than they needed. I included this outline here as a reference.)

<u>Overview:</u>

- Illustrate your primary source chapter with various historically relevant images, maps, and other visual aspects.

Objective:
- Use visual imagery to better contextualize and explain your primary source to the reader and create a more stimulating reading experience.

Assignment Activities:
1. You will need to find at least three different illustrations to help your readers better understand and contextualize the primary source you chose;
   a. These illustrations can be:
      i. Maps from the period when the source was created;
      ii. Paintings from when the source was created;
      iii. Illustrations from newspapers, magazines, and media from when the source was created;
      iv. Student-made maps, timelines, diagrams, or other relevant visual elements from prior iterations of the course.
2. You want to use sources that show clear, relevant, and meaningful connections to your primary sources; you don't want to illustrate randomly.

Assignment requirements:
- Compile this material into a PDF with a short paragraph for each illustration explaining why you chose it and how it connects to your sources.

Primary Source Discussion Questions Assignment Template

(When designing this project, I understood that most of the students who signed up for my course did so for general education credit. In fact, my course might be their last course in History. As such, I developed this project as a means of helping them see History as more than just a collection of facts organized into an interesting story. I wanted my students to practice the skill of asking critical questions about the past, particularly in a context where they had a reasonably deep knowledge of the subject. The act of questioning creates a gateway toward curiosity, critical thinking, deeper understanding, and lifelong learning. This assignment created space for that conversation.)

Overview:
- Develop a series of discussion questions to help other readers explore and better understand the source.

Objective:
- Practice writing questions to dig deeper into the past and use questions to elicit deeper connections.
- Help readers dig deeper into your primary source chapter.

Assignment Activities:
1. Before you start this project, consider what a good discussion question is. This process can be daunting, so consider the following:
   a. Can the question be answered with a "yes" or "no"? If so, then it won't make a good discussion question.
   b. Does the question ask the reader to summarize what they read? If so, then it won't make a good discussion question.
   c. Does it challenge the reader to think about what they read differently? If yes, then this is a good start.
   d. Does your question ask the reader to make connections to their own experiences or preexisting knowledge? If yes, then this is a good start.
2. As you re-read your primary source, annotations, and introduction, start creating a list of questions, and do not worry about the quality. Create as many as you can.
3. With your list, begin developing three of the most interesting ones into your finalized discussions.
   a. For example, you might think about the following types of questions:
      i. Analytic questions: these often begin with "Why . . ." or "how would you explain . . ."

    ii.   Compare and Contrast questions: these begin with "Compare . . . " or "Contrast . . . " or "What is the difference between . . . "

    iii. Cause and Effect questions: these often begin with "What connection is there between . . . " or "What are the causes of/results of . . . ?"

<u>Assignment Requirements:</u>

- Please turn in three discussion questions about your primary source chapter in Times New Roman, 12-point font. Proofread carefully.

Textbook Finalized Chapter Material Template

(These requirements are closely tailored to what this textbook would look like in the context of an introductory History course; it will look different based on the discipline. However, regardless of course content, the project functions the same—it works to simulate academic discourse in a microcosm and, through simulation, helps students practice skills related to critical thinking, problem-solving, management, negotiation, researching, and visual and written communication.)

<u>Overview:</u>

- You will upload your finalized textbook chapter material.

<u>Objective:</u>

- Upload the material so the next cohort of students can edit, transform, and upload it as a finalized chapter.

<u>Assignment Activities:</u>

1. Before uploading your material, please proofread and fix any errors, typos, or issues in your primary source annotations, introductions, and discussion questions.
2. Make sure your illustrations are clear, high quality, and high resolution.

<u>Assignment Requirements:</u>
- Please upload the following material:
    1. Primary Source Introduction (as a .doc file)
    2. Primary Source with your annotations as footnotes (as a .doc file)
    3. Primary Source Illustrations (as .jpegs or .tiff)
    4. Primary Source Discussion Questions (as a .doc file)

Of Dice, Women, and Men:

Roleplaying Simulations and the Immersion Experience in the History Classroom

Daron W. Olson

The Challenge of Teaching History

I study dead people and that can be a problem.

One of the challenges of history is the subjects of the field are mostly dead, and making them come alive or seem real to students is daunting. For more recent history, film clips or movies can help fill in the void, but in the grand scheme of human history only a small percentage has this type of material. Photographs or paintings can be useful, but they are static images. For many students, history can therefore appear dull or frozen; it is something that lacks the energy of the more contemporary humanities.

As a longtime professor of history, I struggled with this quandary. I understood that history was dynamic and tension-filled but had difficulty making that apparent to my students. For many years, I was in a multidisciplinary department that included World Languages, and I enjoyed hearing about my colleagues' efforts to give their students "immersive environments" that would enhance their learning of a foreign language. Immersing students in the past, in history, was an exciting concept, but it seemed destined to fail unless a time-travel machine became available. Then a couple years later, one of my history colleagues, Dr. Justin Carroll, introduced me to the pedagogy known as Reacting to the Past (RTTP). It was an eye-opener, and I found it compelling. Students got the chance through RTTP to roleplay real historical persons.

RTTP bases its pedagogy on the idea that students will filter most historical subject matter through their contemporary experiences. To counter this tendency, RTTP places the students into an immersive historical roleplaying scenario in which they act as historical characters. To do so, the students must play their characters in the spirit of the times; in other words, if a student is playing a character during the French Revolution, they must react to situations based on what the historical character's biases and ideas were. To help students gain the proper historical perspective on their character, RTTP requires them to research the history, including the character, using a variety of assignments that prepare students for the game.[1] Reacting to the Past has proven to be a transferable method of instruction—according to the American Historical Association, more than 350 campuses have adopted its use at universities within the United States and abroad. The Reacting Consortium, an alliance of colleges and universities, serves as a clearinghouse that provides programs for faculty development and curricular change, including conferences and workshops.[2]

I considered using RTTP in one of my classes, but I thought there might be a different way to approach historical immersion. One of my favorite hobbies throughout adult life has been roleplaying, participating in simulations in which one plays created characters. I have always enjoyed such games in the "Sword and Sorcery" genre as *Dungeons and Dragons* or such British games as *Runequest* and *Stormbringer* (based on the novels by Michael Moorcock). During the 2013–2014 academic year, I was scheduled to teach a new spring semester course about the Viking Age. While on semester break, I contemplated whether including a roleplaying component in the course would enhance the immersion experience for my students. I then decided to implement a roleplaying simulation into my Viking Age course.

Since 2014, I have taught the Viking Age course every other year and employed a successful roleplaying simulation as a component of the course.

---

1   Colleen Flaherty, "Minds on Fire." *Inside Higher Ed News*, August 27, 2014. Accessed December 19, 2022. Flaherty discusses the groundbreaking work by historian Mark C. Carnes, *Minds on Fire: How Role Immersion Games Transform College*. https://www.insidehighered.com/news/2014/08/27/book-advocates-reacting-past-pedagogy.

2   American Historical Association, *Reacting to the Past*. Accessed December 19, 2022. https://www.historians.org/teaching-and-learning/teaching-resources-for-historians/reacting-to-the-past.

In addition, the following year I began teaching a course on ancient Greece set during its Golden Age, and I employed a roleplaying simulation in it as well. This chapter will provide an analysis on the use of roleplaying simulations in the history classroom. I will discuss how the roleplaying simulations relate to the study of the subject material, how students are prepared for the simulation, what my expectations of them are, and which learning outcomes the simulations are designed to meet. I will include shell syllabi, course readings, examples of roleplaying narratives I employ, and rubrics I use to measure their success. The qualities of the roleplaying simulation also offer possibilities for courses in other disciplines. A study by Shebli Younus Idham, et. al found that non-native English speakers improved their English skills through the pedagogic technique of roleplaying.[3] Hence, the use of roleplaying in the classroom would be of benefit to courses that seek to improve the speaking skills of students, which suggests many if not most university courses. Over the course of this chapter, I will discuss further how roleplaying pedagogy is transferable to other non-history courses.

I have employed roleplaying simulations in the Viking Age and ancient Greek classes seven times to date. From assessment, I have found the historical roleplaying simulations to be highly effective methods by which to immerse students in historical learning experiences. Students who have taken these courses find the historical simulations empower them to better comprehend the historical context than they would in a more traditional classroom setting.

Roleplaying and the History Classroom

For many years, the favorite courses among the IU East students I have taught have been HIST-B448, Scandinavia during the Viking Age and HIST-C377, Ancient Greece: Persian Wars to Alexander. I suspect much of this popularity originates from both courses employing historical roleplay. My inspiration for this method owes much to my esteemed fellow historian at IU East, Dr. Justin Carroll, who as noted above first introduced

---

3   Shebli Younus Idham, Ilangko Subramaniam, Alla Khan, and Sarab Kadir Mugair, "The Effect of Role-Playing Techniques on the Speaking Skills of Students at University" *Theory and Practice in Language Studies*, Vol. 12, No. 8 (August 2022): 1622–1629.

me to the idea of Reacting to the Past. In the fall of 2013, I engaged him in conversation several times, learning about the concept of RTTP. He told me he was enthusiastic about employing RTTP since it would engage the students in ways that would make the learning experience more fun and exciting. Dr. Mark Carnes of Barnard College had first developed the RTTP format in the late 1990s. What Carnes realized is that students live in a world propelled by social competition, including social online networks, video games, or other forms of competition. Carnes attempted to channel this spirit of competition by making his classroom games competitive by nature. His documentation proved that students responded enthusiastically to the chance to portray historical figures if it meant they could be competitive and have a chance at winning the game. More recent research suggests that RTTP has also been successful as a model of instruction in such disciplines as the sciences, business, and others.[4]

The conversation led me to think about other roleplaying approaches, so I asked him what he thought about using a roleplaying simulation such as *Dungeon and Dragons* or *Stormbringer* and adapting it to my Viking Age course. He was enthusiastic and suggested I talk to the excellent staff at the Center for Teaching and Learning (CTL) at the IU East Campus. When I related my ideas to the CTL, they were likewise supportive, and Gretchen DeHart, one of the teaching-delivery specialists and an avid gamer herself, provided helpful feedback. From these discussions, I soon realized I would need an assistant to help run the roleplaying simulation in the Viking Age course. The CTL staff recommended Andrew Davis, an English major who was known as an active gamer, to assist me. The roleplaying simulation required an assistant because the course looked like it would have about 14–16 students (16 was the final total), and a single gamemaster (the person who operates the scenario for the players/students) can normally handle up to 7–8 players. With the hire of Mr. Davis as a Supplemental Instructor, I worked feverishly to develop the framework for the first roleplaying simulation. The simulation combined aspects of the *Stormbringer* system with *Dungeons and Dragons*, using a hybrid framework I developed in my personal gaming many years prior.

---

4   Christian Garner, "Reacting to the Past Pedagogy in the Classroom." Paper submitted to the Center for Faculty Excellence (United States Military Academy, West Point, NY, 2018), 4–6.

Each time I run the roleplaying simulation in the Viking Age class, I make notes regarding what works well and what doesn't. My overview of the Viking Age course reflects this refinement; the roleplaying simulation in the Greek course is the product of a similar process. In both classes, the first day is the introduction in which I explain my expectations, including key aspects of the syllabus. When I explain the class will have a roleplaying simulation during the second half of the semester, I inform them that the simulation will serve as an assessment of how well they have learned the important aspects of Viking Age and Greek culture and thought processes. The goal is to get them to think like a Viking in the first course and like an ancient Greek in the second. In a history course, context is paramount, and a common problem history instructors face is getting students to think historically and in the context of the studied era's societal values. According to Luciana C. de Oliveira, students cannot learn historical context owing to limited historical knowledge and, increasingly, to limited reading comprehension skills. The traditional approach of having students read about historical context does not work for many students.[5] However, roleplaying provides students with a hands-on approach to learning societal context, and this approach would be beneficial to non-history courses as well.[6] Next, I give them a handout (also available on the Canvas online course site) that provides descriptions of each character class. In gaming parlance, a character class has advantages and weaknesses. Some character classes tend to be martial in character, while others use stealth or intelligence to succeed. I have the students list their top three choices to prevent everyone from picking the same class.

At the next class, the two assistants[7] and I have the students determine their character attributes. These attributes include strength, intelligence, dexterity, speed, power, and others, and they help to shape what the

---

5   Luciana C. de Oliveira, "'History Doesn't Count': Challenges of Teaching History in California Schools" *The History Teacher*, Vol. 1 No. 3 (May, 2008): 368–369.

6   Garner, 4–5.

7   These classes now enroll 22–24 students and require two student assistants to help me run the roleplaying simulation. I usually employ two graduate teaching assistants or one graduate teaching assistant and an undergraduate supplemental instructor. Owing to COVID-19, the 2022 Viking Age class had only seven students, so I was able to run the roleplaying simulation without the aid of student assistants.

character can do well and not so well. A student who chooses to play a warrior-type character will get a bonus, depending on class, in the physical attributes while a character that relies on knowledge will receive bonuses for attributes such as intelligence or wisdom. Once the students have rolled up their characters, I then ask them to come up with their characters' names. Usually, this is the extent of we accomplish on the second day of the course. However, students still have work to do with their characters. I inform the students they have an assignment due in four weeks. I expect them to provide a typed description of their character and their family background. I also require them to come up with the symbol found on the shields employed by their family (I do this in both simulations). Using this method does not require students roleplay specific historical characters as per RTTP, but they do create plausible historical characters.

My preference for plausible over actual historical characters involves the importance of two factors: (1) increasing student ownership, especially increasing the student voice; and (2) increasing student choice.[8] As noted by the National Institute for Excellence in Teaching (NIET), "When students own their learning, they are doing more than just engaging: They are actively taking a role in leading their learning. When this happens, the teacher serves more as a guide for students to take them further."[9] Beth Green's research reveals that pedagogic methods that increase student ownership result in students who develop a sense of autonomy, critical thinking skills, and connections outside the classroom to learn the subject.[10] Students who have participated in the roleplaying simulations observe that they feel invested in and often develop a close bond with their character. In addition, they note the roleplaying simulations are more open-ended than they would be if they played historical characters, and this effect gives them a greater variety of choices. As one student stated, "If I were playing a historical character, I

---

8   Paula E. Chan, et. al, "Beyond Involvement: Promoting Student Ownership of Learning in Classrooms." *Intervention in School and Clinic*, Vol. 50 No. 2 (2014): 105–113.

9   "What is the Difference Between Student Engagement and Student Ownership?" 2021 Learning Acceleration Resources. National Institute for Excellence in Teaching. Accessed December 19, 2022. https://www.niet.org/assets/Resources/523891961b/student-engagement-versus-student-ownership.pdf.

10   Beth Green, "Millennial Students and Democracy: What Happens When Students Have Ownership of Learning?" Doctoral dissertation. Stephen F. Austin State University, August 15, 2009. 118.

would always be thinking that I had to do what he or she did, not what I would do if placed in that situation."[11]

After the students have created their characters during the first week, the course shifts in week two, commencing the historical subject matter's study for the next seven to eight weeks. For the Viking Age course students learn about various topics, including the domestic and intellectual life of the Vikings; invasions and settlements; Viking warfare; the religion of the Norse; and others (see sample syllabus). The Greek course follows a similar format, and students learn about such topics as democracy, the role of women, Greek art, and ancient philosophy (see sample syllabus). The students must understand the era's historical context before they can engage in a roleplaying simulation. These seven to eight weeks additionally provide valuable training time since I am also meeting weekly with the student assistants during this portion of the course, teaching them how to run their sector of the campaign and instructing them on the learning outcomes the course tries to achieve.

Once students have learned the subject matter, the course switches to the roleplaying component comprising the semester's remaining seven weeks. On the first day, I like to have the students roleplay their characters in a group setting. For the Viking Age course, the setting is usually a *thing*, the Old Norse equivalent of an assembly; for the Greek course, the setting is the *ekklesia*, which is also an assembly. During this first session, the students in character will not be participating in any combat or other activities. I do this so they can become accustomed to acting through their character and to get them to think and act in the appropriate historical context. In terms of the game, some dangerous situation has occurred that requires the characters to gather and decide what options can be pursued. At this initial event, the student assistants and myself often play non-player characters, and we are the ones who normally inform the students' characters about the dangerous situation. I encourage students in this setting to act realistically, and a common approach is for their characters to invoke the gods for assistance. Sometimes, they might enhance their pleas with the (imaginary)

---

11   In 2019, three students from my Viking Age course and I participated in a panel discussion about the use of roleplaying simulations in the classroom at the IU East Day on Student Writing. The comments are from these three students.

sacrifice of goods or even animals (the Greeks typically sacrificed a lamb, while the Norse would have sacrificed a cow, a pig, or even a horse).

This initial setting provides the students with the opportunity to get the feel of roleplaying. Since the setting is an assembly, they can take turns and speak out about what they think. While students who have prior roleplaying experience outside the classroom tend to feel more comfortable, those students without prior roleplaying experience catch on quickly. While the students, student assistants, and I are in character, the students through their characters learn quickly that they must converse using concepts the Old Norse or ancient Greeks would have understood. For example, one time in my Viking Age game the community's leader, a jarl (earl) had been killed. Several of the warriors in the group wanted to know who was responsible so they could avenge the jarl's death. In this situation, my character announced the bad news and, within the game, the students' characters had to use the term jarl. If they used the term earl or lord, I would look at them quizzically and ask what they were trying to say. Through this method and throughout the simulation, the students learn key societal concepts related to their studied eras.

For the remainder of the semester, the students are broken into three groups, each one directed by a gamemaster (the two student assistants and I). Each group normally has 7–8 characters. The gamemaster introduces the scenario, providing key details and descriptions to set the background for the characters. The scenario differs in each of the three groups to prevent students from listening in on what is happening at the other two tables. I meet weekly with my student assistants to ensure they are running scenarios that meet the learning objectives for the course. I will discuss what these are later. To provide a sense of how a scenario starts out, here is one example from my Viking Age course:

A Beach Most Red

Olaf was the first to awaken, though his head felt like Thor's whetstone was lodged in his skull—he noted the incessant throbbing. He managed to rouse the others for they had a meeting that morning with Ali Ívarsson, who had recruited them to the cause of Njal Lugaidh, the Norse Gael who would become king of Dyflin, Jorvik, and the Orkneys. The other members, Ulvir, Vak, Finn, Þórrið, Freydis, Alf, and Ellisif grumbled and made a hasty breakfast of boiled trout and cheese. Ali's ale had been as good as advertised, albeit a bit potent.

As they sat around a large table, Ali entered the longhouse with his skald, Eyvind Þórleiksson. "I want to thank you for joining my cause, dear friends. We have a long road to victory, but I know the gods favor us. I need you to make contact with a warrior from the Orkneys named Brandvig Einarsson." He nods as several of the warriors recognize the name—Ulvir, Olaf, Finn, and Alf. He resumes. "Brandvig wants to join our cause and he has informed me he has knowledge of something that will aid us. He says he has the key to our success. I admit it's a bit cryptic, but one as powerful as Brandvig commands our respect. My messenger has told him to expect your group. I must now depart for I have important trade to conduct in the Eastern Sea {the Baltic}. May the gods protect you." Ali departs and the group turn their attention to Eyvind.

They note the skald is in his fifties with graying hair. He is a renowned poet and his words are said to invite favor from the gods, especially Oðin, Þórr, and Freya. You note he carries a skomr at his side and he wears gray clothing. His eyes are a bright blue and seem to sparkle. He begins: "Finn, I suggest the group take your drakkar ship, *The Raven's Feast,* to Halmness, which is where Brandvig will meet us. Yes, I will be coming along. I know many people and I can be sure we stay in touch with Ali, plus our other leaders, Njall and Leif. We will sail to Halmness in the Orkneys and meet Brandvig. He relates to warriors and I suggest the four of you—he looks at Finn, Olaf, Alf, and Ulvir—convince him to join us. Ali and I are not sure what his price for joining us will be, but as Ali says, Brandvig says he holds the key to our victory. I say we should be open-minded and prepared to meet his price, assuming he joins us. He is a respected leader and will bring many men and ships to our cause. Do you have any questions?"

It is Þórrið who speaks up: "Eyvind, do you or Ali have any idea what this knowledge or key that Brandvig possesses is?" The skald looks at the tall spákona, "No, I do not. I tried to dream about it, but nothing came to me. I guess we will learn together. Let's get our provisions and equipment ready and head out. It is a fine day to feel the breeze of the ocean on our faces. And to sail on *The Raven's Feast*, my dear Finn, surely Oðin is pleased. Let us not forget to praise Þórr for good sailing weather, too."

By late morning, the group was aboard *The Raven's Feast* and sailing for Halmness.

By way of this introduction, the students get a sense of the cultural milieu they have entered. This passage names all the students' characters— Olaf, Ulvir, Vak, Finn, Alf, Freydis, Ellisif, and Þórrið—so they know they are involved. The passage also relates two of the NPCs they met at the *thing*, namely Ali Ívarsson and Njal Lugaidh. From the previous meeting at the *thing*, the characters had learned their jarl, who controlled several territories in the north Atlantic, died without an heir and now several factions were competing to control these territories. The characters had chosen to side with the faction of Lugaidh, who is a Norse Gael, one of mixed Norse and Celtic ancestry. His lieutenant, Ali Ali Ívarsson, is of mixed Norse and Arabic heritage. The introduction of these two NPCs highlights the diversity of the Viking Age, dispelling the idea that only those of Norse ancestry could be Vikings. Furthermore, the passage informs the students what is important to their characters: praying for good fortune to their gods; the use of Norse terms such as *skald* or *spákona* (a Norse woman who practiced magic); the importance of food and drink; and the Vikings' love of fierce imagery as indicated by their ship, the *Raven's Feast*.

I also want to present an example from the Ancient Greece course. It sets the background for the characters' next adventure:

The Trial of Metrophanes . . . And Beyond

Only two weeks after Metrophanes' failed attempt to have fellow Naophor Epiphrades exiled, the tables were turned. A trial concerning the Exile of Metrophanes was convened, led by the skillful work of Leumas. Owing to his tenacity both on and off the battlefield, Leumas was now being called Leumas the Lion. At the trial, the smooth-tongued Metrophanes, a philosopher, put up a polished defense but the two letters introduced by Leumas sealed the case by a vote of 527 to 471. The Assembly of Ephres voted to exile Metrophanes for a period of five years. His position as Naophor would remain, though he would not vote, which meant the council now conducted the business of the polis with four—Hermokrates (ally of Metrophanes); Epiphrades (ally of Leumas); Pistarchus (ally of Metrophanes); and Xenophos (ally of Epiphrades). Thus, for almost a year very few new measures were enacted. All around the signs of a pending war between Athens and Sparta were growing. The deadlocked Naophorion remained a sore spot for many, including Leumas and his group, but efforts to exile Hermokrates had come to not, for there was no striking piece of evidence to remove him. When exiled, Metrophanes had cursed the Assembly, saying he would invoke his revenge. Some believed his curse was working.

The group led by Leumas, which included Ezio, Delianis, Arcuis, Amara, Kleio, and Nymphodora, was also trying to collect the various segments and keys of the Epiphania—a device rumored to help achieve peace. And while the group now possessed the First Segment and its key, plus the second key, it was almost certain the exiled Metrophanes now had the Second Segment. Moreover, he was in alliance with Athenaris, the deadly priest of Athena, and he had crossed their path as he seemed to be searching for the segments and keys as well. They were sure that Athenaris had the third segment and its key as his letter to Metrophanes indicated as much.

Another problem, however, concerns the group. During the trial of Epiphrades, Arixantes performed badly in front of the Assembly. He told Leumas he had been threatened with harm to his three sons. Now, the worst has happened, and indeed his three sons have vanished. Arixantes tells you that he had sent his sons to stay with Opthalkydes, since he was a trusted friend of the late Polykarpos. All seemed fine, but one day the mother of the children visited the place where Opthalkydes was keeping the three boys safe. She and the slaves arrived to find the place had been attacked and that Opthalkydes was wounded. He told her armed men had arrived and taken them. Moreover, he heard them talk and they had Athenian accents. Once he learned of the abduction from his wife, Arixantes came straight to Leumas. Though no ransom was posted, it appears the boys were taken by ship—

most likely to Athens. Through the efforts of Amara, the group learned the three boys were in Athens. Leumas asked Amara who her information came from, but she remained coy and would not reveal it. With little else to go on, it was decided the group should enter Athens and rescue the three boys. Fortunately, Amara and Nymphodora were skilled in the arts of disguise; hopefully they could disguise the others.

{Have them devise how they will be disguised as they enter Athens.}

Because this passage comes at a later stage in the Greek simulation, it might be difficult to follow. For our purposes, I offer a few key points. First, the scenario recounts the last roleplaying session in which the student characters, led by Leumas, successfully exiled a member of the Naophorian, the ruling council of their home polis of Ephres. By this time in the simulation, the students' characters have become entangled in the politics of the polis, which is a goal I wanted the simulation to achieve. However, through their actions the group of student characters (Leumas, Ezio, Delianis, Arcuis, Amara, Kleio, and Nymphodora) have made enemies. In this scenario, the three sons of one of their allies, Arixantes, has been kidnapped, and the students' characters are compelled to go to Athens to rescue the three sons. The characters also have the additional concern about retrieving the segments and keys of a powerful artifact known as the Epiphania before their enemies acquire them. The scenario thus creates a sense of urgency for the characters yet places them in the city of Athens where they must use stealth and subterfuge to successfully rescue the sons of Arixantes.

As subsequent gaming sessions unfold, I work with my student assistants to ensure the students experience the key course subject themes I want students to learn through their characters. These themes do not need to be encountered in any particular order, but each one should be addressed at least once during the simulation. In the Viking Age course, for example, the themes covered include the following:

1. The importance of honor and reputation to the Norse;
2. The limits of violence and when violence is appropriate;
3. The importance of trade;

4. How the Old Norse religion shaped people's perceptions;
5. The strategies and tactics employed by the Vikings;
6. The role of women in Old Norse society;
7. The role of slavery in Old Norse society;
8. How Old Norse legal systems functioned; and
9. How the concept of fate shaped the Old Norse viewpoint.

Most of these themes will recur throughout the campaign; since they involve being active learners in the process, students learn these key themes more effectively than through a traditional lecture format because it compels students to think, draw upon evidence, and draw fine distinctions. The study by Howes and Cruz on roleplaying pedagogy argues that the use of roleplaying in science education allows students to obtain a more nuanced understanding of who scientists are and how science is much more complicated than as often presented in everyday life.[12] In a post-simulation evaluation, one student explained that the simulation absolutely increased the students' understanding of the subject since they could openly discuss situations and the simulation helped make the Viking Age "real."[13] The simulation also creates situations in which the students need to consider a variety of solutions. Sometimes, solutions can come by using arguments or persuasion; in other instances, though, combat ensues. The battles within the simulation require the characters to act cooperatively and take advantage of their respective skills. They also learn that killing an important NPC can increase their fame, but it also comes with cries for revenge on behalf of the killed party's family.

Likewise, I aim for the thematic approach in the ancient Greek class, using the gaming sessions as spaces where the students encounter the themes of ancient Greece during the fifth century, B.C.E. through their characters. Those themes are:

1. The importance of honor and reputation in the ancient Greek world;

---

12   William B. Robison, "Stimulation, Not Simulation: An Alternate Approach to History Teaching Games," *The History* Teacher, Vol. 46, No. 4 (August 2013): 584. Elaine V. Howes and Bárbara C. Cruz, "Roleplaying in Science Education: An Effective Strategy for Developing Multiple Perspectives," Journal of Elementary Science Education, Vol. 21, No. 3 (Summer 2009): 40–41.

13   Assessment of Viking Age roleplaying I conducted during the spring 2014 class.

2. The limits of violence and when violence is appropriate;
3. Knowledge of the ancient Greek gods and how to placate them;
4. Employing appropriate strategies and tactics in combat situations;
5. The role of women during the Greek Golden Age;
6. The role of slaves during the Greek Golden Age;
7. Awareness of ancient Greek legal and political concepts, including democracy and the polis system; and
8. Distinguishing how fate shapes Greek perceptions of cause-and-effect situations.

In both simulations, the game mechanics reward students to increase their characters' abilities, a process often known as "leveling up." In a commensurate fashion, the simulation offers greater challenges to the students with greater stakes and rewards. As they progress through the simulation's challenges, students' characters gain in fame and attract their own followers. As a sign of this status, their characters often acquire sobriquets. Some examples from the most recent version of the Viking Age simulation included Finn Ravenblade, Ulvir Shadowaxe, and Þórrið Wolftalker. By the final session of the Viking Age simulation, the students' characters are involved in a large-scale battle against their foes to see whether their faction becomes the new rulers over the north Atlantic territories. If they are successful, the characters are rewarded by the faction leader, usually with land, titles, and great stories sung by skalds. For the Greek simulation, there is a similar process of increasing challenges and corresponding risks and rewards. Given the greater complexity of the Greek polis system, the characters who do well receive political appointments at the end of the simulation. During one of the Greek simulations, a Greek polis rewarded a particularly successful character named Leumas with the tile of Strategoi, or military general.

Reflections on the Efficacy of Historical Roleplaying Simulations

Historical comprehension requires students to grasp the studied era's historical context. However, they often fall short of this goal owing to the tenacity of modern presentism among many students. Simply put, they often fail to realize that cultures separated by time and place usually did not share in modern preconceptions of how the world operates. Roleplaying simulations in the history classroom have proven highly effective as a form of active learning in an immersive environment. By placing students in a historical simulation, "history comes alive" for them, and the experience enables them to gain insights into how cultures of the past held different values and practices from their own. Coupled with a regimen of content study, the roleplaying simulation engages their creative impulses, allowing them to immerse themselves in a performance-based interaction of the past. Because roleplaying simulations allow students to assess their constructed environment by choosing their actions and experiencing the consequences, it places students in complex situations they are not used to experiencing. While authors Alanna Gillis and Brionca Taylor noted that students in roleplaying sociology simulations achieve learning outcomes at a high level compared to those in traditional courses, they also recognize that role-playing simulations are an effective approach in many disciplines.[14]

As defined by Van Ments, role play is a form of communication that involves someone imagining being someone else in a certain situation. Through role play, the individual is required to act out the feelings, words, and actions of that other or to place himself or herself in another person's situation.[15]

Research indicates the use of historical simulations such as roleplaying is a high-risk, high-reward strategy.[16] As noted by Jeremiah McCall, historical simulation offers several advantages:

> The educational advantages historical simulation games can offer may best be thought of as advantages of immersion and provocation. When

---

14   Alanna Gillis and Brionca Taylor, "Social Networks and Labor Market Inequality: A Role-playing Activity to Teach Difficult Concepts," *Teaching Sociology*, Vol. 47, No. 2 (April 2019): 148–149, 154–155.

15   M. Van Ments, "The effective use of role play. A handbook for teachers and trainers" (Worcester, Great Britain, Billing and Sons Ltd, 1983). Cited in Jenny S. Wakefield et. al, "Learning and teaching as communicative actions: Improving historical knowledge and cognition through Second Life avatar role play" *Knowledge Management & E-Learning: An International Journal*, Vol. 4, No. 3 (2013): 261.

16   Jeremiah McCall, "Simulation Games and the Study of the Past: Classroom Guidelines" in *Fastplay: Teaching and Learning History with Technology* (Ann Arbor, MI: University of Michigan Press: Digitalculturebooks, 2014), 228–229. Accessed July 15, 2020.

playing a simulation, as opposed to other forms of instruction, a learner can become immersed in a virtual representation of the past and, in doing so, be provoked to consider how and why humans lived, made choices, and acted the way they did in the past. There are insights about the systemic contexts in which people lived, which is really just another way of saying the network of obligations, necessities, and desires that link individuals to the environment and to the rest of human society.[17]

Another advantage to historical simulation is that it helps students to understand how change works over time. Dan Moorhouse emphasizes how events over time can change circumstances for the student-operated characters in the simulation. Through this form of experiential learning, the historical simulation helps students understand how events (including the agency of the characters) leads to change.[18] A study by David Green and Mary Kay Cassani on roleplaying and STEM education offered three conclusions concerning the impact of roleplaying and student learning. First, students effectively collaborated to evaluate relevant and complex real-word scenarios. Second, student teams formed evidence-driven perspectives to support their positions as stakeholders [the roles assumed by students in the simulation]. Third, students employed metacognitive strategies where they critically reflected on the overall experience.[19] These outcomes would be desirable across academic disciplines, further supporting the applicability of roleplaying in the learning environment.

For students, the appeal of historical roleplaying simulation derives from their ability to shape the narrative through their characters. In pedagogical terms, this process is known as digital composition: the creative process that makes students invested in historical roleplaying simulations. As stated above, before the simulation begins, each student creates a historically plausible character. In the class, descriptions of various character archetypes,

---

17   Ibid, 230.

18   Dan Moorhouse, "How to make historical simulations adaptable, engaging, and manageable" *Teaching History* (December 2009, No. 133): 11.

19   David Green and Mary Kay Cassani, "Scenarios, Stakeholders, Autonomy, and Choice: Using Role-Play to Facilitate Transformational Learning Experiences," *Journal of College Science Teaching*, Vol. 49, No. 5 (May/June 2020): 42–43.

again, usually known as classes, provide students with choices regarding who they want their character to be. Next, the student rolls dice to generate the basic ability scores, which provide a sense of what the character is good at. For example, if a student in a Viking Age game chose to be a Berserker, then his higher dice rolls would likely be designated for the attributes of Strength and Constitution, while the character would assign the lower scores for other attributes.

Through their characters, the students shape the historical narrative that unfolds in the simulation. In attempting this process, the students learn something important about historical causation. As observed by Chapman and Woodcock, students tend to see events and outcomes as inevitable, behaving as if no other options which were considered at the time were available. They stress that "Role-playing positions and decisions in a simulation would make students examine the detailed, shifting evolution of an historical episode" and "help them see that things could have been different; that sometimes outcomes turned on a single moment, or sometimes they were held back by greater forces; that someone *almost* did something different; that a particular outcome was not a foregone conclusion, at least not in the eyes of the participants."[20]

Instructors must carefully approach the potential for violence in a historical simulation. Victoria Lagrange and her colleagues point out that morality inhibits violence in interactive fiction—a process similar to digital composition—and that participants will enjoy violence more if they can create a path of moral disengagement. They note that when emotion is elevated (at the expense of morality) in the creative process of a simulation, the chances for violence increase.[21]

Undoubtedly, a similar phenomenon is present in historical role-playing. It is imperative the instructor, therefore, teach about the constraints of violence within the historical simulation's society. For example, in the Viking Age role-playing, violence is omnipresent, and some students might deem violence something they can wield without regard to penalty. In the

20   Arthur Chapman and James Woodcock, "Mussolini's missing marbles: simulating history at GCSE," *Teaching History* (September 2006: 124): 18.

21   Victoria Lagrange, Benjamin Hiskes, Claire Woodward, Binyan Li, and Fritz Breithaupt, "Choosing and enjoying violence in narratives," *PLoS One* Vol 14, No. 12 (June, 2019): 4.

role-playing simulation, however, Viking Age society imposes its restraints. A Viking Age person who killed another person's thrall (a slave) would be expected to pay compensation. The same would also apply for the killing of a free person, and the compensation would often be quite high. Honor and reputation also reined in violence during the Viking Age. A Viking who killed a foe who had fallen would often be considered cowardly or needlessly bloodthirsty. A captured opponent could bring a ransom and this factor likewise placed limits on Viking Age violence.

Conversely, the students in simulation need to realize that past historical eras, including the Viking Age, were violent and violence often could not be avoided.

When using roleplaying simulations, the instructor must be cognizant of the intellectual milieu of the era. For example, if a historical simulation occurs during an era when the predominant belief system was not science-based, then the simulation will have a component known as magical realism. According to Michelle Witte, magical realism results when a real-world setting is combined with fantastical elements. She notes that within the genre of magical realism everything is normal except for one or two fantastic elements that give the environment an otherworldly feel.[22] While the term evolved within the field of literature, the historical roleplaying simulation—again, a form of digital composition—will often utilize magical realism to present the simulated culture's mythological belief systems. Thus, a Viking-Age simulation will revolve around the normal everyday life of the students' characters, but their characters can on occasion encounter elements of Norse mythology, which would include giants, elves, or dwarves, and possibly even gods and goddesses. During the Viking Age, the Norse would have perceived these beings as real and, through magical realism, the historical simulation places the student characters in a similar mindset. In the Greek course, students can expect similar encounters with beings such as sirens or a cyclops.

The efficacy of the role-playing simulation in achieving learning outcomes is promising. The overall results show that role-playing can be beneficial for many students. In a 2017 literature review, Vlachopoulos and

---

22   Michelle Witte, "What is Magical Realism?" http://michellewittebooks.com/2015/07/what-is-magical-realism/ Accessed July 10, 2020.

Makri state that "simulations provide an environment where students can experiment with different strategies, adopt different roles, and take charge of their own decisions by assuming responsibility."[23] Their study also concludes that games and simulations are powerful approaches for improving cognitive abilities in students, including higher-order thinking or meta-cognitive skills, regarded as "essential elements of in-depth learning."[24]

Additionally, Sheila Anderson Kirschbaum's study identifies how museum simulations induce prolonged engagement, creating a "flow" experience conducive to learning. Moreover, they point to a successful labor simulation in which the emotional context of the simulation helped students to identify with the factory workers whose lives they were simulating. Through this kind of activity, literacy development is fostered by communication in context.[25] For the history instructor, getting students to understand history as a subject in the context of the times is one of the most important learning outcomes. However, this significance also applies to the larger academic world. For instance, Rebecca Jackson specifies how cognitive development, which includes literacy development, is important if college students are to move beyond absolute or dualistic learning (in which all issues are seen as good or bad) and achieve "contextual knowing," characterized by the belief that knowledge exists in context and is judged on evidence relative to that context.[26]

Role-playing simulations also encourage students to engage in more research than they might in a traditional classroom setting. In his classroom simulation on the European Union, Joseph Joswiak concluded that students engaged in research wrote more because it provided an immediate "payoff" in the simulations. He further observes that students should be encouraged

---

23   Dimitrios Vlachopoulus and Agoritsa Makri, "The effects of games and simulations on higher education: a systematic literature review" *International Journal of Educational Technology in Higher Education* Vol. 14, No. 22 (1917): 16.

24   Ibid, 17.

25   Sheila Anderson Kirschbaum, "High School Students' Perspectives about Work, Skills, and Power as Related to a Museum-based Labor History Simulation." Doctor of Education Dissertation, University of Massachusetts Lowell, 2014. 90–91.

26   Rebecca Jackson, "Cognitive Development: The Missing Link in Teaching Information Literacy Skills," *Reference and User Services Quarterly*, Vol. 46, No. 4 (Summer 2007): 28–29.

to write research essays and problem reports in conjunction with such problem-based learning as simulations.[27] Studies show that having them engage in research improves students' skill development. Christiana Cianfrani observes how student-driven research in first year science courses builds the students' scientific skills, including critical thinking, the ability to identify outside information, and the role of working collaboratively in achieving success. The multidisciplinary study by Corony Edwards, et. al demonstrates a research-informed curriculum enhances student learning.[28]

Historical role playing immerses students in an experiential learning environment. Because of the multiple aspects involved in their engagement in a historical simulation, students will often achieve learning across multiple outcomes. Research by Frederick Drake indicates that alternative historical learning assessments, including historical simulation, allow the history instructor to assess student learning in each of three interrelated dimensions: knowledge, reasoning skills, and communication skills.[29] Using roleplaying in the classrooms of other disciplines would also transfer these skills.

When using historical role-playing, it is crucial for students to receive feedback. Usually, this takes place once the class completes the simulation, since it offers the optimum moment for teachable exchanges between the instructor and students.[30] In my classes, I ensure the students get regular feedback on how they play their characters. For instance, if a student in the Viking Age game prays to Thor for good weather before a sailing expedition,

---

27 Joseph Joswiak, "vegelate' and Greece: teaching the EU through simulations" *European Political Science* 12:2 (2013): 227.

28 Christiana Cianfrani, "Student-Driven Research in the First Year: Building Science Skills and Creating Community," *Journal of College Science Teaching,* Vol. 50, No. 2 (November/December 2020): 63; Corony Edwards, Mike Mclinden, Sarah Cooper, Helen Hewertson, Emma Kelly, David Sands and Alison Stokes, "Cultivating student expectations of a research-informed curriculum: Developing and promoting pedagogic resonance in the undergraduate and student learning pathway." Chapter in *Developing the Higher Education Curriculum: Research-Based Education in Practice,* Brent Carnell and Dilly Fung, editors (London: University College of London Press, 2017), see especially pages 23–30 for details on specific discipline case studies.

29 Frederick Drake, "Improving the Teaching and Learning of History through Alternative Assessments" *Teacher Librarian,* Vol. 28, No. 3 (February 2001): 32–33.

30 Tony R. Sanchez, "The Triangle Fire: A Simulation-based Lesson," *The Social Studies* (March/April 2006): 67.

I praise the student on the spot. Likewise, if a group of students who did poorly in a battle had forgotten to pray to Odin for a successful outcome, I will mention to them that the god of battle does not take kindly to those who forget to seek his favor before combat.

To assess how well students have done in the roleplaying simulation, I not only use a rubric but also have students provide qualitative feedback. The forms I use for the rubric can be found at the end of this chapter. My qualitative feedback involves asking students such questions as, "Did participating in the Viking Age roleplaying simulation help you to better understand the concept of honor and oath-taking?" Another question I ask is, "Did participating in the Viking Age roleplaying simulation help you to understand gender roles in the Viking Age?" From these qualitative surveys, students often reveal enthusiasm for the roleplaying simulations. In response to the honor question, one student noted, "I believe that I did. It taught me that it was very important during the Viking Age to honor the people around you and to keep your promises." On the question of gender roles, one student remarked, "Yes. Women played more of a role in the Viking Age and were respected more than other cultures would have in that era. That was shown by how many of the female characters were treated. Example; I was a volva and my advice was taken into consideration, when in other cultures it probably wouldn't have been." Of the 18 students who answered the survey, 17 thought the game taught them more about the Viking Age then they would have learned in a traditional classroom. These 17 also recommended keeping the roleplaying simulation as part of future offerings of the course.[31]

I have also received positive feedback from the official student evaluations. For instance, one student wrote: "The course overall, with the use of the DnD scenarios, was able to help myself and other students learn what it was like for many of these Vikings [sic] during their era." Another student offered this: "Dr. Olsen [sic] goes out of his way to provide interesting and informative literature to read at the beginning of the semester. The second part of the semester where Nornlandia (Viking roleplaying game) takes place, students can enjoy and learn through hands on experience."[32]

31   Viking Age Roleplaying Simulation Survey. Used in the Canvas site of the HIST-B448, Scandinavia during the Viking Age course taught during spring 2020.

32   These comments were taken from the official course survey for the HIST-B448, Scandinavia

Over the years, the students who have participated in the Viking Age roleplaying simulation and the Greek Golden Age roleplaying simulation have spoken enthusiastically about the experience. The simulations effectively allow for a "historical immersion" experience that allows the students to engage with the historical context of these eras through an active learning format that improves their knowledge and comprehension of the subject. Research on active learning indicates it enhances student learning in other disciplines. The study by Scott Freeman, et. al concludes that active learning increases student performance in science, engineering, and mathematics.[33] As an innovate active learning strategy, therefore, a roleplaying simulation of this type offers a viable option to other disciplines.

Sample Syllabus Overview for Scandinavia during the Viking Age

Generic Course Description:

This course covers (1) major events of the Viking Age; (2) modern-day perceptions of the Viking Age; (3) Viking Age religious beliefs and cultural practices; (4) Viking Age technology, including ships and weapons.

This course is an upper-division survey course of the Viking Age designed for History majors and Secondary Education majors with a history concentration. Given the popularity of the Viking Age in contemporary society, the course likewise attracts students who are drawn to the popular imagery and ideas concerning the Viking Age. In the course, I aim for an accurate depiction of who the Vikings were and especially who they were not. I'm a strong believer in active learning for students and I structure the course so the subject matter is learned in the first half of the course and serves as a scaffold to the roleplaying simulation. Because of the roleplaying

during the Viking Age taught during spring 2020.

33   Scott Freeman, Sarah L. Eddy, Miles McDonough, Michelle K. Smith, Nnadozie Okoroafor, Hannah Jordt, and Mary Pat Wenderoth, "Active learning increases student performance in science, engineering, and mathematics," *Proceedings of the National Academy of Sciences of the United States of America*, Vol. 111, No. 23 (June 10, 2014): 8410–8415.

simulation's immersive nature, it is a fun method for getting students to engage with key themes and concepts of the Viking Age. Furthermore, because roleplaying is such an engaging form of active learning, students achieve in such areas as critical thinking, reasoning, communication, and research skills. These skills are not exclusive to history, thus the roleplaying simulation can be used to enhance the student learning experience in the courses of other disciplines.

General Course Learning Objectives (CLOs):

Students who pass this course with a C grade or higher will be able to:

1. Explain the major events of the Viking Age
2. Describe modern-day perceptions of the Viking Age
3. Identify Viking Age religious beliefs and cultural practices
4. Assess Viking Age technology
5. Apply Viking Age concepts to the roleplaying simulation

Suggested Course Reading Materials:

1. Anders Winroth, *The Age of the Vikings* (Princeton, NJ: Princeton University Press, 2014).
2. Angus Sommerville and R. Andrew McDonald, eds, *The Viking Age: A Reader,* 2nd ed (Toronto: University of Toronto Press, 2014).
3. Kevin Crossley-Holland, *The Norse Myths* (New York: Pantheon Books, 1980).

Because this course has two parts, a more traditional exploration of the subject matter and the roleplaying simulation, I aim to address the historical and mythical aspects of the Viking Age. I use the Winroth textbook to largely address the historical aspects, supported by primary-source documents from the Sommerville and McDonald book. Crossley-Holland's book addresses the Norse myths. I find the roleplaying component works best once students have learned the subject matter. The roleplaying simulation serves to assess how well students can apply what they learned. I think this scaffolding approach would work well for other disciplines.

Suggested Course Assignments:
1. Weekly Subject Readings with Reflection Papers
2. Group Discussions over Key Topics
3. Digital Composition for Viking Age Character
4. Quizzes for Subject Assessments
5. Viking Age Roleplaying Simulation
6. Research Paper

As an upper-division course I give occasional lectures, but I rely more on having students engage in group discussions based on readings or other assignments. I use the reflection papers to ensure students complete the readings. I use the quizzes, reflection papers, and research paper to assess their performance in Viking Age subject matter. The digital composition assignments and roleplaying simulation help to assess how well students can apply what they learned. Instructors could tweak the assignments based on their disciplinary needs. The roleplaying simulation is likewise flexible and could be adopted to a variety of contexts.

Suggested Course Schedule:

In my course, which is 15 weeks long, I cover the Viking Age subject matter during the first half of the course (first seven weeks) and then switch the class to the Viking Age roleplaying simulation for the second half (final seven weeks; Week 15 is Finals Week). It is important students achieve an understanding of the Viking Age before they undertake the roleplaying simulation.

Week #1: Course Introduction, Initial Viking Age Character Creation, and Discussion on Why the Modern Era is Enamored with the Viking Age.
1. On the first day, I go over the syllabus and conduct the course pre-test. They also use dice to create their Viking Age characters' attributes.
2. On the final day of the week, students will have read material on modern fascination with the Viking Age. They discuss this concept in small groups and then as a class.

Week #2: Domestic, Economic, and Intellectual Life of the Vikings.

1. I assign portions from Winroth, Chapters 7 and 9. I supplement these with other readings or videos. YouTube has several good videos. I like the ones done by Jackson Crawford at the University of Colorado. I get students to talk about what they expected Viking life to be like versus the historical reality.
2. Assign individual and/or group Reflection Papers.

Week #3: Invasions and Settlements during the Viking Age. Viking Warriors

1. I assign Chapter 3 from Winroth, plus sources from the *Viking Reader*. I often supplement with readings from John Haywood's *Viking Atlas* or Richard Hall's *The World of the Vikings*. One theme from our discussion is how far the Vikings traveled for their various activities. Most students are surprised by the extent of the Viking world.
2. On the final day of the week, I assign them to read Winroth's Chapter 2. I have also found William R. Short's *Viking Weapons and Combat Techniques* to be a solid source on Viking warriors. Again, in discussion, we work to clear up misconceptions about Viking warriors.
3. Assign individual and/or group Reflection Papers.

Week #4: Old Norse Religion Part I

1. I assign Winroth Chapter 8, plus selected readings from Crossley-Holland. We also watch YouTube videos from Jackson Crawford. On the first day of the week, I have students discuss which myths are most historically accurate and why. On the last day of the week, I have them discuss which myths are most historically inaccurate and why.
2. In groups, students create a plausible Viking religious myth
3. Assign individual and/or group Reflection Papers.
4. Have students take the First Quiz, which covers material from the first three weeks of class.

Week #5: Vikings in the North Atlantic and the East. Viking Expansion and the Rise of Kingdoms

1. I assign Winroth Chapters 4 and 6, selections from the *Viking Reader*, plus supplemental readings and YouTube videos. We discuss why the Vikings were so active from the Atlantic to eastern Europe. I also ask them how the Vikings differed as they encountered different societies.

2. In group discussions, students interpret how other societies viewed the Vikings. How might this perspective impact their characters in the roleplaying simulation? They also discuss the reasons the Vikings tried to establish kingdoms. What motivated them?

3. Assign individual and/or group Reflection Papers.

Week #6: Poetry in the Viking Age. Use of Viking Myths in the Modern Era

1. I assign short examples of Viking Age poetry. *The Viking Reader* has some good selections.

2. Have students discuss why poetry and song were so important to non-literate peoples of the Viking Age.

3. Take the Second Quiz, which covers material from Weeks Four and Five.

4. Assign individual and/or group Reflection Papers

Week #7 Use of Viking Myths in the Modern Era.

1. I assign John Greenleaf Whittier's poem "The Norseman" as an example of the Viking in a modern-era poem. I also assign Dag Blanck's "The Transnational Viking: The Role of the Viking in Sweden, the United States, and Swedish America" as an example of modern Viking symbolism.

2. Have students discuss why the Viking works so well as a modern-day symbol.

3. Have students discuss how the Vikings have become identified with white racial supremacy.

4. Take the Third Quiz, which covers material from Weeks Six and Seven.

5. Assign individual and/or group Reflection Papers.

Note on the Roleplaying Sessions: When running the roleplaying simulation, I make sure the key nine themes (see p. 210-211) are all covered, but you can employ some flexibility regarding the order in which you cover them. The simulation is a product of what you present to the students through their characters and how they interact with the simulation. As such, the campaign will unfold in unpredictable ways. Below is a suggested way to present the key themes, but do not be afraid to mix them up if an opportunity presents itself.

Week #8 Viking Age Roleplaying: Old Norse Legal Systems; Honor and Reputation

1. I usually start the roleplaying by having the students participate in a *thing* (assembly) since it allows them a chance to roleplay their characters. It also allows me to see if they learned Old Norse legal concepts.

2. Since the students' characters are starting out as inexperienced, I like to have them offered employment by a powerful Non-Player Character (NPC). The NPC will want them to swear an oath to them, which provides later opportunities for them to test their loyalty to their leader. American students tend to see this process as a choice of convenience and often do not realize the implications of oath breaking, which was sacred to the Vikings.

Another way to think of the initial sessions is as a "test drive" in which the students get to try out their characters. Regardless of the setting involved in the roleplaying, it is important for the students to learn that they control their characters. This process is the beginning by which students establish ownership in the simulation.

Week #9 Viking Age Roleplaying: Strategies and Tactics of the Viking Age. The Concept of Fate

1. By this week, I often like to have the characters engaged in a scenario where they must rescue someone valuable to their cause (the cause can be varied depending on the overarching theme of the campaign). This challenge gives them a chance to learn about

small-scale Viking weapons and tactics. It is also useful for helping them learn to cooperate so they can attain their goals.

2. Regardless of how well the group does, I usually have the target of their rescue killed, including a dumb stroke of luck by the opposition. When doing so, I have ominous portents appear such as ravens or wolves. I will also have an NPC say something like, "Well, Oðin was fickle today and nothing was going to stop him from claiming his prize." These moments help students understand the sense of foreboding fate often brought to the Viking Age.

Getting students to cooperate is a high-impact practice and the roleplaying simulation, if well designed, will offer students numerous opportunities to engage in cooperative activities through their characters.

Week #10 Viking Age Roleplaying: The Importance of Trade and the Role of Slavery

1. In this scenario, the characters travel to a market town to engage in trade, including barter. The goal can vary; sometimes it involves procuring a better weapon such as a sword or looking for rare herbs.

2. At the market town, I often have them encounter the selling of slaves. Often, I have an NPC approach them and offer to sell them slaves that have been freshly acquired. I want them to realize the Viking age was not romantic, but a place where life was harsh, short, and brutal.

From a history perspective, I enjoy how roleplaying allows the students to experience the society they have been studying during the semester through their characters, placing them in historical context. An effective simulation should establish the context in relationship to the discipline for which it is being used.

Week #11 Viking Age Roleplaying: Old Norse Religion and the Role of Women

1. At some point the characters will need to seek help from the gods or goddesses. At this point, I like to have them interact with a Viking woman who practices *seiðr*, a form of Old Norse prophecy. The practitioner will usually aid the party, but she will seek a price, often with a vague prophecy of a future death. This type of scenario allows them to explore the religious dimensions of the Viking Age and understand that women in the Viking Age often had great powers, especially in the realm of magic.

In a non historical roleplaying simulation, the instructor could use this approach to help students learn about elements in society that are more important than their characters are. Thus, in business simulation for instance, the characters would need to negotiate the influence of powerful corporations or government entities. For a science simulation, the characters would encounter the influence of government or perhaps rivals at another university. The instructor can tailor the roleplaying simulation to the milieu that has been created.

Week #12 Viking Age Roleplaying: The Limits of Violence and the Importance of Honor

1. I like to have a scenario where the characters encounter rivals from another faction. This becomes an excellent opportunity to engage in *flyting*, or the Old Norse practice of hurling insults back and forth. At some point, I have the situation deteriorate until it seems a fight is imminent, and the students' characters are outnumbered. They must now decide if violence will solve their problem or if there is another way.

2. A good solution is for a *holmgang*, or an Old Norse duel to take place. The holmgang involves a ritualistic weapons fight where the first to draw blood is assumed to be favored by the gods and thus in the right. This tactic is one way for the student characters to achieve bragging rights if their champion draws first blood, but if the result is reversed it will mean they have to take back what they

have said and eat the Old Norse version of crow. Certainly, their honor will have suffered from this loss.

Placing the characters in a position where they are at a disadvantage offers a good opportunity for them to demonstrate critical thinking. It compels the students to make tough decisions, which can be applied to a variety of simulations, whether historical or otherwise.

<u>Week #13 Viking Age Roleplaying: Old Norse Religion and Legal Systems</u>
1. At this stage, the characters' cause looks bleak, so I have them purse a quest to grant them an advantage. In this scenario, I rely on magical realism and usually exploit something from Old Norse mythology. One of my favorites is that one of the characters has met the Dwarves, who offer to fashion a magical item that will guarantee victory. However, the characters must engage in an epic quest to gain something for the Dwarves before they will construct the magic item.
2. I like to combine a second Viking Age theme in this scenario, so this time I decided to involve Old Norse legal ideas revolving around someone who has been outlawed but is the key to their quest. This type of scenario creates a dilemma for the characters, and they will have to resolve it, weighing it against their greater goals.

A good simulation will place the characters in a situation where they must negotiate, which will test their communication skills, and applies to a wide range of roleplaying simulations.

<u>Week #14 Viking Age Roleplaying: Strategy, Tactics, and Fate</u>
1. In the final scenario I usually employ a great battle. The characters are outnumbered but their magic weapon from the Dwarves gives them a chance. The atmosphere is grim and Oðin's ravens are gathering. The fight goes badly at first, but then the magic item, normally wielded by one of the characters, starts to turn the tide and victory is won.

2. But Fate is ever so fickle and the final scenario often produces an unexpected twist. Perhaps one of the students' characters dies. Another likelihood is the leader of their faction dies in the battle. At this point the spiritual woman from before appears to confirm her prophecy of death. The victory is thus bittersweet and there is an air of uncertainty as to what happens next. The skies are gray and it begins to rain as the clouds move in....

Week #15 Finals Week
1. During the roleplaying simulation, I have been having individual meetings with students to go over their research papers. They are required to submit early drafts that I critique.
2. Students submit their research papers.
3. I meet with the students to "debrief" them about the roleplaying simulation. I will ask them if the roleplaying simulation helped them understand the Viking Age better than a traditional format. This is an important step for all roleplaying simulations.

Sample Syllabus Overview for The Greek Golden Age: Persian Wars to Alexander

Generic Course Description:
This course explores the world of the Greek Golden Age by 1) recognizing the key peoples and events of the era; 2) explaining its major trends and developments; 3) understanding the major historical arguments of the era, and 4) identifying the cultural components of ancient Greek societies.

This course is an upper-division survey course of the Greek Golden Age. The first half of the course has a traditional feel and I aim to have the students learn about the subject matter, history, and historical context of the Greek Golden Age. The second half encompasses the roleplaying simulation. I believe students need a minimal of subject competency before engaging in roleplaying and I would recommend a similar formula for courses in other disciplines using the roleplaying simulation.

General Course Learning Objectives (CLOs):
Students who pass this course with a C grade or higher will be able to:
1. Recognize the key people and events of the Greek Golden Age
2. Explain its major trends and developments
3. Understand and interpret major historical arguments
4. Identify the cultural components of ancient Greek societies

Apply Ancient Greek Concepts to the Roleplaying Simulation

Suggested Reading Materials:
1. Josiah Ober, *The Rise and Fall of Classical Greece.* Reprint Ed (Princeton, NJ: Princeton UP, 2015).
2. Adam Angelos, *Greek Mythology: A Guide to Greek Gods, Ancient Greece, Goddesses, Monsters, Heroes, and the Best Mythological Tales* (Middletown, DE: Create Space Publishing, 2016).
3. Alecos Papadatos, Abraham Kawa, and Annie Di Donna, *Democracy* (Bloomsbury, USA: 2015).
4. Kieron Gillen, Ryan Kelly, and Jordie Bellair, *Three Volume 1TP* (Image Comics: 2014).

I employ the Ober book as the basis of their readings during the first half of the course. It addresses the basic history of the Greek Golden Age. The Angelos book offers a short summary of Greek myths, which are important to learning about ancient Greek society and also as an important backdrop for the roleplaying simulation. The remaining two books help students to understand how democracy functioned in ancient Greece and why many Greek poleis did not have democracy or had very limited democracy. The Gillen, et. al piece was a graphic novel and the students responded well to it. I think it appeals to them as they have grown up in a more media-saturated world. For instructors in other disciplines, they can structure the readings to fit the needs of their students.

Suggested Course Assignments:
1. Individual and Group Reflection Papers
2. Group discussions

3. Group Creative Activities, Individual Character Creation
4. Examinations
5. Roleplaying Simulation
6. Research Paper

Suggested Course Schedule:

In my course, which is 15 weeks long, I cover the Greek Golden Age subject matter during the first half of the course (first seven weeks) and then I switch the class to the Greek Golden Age roleplaying simulation for the second half (final seven weeks; Week 15 is Finals Week). It is important that students achieve an understanding of the era before they undertake the roleplaying simulation.

Week #1: Course Introduction, Initial Character Creation, and Background to the Greek Golden Age.

1. On the first day, I go over the syllabus and conduct the course pre-test. Students also use dice to create their Greek Golden Age characters' attributes.
2. On the final day of the first week, we cover the basic history leading up to the onset of the Greek Golden Age.
3. Assign group Reflection Paper on Why Modern Humans are Attracted to the Ancient Greeks.

Week #2: Democracy in Ancient Greece.

1. Assign Ober, Chapters 1 and 2 and Democracy pp. 8–108.
2. In class, view a YouTube video on Ancient Greece.
3. Discuss how the ancient Greeks viewed democracy versus modern conceptions of democracy.
4. Assign individual and/or group Reflection Paper.

Week #3: Women and Ethnicity in Ancient Greece. Greek Mythology, Part I.

1. Assign Ober, Chapters 3 and 4; Sarah B. Pomeroy, "Women and Ethnicity in Classical Greece: Changing the Paradigms; YouTube video on the Greek Gods; Greek Mythology, pp. 3–25. Continue reading Democracy, pp. 109–236.

2. Have the students discuss gender roles in ancient Greece and how the Greeks viewed ethnicity.

3. Assign individual and/or group Reflection Paper.

Week #4: Greek Mythology, Part II; Greek Society: Citizens, Foreigners, and Slaves.

1. Assign Ober Chapter 5, *Greek Mythology*, pp. 26–68, and Nick Fisher, "Citizens, Foreigners, and Slaves in Greek Society."

2. Have students discuss Greek myths and the various ranks of Greek society.

3. In groups, have students design a Greek myth that is plausible.

4. Assign individual and/or group Reflection Paper.

I enjoy having students create their own Greek myths. I think it helps them to better understand the ancient Greeks' worldview. For instructors using roleplaying in another discipline, I recommend an assignment that helps students discern the key features of the milieu in which the simulation will take play.

Week #5: The Persians and Greeks, Warfare in the Classical Age.

1. Assign Ober, Chapters 7 and 8; YouTube video on the Greek and Persian Wars; John W. I. Lee, "Warfare in the Classical Age" and Karl-Wilhelm Wilwei, "The Peloponnesian War and its Aftermath."

2. Discuss these themes in groups.

3. Group Project: Have half the groups be pro-Greek soldiers and the other half pro-Persian soldiers. Debate ensues: Which area had better soldiers, the Greeks or Persians?

4. Assign individual and/or group Reflection Paper.

5. First Examination Paper over Material in Weeks 1–4.

Week #6: Ancient Greek Art and Greek Relations with Non-Greeks.

1. Assign Ober, Chapters 9 and 10. Steve Lattimore, "From Classical to Hellenistic Art," Robert Rollinger, YouTube video on Greek Art, "The Eastern Mediterranean and Beyond: The Relations

between the Worlds of the 'Greek' and 'Non-Greek' Civilizations" Three, parts 1–3.

2. Discuss characteristics of Greek Art. Which values were reflected in Greek art?
3. In groups, discuss how the Greeks interacted with non-Greeks. How might these attitudes be reflected in the roleplaying simulation?
4. Assign individual and/or group Reflection Paper.

I find assignment number 3 above to be useful for preparing students for the simulation. Instructors in other disciplines should feel free to use an appropriate assignment to achieve the same level of preparation.

<u>Week 7: The Decline of the Greeks and the Rise of Macedonia. Digital Composition of Greek character.</u>
1. Assign Ober, Chapter 11. Three, parts 4–5 and Egypt.
2. Discuss why the Greek Golden Age waned and why Macedonia and Alexander eventually triumphed. What is the legacy of Alexander the Great, including Greek culture?
3. Submit character background (digital composition).
4. Post-Test
5. Second Examination over material in Weeks 5–7.
6. Assign individual and/or group Reflection Paper.

Note on the Roleplaying Simulation: When running the roleplaying simulation, I make sure the nine key themes are all covered. These are:
1. Greek reputation
2. Greek politics and democracy
3. The importance of trade
4. Greek mythology
5. Greek warfare, including small-scale tactics
6. The role of women in ancient Greece
7. The role of slavery in ancient Greece
8. The Greek concept of Fate
9. The role of philosophy and science

You can employ some flexibility regarding the order in which you cover these themes. The simulation is a product of what you present to the students through their characters and how they interact with the simulation. As such, the campaign will unfold in unpredictable ways. Below, I present a suggested template for introducing the key themes, but the instructor should not be afraid to mix them up if an opportunity presents itself.

Week 8 Greek Roleplaying Simulation: The Ecclesia and the Villa.
1. I usually start the characters at an *ecclesia*, or Greek Assembly. The male characters with property can speak freely and vote. Female characters have a harder time since they are not allowed to speak or vote independently. I often have the female students accompanied by a male relative, such as a brother, father, or uncle, who they roleplay at the assembly. This exercise introduces them to the concept of Greek democracy. After the ecclesia ends, I usually have them approached by a noble who wants them to perform a task for him.
2. The task is played out as the characters travel to a villa outside the main city. The owner is another Greek nobleman who is in charge. The characters will have to show him deference and can see how the nobleman treats his slaves, wife, and daughters, who tend to stay inside and are not expected to interact with the group. However, a *Hetaira*, or Greek woman who is both party conversationalist and sexual partner, will lead the table. This situation allows the characters to see that the Greek wife remains isolated, and her entertainment function is fulfilled by an outsider. This dynamic reveals gender roles to the characters.

During the first week, I try to have the characters in situations where they have to communicate. I find this exercise builds student confidence in their ability to roleplay their characters. I would recommend roleplaying simulations in other disciplines employ a similar approach.

<u>Week 9 Greek Roleplaying Simulation: Greek Trade and Greek Battle Tactics.</u>

1. At this stage, I usually have the characters seek a trade item or several items for the noble who hired them. They will travel via ship to a busy port such as Athens and enter the market area. This scenario allows the students to experience the importance of trade as they must enter into hard-earned negotiation to secure the item(s) they want.

2. After they leave the port city, I often have their ship attacked by another ship. They learn that the other ship's leader wants the item(s) they have just procured from the trading center. This scenario introduces students to Greek small-scale tactics, and they must learn to cooperate to fight off the attackers.

I aim for scenarios where students must learn to cooperate through their characters. I have found this exercise enhances the active learning experience. Instructors employing roleplaying for other disciplines would benefit from scenarios that rely on character cooperation.

<u>Week 10 Greek Roleplaying Simulation: Greek Mythology.</u>

1. The characters are unsure who attacked their ship, and they wish to learn why they were accosted. At this point, I often have them seek out the Oracle at Delphi, who was famed throughout the Greek world for her gift of prophecy. I have them travel to Delphi and allow only three characters to seek an audience with the Oracle. The Oracle will answer their questions with references to Greek mythology. If the characters can decipher what the Oracle says, they can they undertake the mythic quest she suggests.

2. This mythic quest takes part in the latter half of the week and the characters must perform some right of passage before they can learn who attacked them. I might have them defeat a famed monster from Greek myth or a famous champion.

Societal context is important to my roleplaying simulations, and I aim to immerse the student characters in these types of scenarios where they encounter the previously studied cultural aspects. Successful simulations, regardless of course discipline, would benefit from this approach.

Week 11 Greek Roleplaying Simulation: Ancient Greek Science and Ancient Greek Politics.

1. From the previous scenario, the characters have learned their ship was attacked by a rival of the noble who hired them. At their leader's suggestion, they decide to bring charges against him. They consult a Greek philosopher who utilizes rudiments of the scientific method to build their case.

2. At the *ecclesia*, the characters bring charges against the rival noble. The scientist is their key witness, and they convince enough members to vote for *ostracism*, or to have the rival noble banned. This week's scenario has allowed the characters to gain insight into how science and Greek justice could interact.

Societies, or milieus, have rules. A successful roleplaying simulation should have the characters placed in situations where they must learn how to operate with those rules or boundaries and understand the limits of what they can and cannot do.

Week 12 Greek Roleplaying Simulation: Ancient Greek Reputation and Warfare.

1. The noble rival refuses to go into exile and instead seeks the protection of the Persians, who see an opportunity to gain further influence (I often use this scenario when the main city is an island in the Aegean Sea). The noble is defiant, and his reputation suffers. However, since the characters presented a legal case, they must show honor and attempt to arrest the defiant nobleman.

2. The characters sail with several ships to a nearby island but encounter a fleet of Persian ships. A naval battle breaks out. The characters realize they are outnumbered but do not want to back down to the Persians. Usually, they are defeated and must retreat. Sometimes, I reward them if during the battle they pray to the

Greek gods, such as Poseidon, god of the sea, for divine aid to escape the Persian massacre.

This scenario is another where characters need to cooperate to succeed. It also creates good opportunities for negotiation, especially in the context of ancient Greece. Successful roleplaying simulations for other disciplines could employ similar scenarios.

Week 13 Greek Roleplaying Simulation: Ancient Greek Mythology and Fate.

1. I bring back the philosopher/scientist who, through his research, has uncovered a myth about a special Item that might help the party win their battle against the rival nobleman and the Persians. They learn they must seek an item on an isolated island or barren shore.

2. The characters travel to the location and encounter a mythical creature (the Greek myths allow for several) that warns the characters if they take the item they will be cursed. Assuming the characters ignore the warning and collect the item, they feel smug for having done so. However, an omen appears as they sail away, such as a blood-run sun or a giant wolf materializes and howls at them.

This scenario serves as a good summative assessment of how well the students have learned about the Greek myths. I recommend those creating their own roleplaying simulation make sure the scenarios become cumulatively more complicated and nuanced. This feature ensures the students are scaffolding their learning through their characters as they encounter the studied subject's milieu.

Week 14 Greek Roleplaying Simulation: Ancient Greek Warfare, Justice, and Fate.

1. The characters engage the rival noble and his Persian allies. The item helps them, and they carry the battle. The rival is captured. The characters receive accolades.

2. At the *ecclesia*, charges of treason are brought against the rival noble. When the noble is condemned to be executed, he declares that he knows the item that brought about his defeat demands a price. He will look at the characters and declare that once he dies, he will take one of them to Hades (Hell) with him. The philosopher who is present scoffs and the execution takes place. The characters notice that nothing happens and they have a banquet that evening to celebrate and toast each other. I usually roll a random dice to determine which character will die after he mutters his toast. (Of course, if the characters refuse to use the special item, they will be defeated and likely captured by the Persians. This outcome can lead to a different ending; that is the beauty of the roleplaying simulation.)

Like a Greek tragedy, there is often an unforeseen twist at the end of the story. I try to employ this technique to reinforce notions of Greek fate. For an instructor creating their own simulation, this method would be optional depending on the milieu they are using.

Week 15: Finals Week
1. During the roleplaying simulation, I have been having individual meetings with students to go over their research papers. They are required to submit early drafts that I critique.
2. Students submit their research paper.
3. I have a "debriefing" with the students about the roleplaying simulation. This is a good time to explain to them what I as the instructor was trying to accomplish. It also allows them opportunities to ask questions and offer feedback on what they thought was effective and what needs to be improved in the roleplaying simulation.

Viking Age Roleplaying Simulation Rubric

Criterion	1	2	3	4	Feedback
The character demonstrates honor and values his/her reputation					
The character realizes violence is context-specific					
The character engages in trade to improve his/her standing in the game					
The character reveals that his/her actions were based on Old Norse religious concepts					
The character employs historically accurate strategies and tactics in combat situations					
The character comprehends the historically accurate role of women in the Viking Age					
The character understands the roles played by slaves in the simulation					
The character shows awareness of Old Norse legal concepts such as *weregild*, compromise, and exile					
The character distinguishes that fate shapes how the Vikings perceived cause and effect situations					

1=standard not met; 2=standard partially met; 3=standard met; 4=exceeds expectations

Greek Golden Age Roleplaying Simulation Rubric

Criterion	1	2	3	4	Feedback
The character demonstrates honor and values his/her reputation					
The character realizes violence is context-specific					
The character reveals a knowledge of how to placate specific gods					
The character employs historically accurate strategies and tactics in combat situations					
The character comprehends the historically accurate role of women during the Greek Golden Age					
The character understands the roles played by slaves in the simulation					
The character shows awareness of ancient Greek legal and political concepts, including the functions of democracy in the polis					
The character distinguishes that fate shapes how Greeks perceived cause and effect situations					

1=standard not met; 2=standard partially met; 3=standard met; 4=exceeds expectations

Nornlandia Character Sheet

Player _____

Character Name _____

Class _____

Homeland _____ Diety _____

Ht _____ Wt _____

Appearance _____

Str:	Level:	Hit Points:
Dex:		

Weapon	To Hit	Parry	Damage
1.			
2.			
3.			
4.			
5.			
6.			

Possessions	Languages	Speak	R/W

Feats

Agility Bonus:	Stealth Bonus:	Manipulation Bonus:	Comm Bonus:
Climb	Ambush	Juggle	Credit
Dodge	Conceal	Pick Lock	Orate
Jump	Hide	Sleight of Hand	Persuade
Ride	Move Quietly	Set Trap	Sing
Swim	Cut Purse	Tie knot	
Tumble			

Perception Bonus:	Knowledge Bonus:	Other Skills:
Balance	Eval Treasure	
Listen	First Aid	
Scent	Make Map	
Search	Memorize	
See	Music Lore	
Taste	Navigate	
Track	Plant Lore	
	Poinson Lore	
	World Lore	
	Craft	

Greek Golden Age RPG

Player: Character Name: God/Goddess: Ht: Wt:	Level: Age: Hit Points: Class:

Attributes	
Str: Int: Dex: Con: Wis: Spd: Pow: Alt: Cha: Siz:	Attack Modifier: Parry Modifier: Damage Modifier: Stealth Modifier: Agility Modifier: Manipulation Modifier: Perception Modifier: Knowledge Modifier: Communication Modifier:

Weapon	Hit	Parry	Damage
1.			
2.			
3.			
4.			
5.			
6.			

Feats:

Weapons and Equipment:	Skills:

* * * * * * * * * * * *

Building Relationships and Deeper Connections in the Classroom

* * * * * * * * * * * *

How and Why to Provide Relational Feedback

Kelly Blewett

Relationships with teachers are generally important in a student's life but particularly so in times of transition. A child's relationship with their kindergarten teacher predicts success in elementary school,[1] and adolescents' relationships with their teachers can have an impact on their attitude toward course content.[2] At hinge moments, when expectations are shifting and environments are new, connecting with trustworthy adults is significant. As people who work in teaching-focused institutions, part of our collective mission is to establish relationships with students that can help them in college, which is, of course, another major transition. Looking broadly at retention data, relationships with faculty are a key component of persistence and success in college.[3] But how are such relationships established?

1   Sondra H. Birch and Gary W. Ladd, "The Teacher-Child Relationship and Children's Early School Adjustment," *Journal of School Psychology* 35, no. 1 (1997): 61–79; Bridget K. Hamre and Robert C. Pianta, "Early Teacher-Child Relationships and the Trajectory of Children's School Outcomes Through Eighth Grade," *Child Development* 72, no. 2 (2001): 625–38.

2   Carol Midgley, Harriet Feldlaufer, and Jaquelynne S. Eccles, "Student/Teacher Relations and Attitudes toward Mathematics Before and After the Transition to Junior High School," *Child Development* 60, no. 4, (1989): 981–92; Roeser, Robert W., Jacquelynne S. Eccles and Arnold J. Sameroff, "School as a Context of Early Adolescents' Academic and Social-Emotional Development: A Summary of Research Findings," *The Elementary School Journal*, 100, no. 5 (2000): 443–71.

3   Buskirk-Cohen, Allison A.; Plants, Aria, "Caring about Success: Students' Perceptions of Professors' Caring Matters More than Grit," *International Journal of Teaching and Learning in Higher Education*, 31, no. 1 (2019): 108–114; Paul D. Umbach and Matthew R. Wawrzynki, "Faculty Do Matter: The Role of College Faculty in Student Learning and Engagement," *Higher Education*, 46, no. 2 (2005): 153–184.

This chapter focuses on feedback as a tool for establishing productive relationships with students that can promote their success within our classes and beyond. Describing feedback as relational may involve shifting our perspective on feedback itself. In this chapter, my aim is to describe the benefits of relational feedback and show what it can look like in practice.

Feedback is a general term for any information on how someone is doing in a particular context. Outside of school, people who research feedback in workplace environments note it can be as unobtrusive and spontaneous as an approving expression or compliment or as high-stakes and formal as an annual review.[4] In the context of the classroom, feedback has been used to describe both formative (coaching) and summative (evaluation) assessment directed to individual students as well as full, class facing interactions that are designed to improve performance on particular assignments (i.e., "In this announcement, I will describe three common problems I am seeing in the drafts…").[5] For the purposes of this chapter, any time you grade work or comment on student performance, whether individually to the student or in a full-class environment, you are providing feedback. In general, effective feedback results in increased engagement with course content and improved understanding of how to meet the learning objectives.

Relational feedback pushes us to consider something more than isolated experiences with feedback: fostering an ongoing conversation with students. Such a vision requires teachers to be purposeful with feedback in ways that align with commonly held best practices for feedback and to think strategically about how to build relationships with students across a 16-week semester or a 10-week quarter. In this chapter, I will talk about how I do that in first-year writing courses. I will include examples of my feedback to Maria, a former student in a general education composition course, throughout the chapter to show situated feedback and an instructional relationship within a particular context.

---

4   Douglas Stone and Sheila Heen. *Thanks for the Feedback: The Science and Art of Receiving Feedback Well.* (Penguin, 2015).

5   Jane E. Pollock, *Feedback: The Hinge that Joins Teaching and Learning* (Corwin, 2012). See also: Maddalena Taras. "Feedback on feedback: Uncrossing Wires across Sectors" in *Reconceptualizing Feedback in Higher Education*, eds. Stephen Merry, Margaret Price, David Carless and Maddalena Taras (Routlege, 2013), 30–41.

My goal as a teacher is to promote student success in my class and to offer myself as an ally for my students, someone to whom they can turn as they continue in their college careers. My hope for you is that you can take what I am doing in this first-year-writing context and see applications to your own courses and will be inspired to think about feedback as a tool for building relationships with students that improve their performance in your class—and can create a connection between you and the student that the student can carry forward.

Ten Guidelines for Effective Relational Feedback

Writing teachers provide a lot of feedback, and a set of best practices have emerged over time that have scarcely changed in the last 50 years. For more on the research underlying these practices, as well as application-focused resources, see the bibliography of further reading at the end of this chapter. My favorite praxis-focused book on the topic is Nancy Sommers's *Responding to Student Writers*.[6] I also really like Richard Straub's point that approaches to feedback are necessarily individualized. He writes, "Different teachers, in different settings, with different students, different kinds of writing, different course goals, and with different time constraints may do substantially different things with their comments and do them well."[7] In that spirit, I offer these ten guidelines about feedback, which align to the best-practices in the field of rhetoric and composition and reflect my own emphasis on instructional relationships:

1. Plan and communicate your feedback routines early on and try to stick to them.
2. Think about feedback not only in terms of content and correction but also of rapport.
3. Create low-stakes assignments where you can get to know students and their individual commitments to the class, especially toward the beginning of a term.
4. Consider how to support process work for bigger assignments,

---

6   Nancy Sommers. *Responding to Student Writers* (Bedford, 2013).

7   Richard Straub. *The Practice of Response: Strategies for Commenting on Student Writing* (Hampton Press, 2000), 4.

which will help you comment on steps along the way.

5. Praise, praise, praise. Look for something to like in the student work. Quote your favorite sentence.

6. Make the feedback dialogic—require the students to write back to you at certain moments (such as generating a revision plan after a conference or writing a note to prepare you to read their final draft). Recognize the value of their reply when they write back to you unexpectedly.

7. Treat disclosures of difficulty with care. Students sharing where they are struggling is a sign the feedback cycle is working well.

8. Try to match your feedback modality to student preference. Experiment with the affordances of audio/video feedback.

9. When offering corrective feedback, be encouraging and specific. Use the assignment's evaluation criteria (which should connect clearly to the course learning objectives) as your guide.

10. Try to teach one lesson at a time—and give the students what they need to attend to their own writing process beyond your class.

These ten guidelines help focus my feedback, and they are attentive to the underlying social-emotional dynamics of learning. As research has demonstrated, when students receive critical feedback they may feel their desired self-image is being called into question, which can in turn prompt disengagement.[8] As Chris Anson and his co-authors write, "teaching is inherently a face-threatening process."[9] This begs the question: how can teachers provide the genuine critical feedback students need while still being attentive to facework? This is not an ancillary question but a foundational one.

As Lad Tobin points out, "fostering productive working relationships in the writing classroom is not another nice thing to do, but it is the primary thing we must do."[10] He suggests productive working relationships

8   Thomas Newkirk. *Embarrassment and the Emotional Underlife of Learning* (Heinemann, 2017).

9   Chris M. Anson, Deanna P. Dannels, Johann I. Laboy, and Larissa Carneiro. "Students' Perceptions of Oral Screencast Responses to Their Writing: Exploring Digitally Mediated Identities" *Journal of Business and Technical Communication* 30, no. 3 (2016): 378–411.

10   Lad Tobin. *Writing Relationships: What Really Happens in the Composition Class* (Heinemann, 1993).

must be established, monitored, and maintained.[11] For me, these keywords speak to the different kinds of practices we can do at different points in the semester: establishing relationships early in the term, monitoring relationships in the long middle of the term, and maintaining relationships at the end of the term (and beyond). Thinking about the timeline of the course as unfolding in relational stages has helped me purposefully attend to the social-emotional component of feedback and, in turn, to fostering productive instructional relationships.

Below I describe these stages as they played out in my spring 2021 first-year writing course. First-year Writing, or Freshman Composition, is one of the largest general education courses in the country. Students often enter this curricular space skeptical of the value of the class—or even with some negative past experiences related to writing (perhaps they did not pass a college-prep course or AP exam that would have enabled them to skip the course). They may perceive the course as irrelevant or remedial; they certainly won't approach it with the enthusiasm of a core-course in their major. For these reasons, effective instruction is of heightened importance in this course.

Maria took this course online during her first year at Indiana University East. In her student profile, she uploaded a smiling selfie, which appears to have been taken in a car. Her eyes gaze directly at the camera; her head is wrapped in a soft pink hijab. Her smile is wide, displaying a set of silver braces over the top row of her teeth. The first line of her introduction read, "My name is Maria. I am twenty years old and I was born and raised in Freetown Sierra Leone." Through Maria's introduction, I learned that Maria was in a very different time zone—and on a different continent. English was not her first language. She did not particularly gravitate toward writing as an activity and was majoring in mathematics. Finally, she was working full-time while also taking the class. Given this information, I anticipated Maria might need extra support throughout the semester, which proved to be true. What I didn't expect was Maria's tenacity and persistence—and the way she'd find unique ways to connect with me, an instructor who lived and worked on the other side of the world. If I invited Maria into an instructional relationship, then Maria more than reciprocated my invitation.

---

11   Tobin, 5.

The composition course I describe here is themed around literacy. Students are introduced to important concepts about writing and then asked to explore their own literacy past (module 2), analyze an academic article (module 3), and report on the literacy practices of a community of which they are a member (module 4). Finally, they gather their favorite writing across the course and reflect on their learning in a portfolio (module 5). I like this course design because it's suitably rigorous, emphasizes research-based ideas about writing, and makes lots of room for students to explore their own connections to course content, which tends to increase engagement. Below I explore the relational stages of the course in more depth.

Early Term: Establishing Instructional Relationships, Fostering Rapport

As I write this chapter, I am reminded of the comment of an experienced teacher whose feedback practices I studied several years ago. She said, "Get the first weeks right and the rest of the semester is a cake walk." I agree that the beginning weeks are among the most important in the term. Early in the term, students will be working hard to get a read on the class and on your instructional approaches.[12]

In week one, it's important to drive clarity on what the course is all about, as well as how the different parts of the course fit together to help the student be successful. When I first started teaching, I would do this informally, for instance through a quick talk on the course learning outcomes and how they related to the different projects. Over time, and thanks to resources like Quality Matters,[13] I now provide an alignment map for students that shows how all learning activities and assessments connect to the outcomes. Whatever your method, and knowing that your method may change over time, the main thing to consider is how the work students will do in your course connects to the achievement of the learning outcomes.

---

12   See Center for Innovative Teaching and Learning, "First Day of Class," *First Day Strategies*, Indiana University Bloomington, https://citl.indiana.edu/teaching-resources/teaching-strategies/first-day-strategies/index.html (Accessed 6-10, 2022).

13   To learn more about Quality Matters, see "Course Design Rubric Standards," *Quality Matters*, https://www.qualitymatters.org/qa-resources/rubric-standards/higher-ed-rubric (Accessed 6-13, 2022).

Discussing this aspect early on will help with your feedback, because you can get students on board with the course learning objectives (from which your evaluation criteria should flow).

Aim to communicate feedback routines in thoughtful ways. Below are two policies from my first-year writing class, where you can see I attempt to communicate the weekly rhythms of the course.

- Grading: Regarding grading, you can generally expect to get short assignments (i.e., discussion board writing assignments) returned within 72 hours, with both qualitative (a sentence or two of informal feedback) and quantitative (a point grade) feedback from me. Longer assignments (drafts and unit papers) may take up to one week to grade.

- Announcements: I post weekly announcements on Mondays. These announcements will review upcoming due dates, offer full-class feedback on recent work, and/or share timely updates and information. You will see the announcements on the top of our course homepage and they will be sent to your email.

In this class, I want students to understand that full-class feedback will be communicated on Monday via announcements, while I intend to offer individual feedback on Tuesday and Friday mornings. When I have longer assignments (drafts and final papers), I guarantee students will hear from me within a week; this timeline enables me to only grade a handful of papers at each sitting. For me personally, I aim to grade around five papers at a time, and I spend about 20 minutes per paper. I've found setting a timer when I sit down to a grade a paper helps me relax and just focus on the paper. Longer papers, of course, take longer. If I taught additional sections, I would adjust my process. In discussing feedback with experienced teachers, I've found most think about feedback routines in this way, that is, both what the weekly rhythm will entail and how many longer assignments they can grade in a sitting. Again, all of this is about planning and managing student expectations and your time.

During this week, I also introduce myself to students. For Maria's class, the introduction occurred via online video. Studies of instructional relationships find students respond best to professors whom they regard as experts in the field they are studying.[14] For this reason, in my introduction, I explain that I like teaching first-year writing, regard the course as an extremely important component of an undergraduate education, and have taught first-year writing for over a decade and researched how it tends to work best. As you think about your introduction, consider ways to demonstrate your interest and expertise in the course content, as that will help students be more receptive to your feedback throughout the course.

To get to know students, I ask for a self-introduction in which they identify which of the learning outcomes interest them most and, because this is a writing class, what three words they associate with writing. I then take the information students provide about the words they associate with writing and create a Word cloud to share with the whole class in my first announcement (see Figure 1).

Figure 1: Words associated with writing in Maria's class (Spring 2021)

---

14   Philip C. Abrami, Sylvia d'Apollina, and Steven Rosenfeld. "The Dimensionality of Student Ratings of Instruction: What We Know and What We Do Not" in *Effective Teaching in Higher Education: Research and Practice*, ed. Raymond P. Perry and John C. Smart (New York: Agathon, 1997), 321–67.

As you can see, students in this section primarily connect writing with communication, knowledge, organization, and imagination. My Word cloud, while not evaluative, offers a kind of descriptive feedback to the full class. It says, "here we are, at the beginning." This kind of feedback, in which you mirror what a class is saying, can be very effective at fostering critical thinking.[15]

I do this assignment for a few reasons: first, so that students feel heard and seen, can start to get a sense of the class community as a whole, and can start to think about their conceptions of writing, which we discuss the following week. Also, students will return to this introduction at the very end of the term, when they are working on their portfolios, to think about how their impressions of writing have changed. So this assignment, while small and low-stakes, sets the stage for the course, begins to establish our unique online community, and provides a useful artifact for a future assignment. This online activity meets the goals of many first-day activities in in-person classes, as described in the Chronicle of Higher Education.[16]

I also respond to each student individually, just to welcome them to the class. Below is my response to Maria's initial post.

Hi Maria,

I really admire your goal of teaching mathematics! One of my friends here at IUE, Dr. Nayeong Kong is a super dedicated teacher, and I've had conversations with her about the importance of writing in mathematics. You are so right that math helps you "learn to pay attention to all assumptions given in solving a problem" and requires systematic and clear communication. I hope you are enjoying IU East so far and I look forward to working with you this semester.

Dr. Blewett

---

15   For more on techniques to foster critical thinking that are similar to this one, see Stephen Brookfield's *Teaching for Critical Thinking* (Jossey-Bass, 2011).

16   James M. Lang, "How to Teach a Good First Day of Class: Advice Guide." *Chronicle of Higher Education*, https://www.chronicle.com/article/how-to-teach-a-good-first-day-of-class/ (Accessed 6-13, 2022).

As I look at this response now, I notice many of the moves I make align with rapport-building strategies described by Nathan G. Webb and Laura Obrycki Barrett.[17] I open with Maria's name (attentive behavior), offer a specific compliment (connecting behavior), quote directly from her writing (attentive behavior), and attempt to draw connections between her interests and our course content as well as to other people I know on our campus (information-sharing behavior). Several of the early discussion assignments in my course facilitate feedback like this, as they expressly ask students to share about their own lives and experiences, which then opens the door for me to connect with students and understand them in a more individual way. When possible, I think it's effective to begin a course by inviting students to use their experience as a bridge to course content, as that can open the door to fostering connection through feedback.

Throughout this early period, my instructional goals are promoting student self-reflection, enhancing students' investments in course content, encouraging students to articulate and examine their assumptions about writing, and fostering a regular writing practice. I also want to get them used to hearing from me, and I aim to find specific ways to encourage their ideas. A lot of this work also builds rapport, as I try to communicate encouragement, respect, and understanding to students through the feedback. These qualities align with research about how rapport is perceived in online courses.[18] Some of my assignments during this time include the following: draw a picture of your writing process, identify a strong literacy memory, apply Brandt's concept of literacy sponsorship to your own life, and think about how our course textbook aligns with your own experiences of writing. Below, I'll share Maria's response to this last assignment on the list and my response to it, just to give you a sense of what this exercise looks like in action.

In the discussion post below, which was written during week two of a 16-week term, Maria was asked to consider what she thought about the

17   Webb, Nathan G. and Laura Obrycki Barrett, "Student Views of Instructor-Student Rapport in the College Classroom," *Journal of the Scholarship of Teaching and Learning*, 14, no. 2 (2014): 15–28.

18   William J. Lammers and J. Arthur Gillaspy Jr., "Brief Measure of Student-Instructor Rapport Predicts Student Success in Online Courses," *International Journal for the Scholarship of Teaching and Learning*, 7, no. 2 (2013).

textbook so far, how it compared to the way she studied writing in the past, and how she personally related (or did not relate) to the concepts it described. Maria wrote:

> At first, when i read the title *"Writing about Writing"*, i thought it was going to be uninteresting to read but it seemed very fascinating and it explains about many concepts that are taking place at the moment. After reading it, i now know why i was struggling in the past while writing as i did not think much of it. Writing has not been my strongest point in the past but after reading this book, i am glad to be a part of this class in order to dig deeper in the concepts of writing.
>
> There's a huge difference between the way i have studied writing in the past and the present. Throughout the years, i always thought that writing was just based on grammar. I remember always focusing on grammar topics such as present tense, past tense, subject and object of a sentence, etc. Even though it is important to have the right grammar, it is also important how you think about the question given and how you are going to present it in order for the reader to receive the right ideas. After reading this book today and seeing how it got stuck in my mind for good, i now know that when it comes to writing, i should just write what i am feeling/thinking about and be confident.
>
> The threshold concept that i relate to the most is "People collaborate to get things done". This shows how important it is to communicate in order to understand the main point/ideas. In order for us to understand writing as a process we must collaborate. It helps people to learn from one another as they introduce you to different skill sets and one can also share knowledge, ask for opinions and get responses. I also find "Writing is process and all writers have more to learn" very truthful. As you keep growing, the way you write changes and you can explain and understand more. We all are being corrected as we are not perfect in writing but day by day we learn more and if we are really passionate about writing then we are ready to face more. As my mother once told me "No one was ever born smart or ready, we all go through the same phase and we keep on practicing."

The purpose of this assignment is to get students thinking toward the first writing project, the literacy narrative, so I want to comment on the students' ideas as related to that purpose, as opposed to discussing surface errors regarding punctuation and grammar.[19] I want to demonstrate that I am listening to them and responding to their ideas. I want to find something I like in the work. I am also mindful of the amount of time the feedback will take, so I try to use technologies that will help me manage my time effectively. In this case, since I know I want to respond to an entire class on Friday morning, I aim to spend about five minutes per student response. With all of this in mind, I provided both a textual and an audio response to this post from Maria. Here's my textual response:

> Maria,
>
> Click on the white triangle in the blue square to hear some audio feedback on your post. Let me know if you have trouble accessing this feedback.
>
> Dr. Blewett

I've found that when using a non-alphabetic modality in my Learning Management System (Canvas), it's helpful to give students some instructions. Below is a transcript of the audio feedback I left for Maria, which was about one minute and 50 seconds long. I've edited it very lightly for clarity:

> Hey Maria, this is Dr. Blewett, here to respond to your discussion board post. I am glad you found the opening to be so interesting and different than how you studied writing in the past. I absolutely love the quote from your mom, "no one was ever born smart or ready." That's a *great* quote, a *great* thing to keep in mind. I wanted to kind of

---

19 As you read this example of feedback, you might be wondering why I did not discuss the surface-level errors in Maria's writing. I did not discuss them because they did not impede my ability to understand her text. As the term progressed, I encouraged Maria to send her papers to the writing center before submitting them for review. Maria began to send both her discussion board posts and her longer papers to the writing center in March, and by the end of the class the submitted writing had fewer surface-level errors. For more information on responding to surface-level errors in student writing, see Sommers *Responding to Student Writers*, p. 31.

help you look forward a bit. You mentioned two threshold concepts you liked were people collaborating to get things done and writing being a process. As we move toward literacy narrative, you might think about uncovering some of the ways that you've approached writing as a process in the past and kind of investigating those a little bit for the literacy narrative. These little memory activities are intended to get us to the literacy narrative, and you can actually explore writing being a process for that paper. As you look back at Chapter 1, some of the blue boxes where the writers invited you to reflect on your life might help you to springboard into some memories that would help you talk about writing as a process for the literacy narrative. That's something to keep in mind that could help you get closer to the threshold concept about process. The other threshold concept you like, about collaborating to get things done, is something we will looking at for the third paper in this class. Thanks, bye!

In studies of audio feedback, two major affordances are consistently noted: first, students can hear the instructor's tone of voice, which, as Anson, et. al describe, emphasizes the distinct identity of the respondent and offers affective cues that help mitigate face threat.[20] Second, it's possible to offer a greater volume of feedback when speaking than when writing.[21] While you are unable to hear my tone in this feedback, the second affordance is very much on display in the selection above. In under two minutes, I was able to offer Maria about 250 words of feedback. Some of the strategies I used to achieve my goals include offering a specific compliment and quoting from her writing (this is one of my favorite ways to demonstrate listening to students; also, research indicates that praise is an often underused tool[22]). I also tried to help Maria connect the dots between these small assignments and the major writing assignment. I direct Maria back to the text to note a few specific areas she might want to review more closely, and I also draw

---

20   Anson, et. al, p. 376.

21   Sommers, Jeffrey. "Response Rethought . . . Again: Exploring Audio Comments and the Teacher-Student Bond," *The Journal of Writing Assessment* 5, no. 1 (2012): paragraph 2.

22   Daiker, Donald A. "Learning to Praise," in *A Sourcebook for Responding to Student Writing*, ed. Richard Straub, (Hampton Press, 1999), 153–65.

a connection between her favorite threshold concept and our third writing project. Through these snippets of feedback, I am trying to build rapport with Maria personally and increase her investment in the course.

If you haven't considered how utilizing LMS technology could simplify your feedback practices, this is one example of how it has simplified mine. Early in the term, I ask students to let me know if they do not like audio/video feedback, or if they have other preferences they'd like to share. Usually some students opt out of getting audio/video feedback, while most indicate they like it. Maria was a student who liked audio/video feedback. In her case, out of 23 low-stakes assignments, I offered video or audio feedback 10 times. On formal assignments, I supplemented text feedback with audio or video feedback three out of four times. Generally speaking, I try to limit the amount of audio feedback to five–six minutes (for longer assignments) or two–three minutes (for shorter assignments).

I notice that I offer more audio/video feedback when teaching online than when teaching in person, as I believe it helps build that relationship with students I am seeking. I hope my students feel like this student, who was quoted in a research study about audio feedback:

> When listening to the tapes, I get a sense of being the professor's equal . . . on the tapes he spoke to me as if to a fellow writer. That can be an automatic ego boost—or at least somewhat of a confidence builder—for a student listening to the tapes. Along with this, the professor communicated in a more personal way on the tapes than he did in class. I would assume this is a natural outcome of being able to speak so freely to one person concerning her work, unlike in a classroom setting. [23]

Toward the end of the second module, Maria and I had our first synchronous conference. When she logged onto Zoom, at first I was completely taken aback by the volume of the background noise on her end. "What's going on?" I asked. She laughed and said it was a busy time at the market on the street below her apartment. After we discussed her paper, she carried her laptop over to the balcony and pointed the camera down to the street.

---

23   Jeff Sommers and Cheryl Mellen. "Audiotaped Response and the Two-Year Campus Writing Classroom." *Teaching English in the Two-Year College* 31, no. 1 (2003): p. 35.

Dozens of small vendors under tents became visible, and the noise was louder yet. I was amazed by the view; from then on, Maria's showing me what was happening in the market became a part of what she and I did when we conferenced.

In all, as I understand the purpose of *establishing relationships* with students, a lot of the work happens before they enter the course site or classroom. By doing this kind of work carefully, you can communicate your identity, course design, and feedback plans to students in ways that will help them be receptive to you. You can also invite them to share relevant information about themselves, and to connect their individual interests and motivations to the course content. Developing rapport with students is about demonstrating understanding, care, effective communication, and respect. Not all students will want a close instructional relationship with you, but if you open the door, some students will use that space to show you things that will surprise you—like the view from Maria's balcony surprised me.

Middle Term: Monitoring Relationships, Pushing Students to Think Harder, and Performing Immediacy

If the beginning of the term is about setting expectations, establishing rapport, and creating pathways for students' experiences to connect to the course content, the middle of the term demands that students work a bit harder to understand the content as it stands apart from their experiences. My instructional goals at this point revolve around getting students to demonstrate reading comprehension and improving their ability to accurately summarize an academic article. The final project during module three is an analysis of the scholarly text; the final project during module four is a report on the literacy practices of one of their communities. Performing well on module three will help students be successful in module four, as the article they are analyzing in module three is all about researching literacy within a community.

During this part of the term, I expect students to struggle. I know when students are struggling, various kinds of difficulty can emerge. So while I have general feedback strategies I use with the assignments, I also make myself available for more individualized support for students, whether in office hours or over email. It turned out Maria benefited from this kind of exchange. In the sections below, I'll talk through how Maria and I navigated an assignment during this middle part of the course—and how my feedback strategies shifted from relating, looking forward, and describing to pointing back at the reading, clarifying muddy points, and raising difficult questions. Next, I'll share a bit about how exchanges outside the course content facilitated the feedback cycle between Maria and me during this part of the term.

Pushing Students to Think Harder

Early in this chapter, I shared that one good way to push students through feedback is to break bigger assignments into smaller parts, which can in turn help an instructor provide targeted feedback on specific skills. In this part of the term, I use several scaffolding steps to move students toward their module three paper, the article analysis. The project progresses in a series of low-stakes assignments that make space for students to grow in their understanding of the article (which is especially important, considering that students come into the class with a wide range of capabilities in academic reading; some, like Maria, are reading in a second language even though they are in a class with many first-language speakers). In the assignment discussed below, Maria was asked to respond to a discussion question about Tony Mirabelli's "Learning to Serve." I've opted not to include her original post here but to cut directly to my feedback. My comments, provided via audio, attempted to correct her perspective in a way that would help her engage with the article more productively in the remaining assignments in the sequence. This audio comment is about three minutes and thirty seconds long:

> Hi Maria, this is Dr. Blewett. I'm really glad to hang out with you a bit this morning to talk about your response to Mirabelli's article. It's clear that you read it carefully and maybe a couple of times. That said, I think there are some places where you aren't responding in a totally correct way. I want to help you think one more time about the article. That's my goal.
>
> You write, "Mirabelli's question seems to be 'how does the status of the workers effect the way they use language.'" I think the second part of

that sentence is the most important—how do they use language? What are the literacy practices of food service workers? And Mirabelli answers that question and gets at the creative, innovative things that they are doing. He basically says, "hey, their low status doesn't make sense, they have more skills than a 9th grade education," but your over emphasis on status has impacted the way that you talk about his analysis.

He does use the website Bitter Waitress, that's true, but his main section isn't about Bitter Waitress, it's about the menu. Bitter Waitress is just an appetizer, just the first little piece that he uses to get into the main thing—the comparison of the two waiters, John versus Harvey. Why is John stronger than Harvey? What is he doing? Mirabelli goes to great lengths to show what John is doing and he shows how Harvey doesn't. Remember my annotations? I wrote, "Harvey mishap 1, Harvey mishap 2." Harvey misses things because he's not as experienced as John, and that's an example how you need to have specialized literacy knowledge within a particular community. Though Harvey is an experienced waiter, he doesn't know this menu, this place.

So Mirabelli's finding is not about the lack of adequate education and status, but rather the innovative and creative ways that workers use language and how that demonstrates multiliteracies. I hope this feedback makes sense. This is a tough article and it's clear you read it carefully. Take time to let this comment reorient how you are seeing things.

In this long comment, which I've lightly edited for clarity, I notice that I am using different feedback strategies, while still attending to rapport. I infer and acknowledge the work Maria put into her response (which helps her save face), and I try to locate the specific problem in her comprehension (I suggest that her over emphasis on the opening example of Bitter Waitress has skewed how she sees the article). I then redirect her, noting how supplemental class resources (the copy of the article I annotated) can help correct her misunderstanding. I also pose some questions designed to get her thinking about the article again ("Why is John stronger than Harvey? What is he doing?"). To this audio comment, Maria responded, "Thank you Dr. Blewett for this feedback for pointing this out. I will review it more."

In the next step of the assignment sequence, Maria's writing demonstrated a stronger understanding of the article. She was able to articulate more of Mirabelli's main argument, and she did not over emphasize his introduction (I find that many first-year students make this error, which reflects a tendency to read the first few pages carefully and then start to skim). Responding to Maria's misunderstanding early in the unit helped her be more successful later in the unit. In other words, the feedback strategies were working, but some other issues were emerging.

Responding Quickly as a Way of Demonstrating Care

Early in the term, Maria shared that she tended to worry over directions for assignments. Up to this mid-point in the term, we had emailed privately seven times—two of which were purely personal emails (a thanks for an effective conference and sharing pictures of a busy day at the market accompanied by a nice note: "Hi Dr. Blewett, I thought I would show you how it looks on a busy day. As you zoom in, you can see what most people sell. Sincerely, Maria"). Now, though, as Maria began to struggle more with the course content, she began to email more frequently. Sometimes we had little bursts of emails. Below is an example:

- *Maria Email:* "I am kind of stuck on how to start. Can you please give me an example or a hint"
- *Kelly Response (3 hours later):* "I see you already submitted the draft—do you still want to connect, or do you feel good at this point? I recommend signing up for a conference next week & we can discuss your work."
- *Maria Email (12 minutes later):* "I didn't submit yet. I hope it wasn't a wrong one."
- *Kelly Response (1 minute later):* "On my end, it looks like you have already submitted, but you should be able to submit again without penalty, so it should not be a big deal. My advice with getting started is as follows . . ." (four ideas are then shared)
- *Maria Email (3 minutes later):* "Can you tell me what appeared to you ? Which document ? And thank you. Your advice did help on how to start the paper."

- *Kelly Response (6 minutes later):* "Sure . . . actually, it's a little odd. My gradebook notification indicates there is a submission from you, but when I click on the link, it's blank. I think we should not worry about it. I am glad my advice helped you get started on the draft!"
- *Maria Email (14 minutes later):* "I'm sure my computer is having some technical issues as I didn't submit at all. Thank you for understanding"

As you can see in this example, a range of issues are coming up, some of them dealing with navigating the learning management system and some of them dealing with assignment difficulty (feeling stuck). As I looked back over our correspondence, I realized that I tend to field a lot of messages from Maria and other students quickly over email. Other topics I addressed with Maria involved how to open a .JPEG, answering questions about Adobe, and helping her navigate our course textbook.

I have a mental framework that helps me not get terribly bogged down in these responses, and that is simply to remember that a quick reply is a demonstration of care in an online class setting. If establishing rapport is an important quality to foster early in the term when relationships are new, it is good to be aware of quickness in response, especially when coursework gets harder. When it's possible to quickly respond and resolve situations, such as by telling the student whether their assignment appeared in the gradebook, that small conversation can contribute to the positive instructional relationship in measurable ways.[24]

To underscore this point, I'll mention that as the term progressed, Maria used these email exchanges to share some larger concerns and some more personal updates:

- "It seems I'm still not quite on the right path."
- "I want your advice. Is this a good start?"
- "Please help me in explaining more because I do not want to fail by misunderstanding."

Students disclosing this kind of concern is generally a good thing. It reflects that Maria is highly motivated and she trusts I will reply. Maria

24   Vivian C. Sheer and Timothy K.F. Fung, "Can Email Communication Enhance Professor-Student Relationship and Student Evaluation of Professor?: Some Empirical Evidence," *Journal of Educational Computing Research* 37, no. 3 (2007): 289–306. https://doi.org/10.2190/EC.37.3.d.

was an unusually engaged student who required a high level of support. But, for the most part, I was able to answer questions Maria had quickly, and it wasn't too much of a burden. For me, in this case and in most cases with students, understanding the value of speed in an educational setting helps allay feelings of irritation. And if I'm in a moment when I can't respond, I find a quick "Thanks for this note. I'll get back to you soon" can be effective.

As the term transitioned to the final weeks, I communicated to Maria over email that she'd need to find new strategies for interacting with instructors, some of whom might not be as available as I was. I encouraged her to think about office hours as times when she could have the kind of quick conferences and email exchanges that helped her succeed in our class, and she replied graciously: "I will be attending office hours for sure." For me, this is an effective feedback exchange because I was able to attend to Maria's needs during the course and begin to look forward to the time when Maria would not be in my course anymore.

End of Term & Beyond: Maintaining Relationships

In the final week of the term, the curriculum in the writing class turns to revision and reflection, as students work on their final portfolio. At this point, my particular role as a reader and respondent to the student's writing takes less prominence, and the student's curation and presentation of their learning is up to them. Like the other modules, I have short process-pieces that help students gather their thoughts for the reflections, as well as models of successful portfolios so they can get a sense of what the final product could look like. I also direct them to earlier assignments in the term, like that first discussion board, so they can get a sense of how they've developed as writers. Below is a short snippet from Maria's final reflection, where you can read what she is taking away from the course (and, interestingly, seems to loop back to her early interest in the writing process):

> After the first writing project and feedback, I gained confidence and I'm proud of myself for a lot of things I've accomplished so far. One of them would have to be allowing others to read my essays and provide

feedback. I used to be adamant about not allowing anyone to read my essays. Receiving feedback proved to be useful. I learned how to organize my work and ensure that it is comprehensive by using opinions. During my high school years, all I could think about was how writing needed to be more grammar-focused. Since taking this class, my outlook totally shifted. I'm also proud of the amount of commitment I'm putting forward. Normally, I would just hand in my paper, but for this class, I have been writing several drafts and thoroughly analyzing my work. I discovered that writing is a method.

Maria's openness to receiving critical feedback will serve her well in future courses. Her plan to visit the office hours of her future professors will help her continue to receive the individual support she needs. And her routine of sending her writing to the writing center provides a feedback loop that can continue as she matriculates to other courses at IU East. Also, some of the writing projects she completed for this course have set the stage for future learning. While I didn't have space to explore it in this essay, Maria's third writing project explored the Psychology major at IU East, and she ended up transitioning to that major by the end of the term. (Her experience is not unique; most of us who teach early-career courses know many students will change majors as they settle into the university.) As of the writing of this chapter, Maria is still a Psychology major—and she's become a mother. She looks forward to finishing at IU East while also taking care of her daughter. When she heard I was writing this chapter and I asked permission to quote from her writing, she replied:

Hello hello Dr Blewett,

I can't tell you how happy i am to hear from you as i have missed you and our conversations. I always remember you when i look at the view outside of my house. You are someone who stays in my mind all the time. I would love to work with you on your project. Of course you have my permission to publicly quote from my writing. Feel free with whatever you need to do. I really hope i can call you whenever you're free and chat with you. You had a huge impact on my life and also in my writing career. Please please let's communicate more often. I

truly believe we had a special connection last semester and i myself can't believe it's about to be a year.
Sincerely,
Maria

The instructional relationship that developed between Maria and me last spring was special, but there was also room for it to grow because of the practices I developed as a responder: making room for connecting with students via conferences and email, designing assignments in ways that encouraged students to see the course's relevance for their future goals, providing timely responses to questions, being sensitive to the embarrassment students could feel when receiving criticism, and finding things I genuinely liked in their writing. These strategies rarely result in emails like the one I received from Maria above, but they often help me feel more connected to students as they go through the course, and I believe that for students looking to connect with a professor, they communicate availability and caring.

Conclusion: Becoming Weak-Tie Relationships for Students

The way we provide feedback to students is necessarily tailored to the specifics of our situation—our subject, our instructional goals, our workload, our students. There are many ways to give feedback well. Whatever our methods, we serve our students best when we respond with care, because learning how to receive critical feedback is an important skill students will need to use throughout college and their working lives.[25] Attending to the social-emotional dimensions of learning helps us create conditions where students will be more likely to learn how to receive critical feedback. They also create conditions where we might be able to stay in touch with students after the class is over. The concept of weak-tie relationships is one way we could think about these post-term connections.

The term "weak-tie relationship" was established by sociologist Mark Granovetter, who was studying people working in Boston in the 1970s.

25 See Nancy Sommers "Across the Drafts," *College Composition and Communication* 58, no. 2 (2006): 248–57.

As Ian Leslie explains, Granovetter's "central insight was that for new information and ideas, weak ties are more important to us than strong ones."[26] Granovetter found 84% of study participants found their job through a weak-tie relationship, not a strong one. The reasoning is that strong tie relationships have too much in common; they share the same information pool. Weak-tie relationships, on the other hand, connect individuals to other networks with whom they would otherwise have minimal contact.

Weak-tie relationships have since been studied to determine the connectedness of a person to their community—a customer and a barista, two people who walk their dog at the same time of day and consistently acknowledge each other with a wave, a trusted professional acquaintance who can help someone find new opportunities for development. As this last example demonstrates, a productive weak-tie relationship can go beyond establishing a kind of benevolent acknowledgement to connecting each other to resources. A particularly good weak-tie relationship is one where both parties benefit from knowing each other's networks.

As teachers in teaching-focused institutions, we have a powerful network our students will benefit from as they move through the institution. We should consider ourselves resources for our students—people with whom they could connect when confused about something happening in school, trusted mentors who could help them take the next step they need via a letter of recommendation, or people who could help connect them to opportunities within their institution that they don't know about. My goal as a teacher is to connect individually with each student well enough that they will succeed in the course and see value in what they are learning *and* that I can be a productive weak-tie relationship for them beyond the class.

Research on weak-ties indicates they enhance feelings of connectedness, security, and belonging. Though the term "weak" might sound unappealing, there is a true durability to these ties, and having a wide number of them will connect the student to campus as a place where they know others and

---

26   Leslie, Ian. "Why Your 'Weak-Tie' Friendships May Mean More than You Think." The Life Project, *BBC*, 2 July 2020, https://www.bbc.com/worklife/article/20201202-why-our-reliance-on-cars-could-start-booming (Access 6-13 2022).

they are known. A few practical ideas on what weak-tie relationships can look like in practice:

- Reaching out to students when you hear about an opportunity or event you think would interest them;
- Nominating students for appropriate campus-wide opportunities, such as a Celebration for Student Writing;
- Writing a short email of congratulations to students when they make the Dean's List or have any kind of public success;
- Being available to write letters of recommendation or to serve as a reference; and/or
- Touching base with students, especially if you see them on campus or in a virtual space such as a public Zoom event and asking how their courses are going this term.

It's likely these are already things you are doing, but you might not have considered how your feedback practices during the course could be connected to—and pave the way for—these post-class interactions. Students will need lots of weak-tie relationships to be successful in college; it is productive for us as teachers to design our feedback practices so we can join what is hopefully a wide and varied group of trusted adults and enhance our campus communities.

Appendix 1: Feedback Strategy Sheet

Considering Relational Feedback: Questions for Reflection

The chapter suggests that focusing on the relational dimensions of feedback productively shifts an instructor's attention from student writing to student writers. Below are prompts to put yourself in a relational-feedback mindset:

- *How do I typically feel when I respond to student work?*
- *How do I want students to feel when they read my response to their work?*
- *Do my students know there's a human behind this feedback?*
- *Am I treating this work as though it's by a human—inferring the process, looking for the logic of errors, reading generously? Referring to*

my students by name and making connections between their interests and my course content?
- *Am I finding things to like in this student work and communicating my appreciation?*
- *If I am offering critical feedback, am I doing so in a way that is sensitive, clear, and actionable? Have I thought about offering difficult feedback using audio or video feedback?*

Considering Workload: Questions for Reflection

As the chapter points out, every writing-intensive class will have feedback rhythms, which can be purposefully transformed into routines that enable you to direct your attention to student work in a more focused way. Below are a few questions related to managing the feedback workload:
- *Do I have a routine for providing feedback?*
- *Have I communicated my routine to students?*
- *Is that routine sustainable?*
- *Am I getting too tired when I grade? Is that impacting the way I receive student work?*
- *Is there anything I can do to create conditions where I can focus deeply on student work for a short period of time?*

Considering Availability: Questions for Reflections

Many times at teaching-focused institutions, our students will be in touch with just-in-time questions. In the chapter, I share how I see responding to questions as a gesture of care and explore how it may impact the feedback cycle. Here are questions related to availability to consider:
- *How available am I to students?*
- *Am I considering how speed of reply is read in an online class?*
- *Have I created resources to respond to frequently asked questions that could help students?*
- *What can I do to communicate availability in ways that are sustainable for me?*

Quick List: Six Ways to Respond to Student Writing that Isn't Evaluative

The chapter notes that responses to student writing can move beyond evaluation (good/bad) and should be more engaged with students' ideas than surface-level errors. Below is a quick list of moves you can make as a responder to student writing that step beyond evaluation:

1. *Describe: What moves do I see the writer making?*
2. *Respond as Reader: What are my reactions to specific parts of the piece? Where do I feel excited or confused?*
3. *Praise: What's one thing I really like? What's my favorite sentence?*
4. *Connect: Can I connect my feedback to other documents, like the assignment prompt, course readings, or past writings of this student?*
5. *Mediate: Can I put my feedback in conversation with peer, course assistant, or writing center feedback?*
6. *Question: Is there a meaningful question that would develop my student's thinking?*

Quick List: Six Ways to Make My Feedback More Responsive and Dialogic

Feedback is only effective if students can engage with it productively. Below are six options for individualizing the feedback and enhancing the dialogic elements of a feedback cycle in a writing-intensive course.

1. *Requesting preferred feedback modalities—and following where I can*
2. *Asking for a response within Canvas; seeing if students are really hearing what I'm saying*
3. *Triangulating my feedback with peer feedback, writing tutor feedback, course assistant feedback*
4. *Asking for a process letter/self-evaluation at key moments in the term*
5. *Asking students to pose questions that I respond to in the feedback*
6. *Providing full-class feedback to help students where they stand on a continuum*

Appendix Two: Additional Resources

Strategies for Responding to Student Writing

Elbow, Peter. "Ranking, Evaluating, and Liking: Sorting Out Three Forms of Judgement." *College English* 55 no. 2 (1993): 187–206.

Ferris, Dana. "Preparing Teachers to Respond to Student Writing." *Journal of Second Language Writing* 16, (2007): 165–93.

Sommers, Nancy. *Responding to Student Writers.* Bedford, 2013.

Straub, Richard. "Managing the Paper Load, Or Making Good Use of Time." *The Practice of Response*, 253–61. Edited by Richard Straub. Hampton Press, 2000.

---. "Guidelines for Responding to Student Writing." *The Practice of Response*, 245–52. Edited by Richard Straub. Hampton Press, 2000.

Social-Emotional Dimensions of Feedback

Anson, Chris M., Deanna P. Dannels, Johann I. Laboy, and Larissa Carneiro. "Students' Perceptions of Oral Screencast Responses to Their Writing: Exploring Digitally Mediated Identities." *Journal of Business and Technical Communication* 30, no. 3 (2016): 378–411.

Daiker, Donald A. "Learning to Praise." *A Sourcebook for Responding to Student Writing*, 153–65. Edited by Richard Straub. Hampton Press, 1999.

Sommers, Nancy. "Beyond the Red Ink: Teachers' Comments through Students' Eyes." *YouTube*, Uploaded by MacMillan Learning, 5 April 2016, https://www.youtube.com/watch?v=PKfLRz7h7gs.

Modality and Feedback

Anson, Chris. "Talking about Text: The Use of Recorded Commentary in Response to Student Writing." *A Sourcebook for Responding to Student Writing*, 165–75. Edited by Richard Straub. Hampton Press, 1999.

Sommers, Jeffrey. "Response Rethought . . . Again: Exploring Audio Comments and the Teacher-Student Bond." *The Journal of Writing Assessment* 5, no. 1 (2012): np.

A Laboratory of Memory:

An Experiment with Difficult Knowledge in a Spanish Civilization Class

Félix Burgos

Contemporary Hispanic culture, history, and society classes are an exciting teaching challenge. They provide opportunities for educators in the humanities, more specifically, language, history, literature, critical pedagogy, or cultural studies, to analyze with our students the explosion of cultural expressions that take place during periods of political and militaristic chaos that are still part of those societies. Such expressions are mechanisms communities use to deal with their troubled pasts directly or indirectly. In this sense, the humanities provide venues to reflect and think together with our students about human resilience and dignity. This chapter explains the creation and execution of a pedagogical experiment that appeals to cultural studies and social justice frameworks to engage educators and students in discussions about interpreting and establishing connections with difficult pasts. Although the materials and reflections I discuss below are specific to one of my Hispanic civilization courses, the chapter is an invitation to educators in the humanities to reflect on how we address issues related to social justice, human rights, and resilience in our courses while creating or interpreting cultural productions.

During the 20th century, the Spanish-speaking world entered a process of transformation characterized by the awakening of different societies towards the construction and consolidation of their national projects. Nonetheless, many of those nations faced violent episodes that defined the fate of those societies. The violent history of the dictatorships in Spain, the South Cone, and the armed conflicts in Central and South America are challenging topics to address, mainly because of how these conflicts still impact the realities of people in those territories. Undoubtedly, I am responsible for discussing how these violent pasts left deep scars in Latin America, contextualizing its societies' responses to the economic, political, and moral reconstruction of their societies. Moreover, students in the United States must identify how the country contributed to these conflicts, considering the ideological and militaristic actions taken due to the Cold War and the War on Drugs. Even though the materials available provide ample information about these histories, I find it challenging to present them in a way that helps students comprehend the causes and effects of violence in those contexts and the resilience and resistance of these conflicts' victims. Moreover, the challenge becomes significant when I invite students to think about the impact of violent confrontations and the importance of memory when they belong to a different generation and place.

My approach to teaching these complex histories is to observe these events from the cultural responses that locate memory practices at the core of narrating the past. In other words, more than focusing on the textbook-like description of the atrocities, I present the events using artistic representations, literature, films, or materials that have functioned as vehicles of expression to name what cannot be named.[1] Presenting those historical narratives using those instruments is certainly not a novel approach. However, I have witnessed in my classes how many students become confused, disengaged, and almost apathetic when accessing those representations.

Part of my labor as a professor and researcher encompasses understanding how post-conflict societies learn about their past. I have learned, for example, about social studies teachers' efforts in my native Colombia to teach younger generations about the country's ongoing armed conflict. The main challenge these teachers have faced is that teaching Colombia's history of violence ranges from exchanging culpabilities between factions,

---

1   The original expression in Spanish is "nombrar lo inombable." The expression refers to artistic efforts to represent violence and repression using the arts as an instrument of reflection. For example, Doris Salcedo, a Colombian artist, uses counter monuments that represent victims' suffering, trauma, and testimony. For further information about Salcedo's work, see Gina Beltrán Valencia, "Doris Salcedo: Creadora de Memoria."

glorifying or demonizing actors, or keeping silent about the victims' sufferings.[2] One way to solve that challenge is to establish a framework incorporating historical memory approaches within the curriculum. This stance means teaching about armed conflict from a place of connecting collective, historical, and personal memories in the classroom to represent the plurality and conflict among different ways to remember and interpret the past. This approach is not different from critical pedagogies educators in post-conflict societies have implemented to address the construction of historical and collective memories as both the means and ends for justice and reconciliation. Learning about the past by creating a common ground where different memories and perspectives about justice and forgiveness interact is an ideal scenario for sharing experiences and thinking differently about the present and future.

All these processes of learning about difficult pasts make sense to students who have a direct connection with or live in those societies. But what is the value of learning about violence or suffering in a distant place and time? More specifically, how do I engage my students who live in the United States to think about state violence or armed conflicts in countries they have not even visited? Furthermore, how do I treat these topics responsibly so my students recognize themselves in the testimonies of suffering and resilience from people living on different latitudes?

Frameworks of social justice in the foreign language classroom and how teachers engage students with difficult knowledge in the classroom became an inspiration for the materials I prepared for my Hispanic Civilization (SPAN-S 383) course at IU East in fall 2021. Before getting into the details about the class, its objectives, and the assignments I prepared for a particular module on historical memory, I would like to briefly describe the functions of the frameworks mentioned above.

Social justice is not a new term in education. For decades, many educators have specialized in introducing topics about power, privilege, justice, and equity in various disciplines to sensibilize students about structural issues in the world, promoting their critical thinking skills and inviting them to

---

2   Maria Emma Wills Obregón. "Queridos Maestros y Maestras." Introduction. In Los Caminos De La Memoria Histórica, 8–13. Bogota, Colombia: Centro Nacional de Memoria Histórica, 2018.

be active social change agents.[3] World language educators have also found ways to connect the essential aspects of language learning with critical perspectives to help students explore and understand the social realities of the communities they hope to interact with while learning the language. In the United States, world language education is mainly based on world-readiness standards that emphasize five areas (also known as the five C's: Communication, Cultures, Connections, Comparisons, and Communities) that go beyond the instructional setting.[4] While they do not directly address social justice within the world-readiness standards, the five C's, especially the community and cultural areas, provide ample opportunities to engage with topics that help students reflect on their position regarding problematic issues around the world. Randolph Jr. and Johnson argue "the language education classroom provides the ideal context for entering critical, transformative spaces of culture and community study informed by a social justice framework."[5] Indeed, there have been many occasions in my experience as a language educator when I have momentarily interrupted conjugations, vocabulary, or grammar activities to answer my students' questions about cultural, social, or political differences between the U.S. and Latin America. These significant moments of reflection have helped my students and I build bridges of understanding about our backgrounds and experiences with the world. However, designing lessons or strategies in the world language classroom is not an easy task. Foreshadowing the conclusion of this chapter, I have experienced challenges in navigating topics with my students, especially those in advanced classes, that include episodes of state violence or discrimination. Nonetheless, it is important not to shy away from proposing and debating these topics with students since they "not only look at how these themes are relevant in the target communities and

---

3   Beth A. Wassell, Pamela Wesely, and Cassandra Glynn. "Agents of Change: Reimagining Curriculum and Instruction in World Language Classrooms through Social Justice Education." Journal of Curriculum and Pedagogy 16, no. 3 (2019): 263–84. https://doi.org/10.1080/15505170.2019.1570399.

4   American Council on the Teaching of Foreign Languages. n.d. "World Readiness Standards for Learning Languages." World Readiness Standards for Learning Languages. Accessed May 2, 2022. https://www.actfl.org/resources/world-readiness-standards-learning-languages.

5   Linwood J. Randolph Jr. and Stacey Margarita Johnson, "Social Justice in the Language Classroom: A Call to Action," Dimension (2017): 101.

cultures, but they also turn a critical eye to their communities and cultures and examine how the intersections of some of those themes affect various groups of people."[6] In this sense, it is appropriate to present the claims for justice, reparation, and reconciliation of various sectors in Spain and Latin America across history as a matter that intersects with the struggles of people in the United States.

Difficult knowledge teaching is another framework that has helped me reflect on the importance of discussing themes that involve histories of vulnerability and social traumas. James Garret proposes a helpful definition of difficult knowledge as a concept:

> [d]ifficult knowledge is a recognition of the unsteadiness of one's understanding of the world and our place in it that comes about through learning. In learning what we did not want to know, sometimes we lose our balance. Difficult knowledge is an orientation toward learning about the tumultuousness of society, recognizes the tumultuousness of our orientation to it, and further takes uncertainty as a central feature of the learning encounter. Difficult knowledge is a walk toward the ways in which that tumult can make one feel diminished, worried, guilty, sad or, alternatively, victorious, justified, and certain about a course of action.[7]

In other words, violent and traumatic episodes in the histories of communities may differ from the realities of those outside them. Having access to these histories and recognizing their incomprehensibility is already a step toward activating a critical perspective about the world. The goals of difficult knowledge studies never intend to provide teachers and students with a framework to see the world from one perspective. On the contrary, uncertainty and conflict are essential values in a type of pedagogy that puts incomprehensibility at the center of the discussion. Of course, one expects that using this conceptual framework in the preparation of a course or lesson may cause feelings of anxiety, resistance, or apathy among students. Our responsibility as teachers is to select the means of representing

6   Ibid, 110.

7   H. James Garrett, "Learning to be in the World with Others." *Difficult Knowledge & Social Studies Education.* (New York: Peter Lang Publishers, Inc., 2017): 19.

violent episodes carefully to avoid extreme responses that could derail the discussion's objectives. The value I find in difficult knowledge is it helps teachers and students think about our ethics, privileges, and ways to make sense of the world.

As previously mentioned, these frameworks allow me to think and question my approach toward teaching State repression and violence in the Hispanic world during the 20th century. What follows, however, should not be applied only for such a course but also to any kind of approach that puts at its core the study of societal changes and cultural responses to atrocities, natural disasters, or global emergencies. Thinking and discussing about difficult knowledges with lenses of social justice is a step towards affirming and empowering students. In what remains of this chapter, I will discuss the objectives, assignments, and reflection about a content module in the fall 2021 SPAN-S 383 course.

Course Description

Hispanic Civilization III is the third in a four-course sequence which provides a transatlantic view of history, literature, and cultural developments in Spain and Latin America from prehistoric times to present. Students who take this class are majors or minors in Spanish or take it as an elective course. In some cases, students are native speakers or heritage learners of Spanish. Most students are proficient enough to read and write complex texts in Spanish, but some are still improving their linguistic proficiency. I must highlight that the Spanish program does not require students to take the four-sequence Hispanic civilization courses in any specific order. This is a great advantage for students interested in taking the courses at any point during their college experience. In some cases, such flexibility impacts the students' knowledge about historical or cultural episodes that could be relevant for context.

Course Overview

SPAN-S 384 explores cultural manifestations, literary texts, and societal practices in Spain and Latin America during the 20th and 21st centuries. This transatlantic perspective allows us to examine the Spanish-speaking regions' cultural contributions and global connections. The main topics the class introduces are:

- U.S., Spain, and Latin America in the early 20th century
- The Mexican Revolution: its political and cultural impact
- Spain: The Second Spanish Republic, Civil War, and Franco's Dictatorship
- Spain: The transition to democracy
- Latin America in the Cold War: Revolutions, armed conflicts, and the Operación Condor
- ¡Basta ya! / ¡No más! / ¡Sin Olvido! Politics of memory after the atrocity
- Spain and Latin America in the 21st century

Since this course is not a survey on Hispanic history, I prefer to provide concise readings or videos that allow students to become familiar with the themes I teach. To do so, I use infographics, short readings, or online videos to give students essential information to understand the historical context of the cultural products we analyze. Afterward, depending on the theme, I provide literary texts, music, films, or documentaries that become the main instruments to understand the social and cultural environment around the events I teach. The overall goal is for students to connect the events and cultural representations to critically analyze those products and compare and contrast the events with global issues at large. For the last assignment of the course, students choose one of the main themes from the class and analyze a series of cultural artifacts considering contextual information they have already accessed during the course.

I structure the class by modules using Canvas, our university's Learning Management System. Each module, which students must complete within two weeks, includes reference materials, video or written discussions, reflection blogs, and an assessment component (e.g., quizzes, written reflections, or short summaries).

An Experiment in Action

In the Fall of 2021, I introduced the module, "¡Basta ya! / ¡Nunca más! / ¡Sin Olvido! Politics of memory after the atrocity." The title includes phrases that various social movements and organizations used in artistic performances, demonstrations, or publications to demand justice for the victims of authoritarian governments or internal armed conflicts. When looking at them carefully, these claims do not only demand but also invite their respective societies to reflect upon complicit silences, apathy, or forgetfulness. [8] The module comes immediately after exploring the rise of dictatorships, their impact in Argentina and Chile, and the origins and consequences of the armed conflict in Colombia. For years, I analyzed and interacted with study cases or theories about historical and collective memories in these countries. However, this module became an experiment because it was the first time I transformed cultural theory into a pedagogical experience for my students.

In the past, I had used some of these materials for my Spanish composition class. At that time, I asked students to write about the power of collective memory as a narrative device for the construction and consolidation of communities. However, for SPAN 383, I wanted to present the topic more robustly and in a contextualized way. In this sense, the overall goals of the lesson were to:

- recognize the concept of historical memory in Latin America by analyzing different ways of narrating and representing the past;
- analyze processes of resilience and social justice in memory demands; and
- establish parallels regarding the importance of memory in the United States and Latin America.

For the materials, I selected and curated a series of texts and videos that provided students with background about the struggles, victories, and loss of victims' communities in Spain and Latin America that have

---

8   For instance, ¡Basta ya! (It's enough!) has been commonly used in manifestations against violence in Colombia. It is also the title of a report the Colombian National Center for Historical Memory published in 2013 about the impact of the armed conflict in Colombia. ¡Nunca Más! (Never again) and ¡Sin Olvido! (Without forgetting) became part of the chants in protests against amnesty policies in Spain, Argentina, and Chile.

defended historical memory as a right and moral duty. The primary source materials came from Chile's Museum of Memory and Human Rights,[9] newspaper articles from Spain that discussed the country's controversial historical memory law,[10] and documents from the Mothers of the Plaza de Mayo organization in Argentina.[11] I also included some sections from *¡Basta Ya¡*, the report the Colombian National Center for Historical Memory released in 2013 to provide an account of the country's armed conflict. Since the language of these texts is either too theoretical or too technical, I selected some of the most relevant pieces to create a 25-slide PowerPoint presentation I later used in a video. The audiovisual materials in this module were the Argentine film *La Historia Oficial*, some sections of the Colombian documentary *No Hubo Tiempo Para la Tristeza*, and two songs that would later serve as the cultural products to analyze in reflections and discussions.[12]

Because of the complexity of the materials, I split the module into two sections. The first section was a contextual and theoretical component that included the PowerPoint presentation and some infographics on the topic. In this first section, students completed four activities: (a) a note-taking exercise, where they would summarize the main ideas from the presentation video; (b) a reading comprehension activity of an article that contextualized the Madres de la Plaza de Mayo movement and the film *La Historia Oficial*; (c) a guide students had to complete while watching the film, and (d) a

9   During the module's development, I provided students with short videos about the foundation of Chile's Museum of Memory and Human Rights, which became the main repository of victims' memories after the Chilean dictatorship and transition to democracy.

10   Spain's 2007 historical memory law introduced a series of restorative measures for the victims of the Spanish Civil War (1936–1939) and subsequent dictatorship (1938–1973). In 1975, the transition to democracy guaranteed that none of the involved parties during or after the Civil War would be prosecuted. However, in 2007 the Spanish Socialist Worker's Party proposed and passed a law recognizing the victims of the war and the dictatorship and provided economic and symbolic retribution to the victims' families. Critics of the law considered that the measures affected not only the social and political relationships in the country but also represented the re-writing of Spain's history.

11   Madres de la Plaza de Mayo is an Argentine association of women who lost their children to the dictatorship between 1976 and 1983. The story of the mothers became the most important example of grassroots organization against crimes committed by the dictatorship. The document I shared with the students is a comic about how the organization defied the prohibition of public protest in the 80s.

12   The complete bibliography of these materials can be found at the end of the chapter.

discussion forum where students would reflect upon the main themes from the movie.

The module's second half provided ideas about the connection between historical memory, self-determination, and justice. In this module section, students learned the process that some communities of victims in Colombia followed to maintain and transmit the memories of their suffering and resilience. I selected some short testimonies and readings from Colombia's *¡Basta Ya!* report and complemented them with excerpts from the documentary *No Hubo Tiempo para la Tristeza*. The main goal of this section was to provide students with ideas about how different organizations think about the past, present, and future. Instead of delivering shocking imagery about victimhood, I wanted students to attend to voices that talk about memory as a vehicle to understanding their pain while communicating it to the whole society. This second part of the module included (a) a reflection activity where students explained their reactions toward the testimonies; (b) the analysis of the messages found in two songs; and (c) a final discussion to compare and contrast how people in Argentina, Colombia, and the United States remember complex or violent stories in the past and present.

I consider this module an experiment, not in the traditional way of using subjects to observe their reactions and give an assessment of their behaviors. On the contrary, this learning module attempted to determine how students can be encouraged to think and reflect critically on episodes not within their range of experience. My objective was not to evaluate the students' reactions to testimonies of a reality that does not belong to them, but to invite them to think about how the language communities view the world in the face of violence, injustice, and incomprehensibility.

In this sense, my students' responses to the assignments met some of the objectives I set for the module. On one hand, most of their reflections displayed a language and attitude that showed respect and sensitivity toward the histories they read. For example, students provided hopeful insights when discussing the victims' efforts to claim and obtain justice. In addition, I was fascinated to read their analysis of the songs since they established important connections between the themes and historical contexts. Some students expanded this analysis by bringing examples of other songs (mainly in English) to the discussion that resonated with materials in the module.

On the other hand, some students expressed the horror, uneasiness, and sorrow they confronted while interacting with the materials. I remember some students displayed resistance toward the content. It is not that they did not want to complete the activities, but they felt the topic was too depressing and difficult to discuss, especially when all of us were still working through the effects of the global pandemic. Within the framework of difficult knowledges, I understood these responses as part of the process that students go through when faced with others' traumatic stories. Not being sure what to do with an emotional charge that does not belong to you is a step towards understanding the incomprehensible. This concept is something I will address toward the conclusion of this chapter.

In the last activity of the module, I was glad to see that students could establish some parallels between the construction of historical memory in Latin America and the United States. It was great to hear the students' reflections on the gaps in American culture regarding historical memory. Students identified, for example, that our societies prefer to commemorate the victor but not the victims' struggles. However, the reflections on that last activity helped students determine the importance of historical memory in various contexts but not use their imagination to think about what their society can do about it.

As I mentioned before, one of the main assignments of the course requires that students choose one of the themes introduced in the class and write a final essay, expanding the topic by focusing on historical contexts or cultural artifacts, such as literary pieces, music, or film. I must admit I felt slightly disappointed when my students decided to work with other themes, avoiding the politics of memory after the atrocity module. I think I missed the opportunity to ask them why they did not consider this topic relevant or exciting for the conclusion of the course.

So, as I prepared this chapter, I returned to the course to revise the content and materials, establishing ways in which the assignments and activities become more effective and valuable for students' careers and personal lives. Reconceiving content and activities is the natural process of our labor as educators, especially if the learning objectives we propose intend to reach students' capacity for empathy, reflection, and imagination. As a conclusion, I offer a series of observations that allow me to adjust plans and materials that will have an impact on classes where social justice plays a central role.

Conclusion: An Experiment Redux

After reflecting and sharing my experience with other colleagues, I realized my so-called experiment had little success in three areas. First, the module must help students demonstrate that they are learning new information by contrasting their previous knowledge. This process is obvious for most seasoned faculty. However, it is essential to remember that selecting information and curating it in an accessible manner is no guarantee that students will successfully comprehend it. For instance, I devoted too much time and effort to designing materials to explain contexts and concepts clearly. Still, I did not prepare a space to include my students' living experiences, thoughts, and ideas.

Second, the material I selected for the class was significant but overwhelming. Because of the nature of the topic, students must have an opportunity to reflect carefully on the testimonies and messages. One of the principles in social justice and difficult knowledge education is teachers must provide students with enough time to comprehend the content, reflect carefully on their thoughts, and be prepared to participate in conversations that do not always end up in agreements. Not allowing the students to think carefully may have impacted the last reflections in the module and the students' decision to avoid working with the topic for the course's final assignment.

Finally, it requires imagination, effort, and preparation to compare people's responses to historical pain or trauma situations. When working on the activities, I did not want students to focus on the traumatic experiences the victims narrated through the texts but on their resilience and effort to transmit their testimony as part of a broader historical memory project. It is easy for me and the students to get enraged or sad after seeing or reading some testimonies. Still, it is difficult to focus on the strength of those who have decided to share their stories to claim justice and change their society. In this regard, the main objective of the final activity is to transform these pieces of difficult knowledge into a possibility to see the world differently.

Based on these short observations, I made significant changes to the activities' structure, material, and assessment. Compared to the experience I previously described, I decided to give more space for my students to reflect and analyze the material and their responses. Students' success does not depend on the quality of the material or the scaffolding of activities but on the time I give them to ask questions, think carefully about their answers, and craft responses that exceed or approach the activities' objectives. Indeed, discussing these topics takes more than an entire semester, and I reckon students will continue finding challenges in grasping the value of commemorating difficult pasts that do not belong to them. However, I opted to have students take their time to think individually and with the group about these topics through the discussions, analyses, and interactions with the materials.

I realized that *La Historia Oficial* was a shocking instrument that did not allow my students to look at memory as a vehicle of self-determination and justice. I realized that helping my American and Latino students reach the module's objectives did not require a film that would activate uneasy feelings against the topic. This realization does not mean those materials have no space in the classroom. On the contrary, films and documentaries are the main allies for language educators since they provide semi-authentic communicative and cultural experiences. In this regard, the videos and songs I kept for the module provide a real vision of the realities of organizations in Colombia and Argentina, but with a tone that aligns more with themes of resilience and social justice. Put differently, the short videos I selected do not show women as victims but as survivors who have decided to denounce the past and transform the present.

Instead of waiting for students to use the theme of historical memory to understand the realities of post-conflict societies in Latin America, I decided to offer an activity, a laboratory of memories, where they could recognize and contrast how memories work in different territories. In other words, I want students to identify that how we commemorate depends on our cultural perspectives and experiences. Indeed, atrocities leave painful imprints in the bodies and minds of victims, leaving them numb or silent. This concept applies to all people around the world. However, mourning and commemorating take different shapes according to the worldviews of the communities who decide to work through the past. Therefore, the last activity of the module precisely focuses on contrasting different ways of claiming justice by remembering tragic events. In that "laboratory of memories," I ask students to look for examples of commemoration in the U.S. and connect them with the ones we studied in the module. In the activity, I ask them to avoid looking at atrocities like the 9/11 terrorist attacks or global wars. Instead, I invite them to explore ways of commemorating daily losses due to school shootings, police brutality, drug consumption, deaths on the south border, car accidents, poverty, etc. I predict that some students will find it challenging to find examples that provide a complete picture of how American society works through difficult pasts. And that is precisely the point!

The following pages provide an overview of the changes I made for the new version of the course, which I will teach in Spring 2023. For readers from other disciplines, I include footnotes that provide suggestions or ideas for content that deals with components of social justice or critical pedagogy. Each assignment contains a description, the objectives, and procedures the group will follow to complete the activities.

Course Overview

SPAN-S 383

¡Basta ya! / ¡No más! / ¡Sin Olvido! Politics of memory after the atrocity[13]

Introduction

After establishing the historical contexts that gave way to and maintained the dictatorships in Spain, Argentina, and Chile. In the following three weeks, we will explore how the transitions to democracy took place and how the cultural responses of memory demand justice and dignity. At the same time, we will analyze the case of Colombia in which the work of the victims' memories compete with an armed conflict that continues.[14]

---

13   The readers will find the module's translation from Spanish to English.

14   Certainly, topics that deal with trauma and atrocities could take a long semester to develop. While the prompt establishes that the module will take three weeks, readings related to the topic you choose

Duration

Students complete all activities in this module in three weeks. During the first week, they will complete the readings and some individual actions that they will post according to the schedule (see below). At the beginning of the second week, they will attend an online session (synchronously or asynchronously) to ask questions and provide some initial reactions to the material. Afterward, students will combine individual and group activities to reflect on the topic.[15]

Module Objectives

By the end of this module, you will be able to:

- explain the value of historical memory from your perspective and for the victims of violence in Latin America;
- establish the difficulties of memory work in post-dictatorship (Argentina) or post-conflict (Colombia) contexts;
- compare memory struggles in your community with those in the countries studied through discussion and reflection; and
- use vocabulary in Spanish regarding social struggles and memory in spoken and written forms.

Materials

- Videos:[16]
  - "Madres de Plaza de Mayo. La historia: Resistir es resistir," September 5, 2020 *Canal Encuentro*. https://youtu.be/ qjhGyQXSL14.
  - "No Hubo Tiempo para la Tristeza," November 27, 2013.

---

could be introduced at early stages of the course. For instance, there can be short readings or general reflections in which the concepts of social justice, transition, or reconciliation become part of the course's vocabulary.

15   Due to the nature of the material, it is important that the instructor is available for discussion or questions about the topics introduced. The online session I propose allows me to see what students are thinking, the ways they are engaging with the material, and the effect the topic has on the students.

16   One of the main issues about using short videos for these topics is they provide information with little background about the issue at hand. For the videos, I have used Kaltura's quiz tools that allow me to provide annotations to complement information and questions that keep students' attention on specific details. I also provide short video guides providing vocabulary or other relevant information.

Centro Nacional de Memoria Histórica. https://youtu.be/das2Pipwp2w.

○ "Falsos Positivos: ¿Quiénes son las madres de Soacha y cuál es su lucha?" June 15, 2021 *Clash Medios* https://youtu.be/hR54VUgvX4Y.

- Readings:
  ○ Iramain, Demetrio. "Capítulo 1. Del Patio de Casa a la Historia Grande del País." In *Una Historia de las Madres de la Plaza de Mayo,* 11–15. Buenos Aires: Editorial de la Universidad Nacional de la Plata, 2017.
  ○ Grupo de Memoria Histórica. "5.3 Las Labores de la Dignidad y Resistencia." In *¡Basta Ya! Colombia: Memorias de Guerra y Dignidad,* 359–395. Bogota: Imprenta Nacional, 2013.
  ○ Gómez Garcia, M. Victoria, Magdalena Díaz Gorfinkiel, Vicente Díaz Gandasegui. *The Conversation* "¿Por qué es necesaria la memoria histórica?" November 18, 2018, accessed June 30, 2021. https://theconversation.com/por-que-es-necesaria-la-memoria-historica-105670.

- Music:
  ○ Sosa, Mercedes and León Gieco. "Sólo Le pido a Dios," April 10, 2012, music video, 4:37, https://youtu.be/as9xXqxtq88.
  ○ Juyó Rodriguez, Javier Alirio. "La Memoria," recorded October 2015, on *Tocó Cantar (Travesía Contra el Olvido),* streaming audio, accessed June 31, 2021, https://centrodememoriahistorica.gov.co/podcasts/toco-cantar/.

Course Schedule

Week one:

The first week combines students' current knowledge and comprehension activities about the topic. The first week of activities allows students to provide initial conceptions and definitions on the topics they are learning.

- Day one:
  - Assignment #1: This assignment is an initial reflection on the topics. Students will write, in Spanish, about the meaning of memory, resilience, and community. Also, they will start learning some of the vocabulary they will be using during the following weeks.
- Day three:
  - Assignment #2: This activity is based on the reading "¿Por qué es necesaria la memoria histórica?" Students will contrast their initial thoughts with the reading and complement their initial responses.
- Day seven:
  - Assignment #3: By this time, students should have read and watched the two reports about Madres of Plaza de Mayo and Madres de Soacha. Students will establish similarities and differences between the two cases using a video discussion tool (e.g., Canvas discussions or Voice Thread).

Week two:

Week one ends with materials that include complex information about the topic proposed. In this case, students will read reports and testimonials about mothers who have lost their children due to the state's violence. Materials that provide unsettling information about victimhood, atrocities, or natural disasters will undoubtedly create negative reactions. It is essential, however, to use the incomprehensibility of those episodes as the core of the reflection and discussions. In other words, the materials we use should help us question the power dynamics of the actors involved or the resilience of the communities affected by those episodes. It is important to hear students' ideas and feelings about the topic in the online discussion and to provide them with tools to appropriately react to actions that have taken place in the past or on other latitudes.

- Day one:
  - Assignment #4: Students will attend a synchronous or asynchronous meeting to discuss the first part of the contents.

The instructor will introduce the central assignment students will submit by the end of the module.

- Day three:
  - Assignment #5: Students will start an analysis of two songs (Mercedes Sosa's *Sólo le Pido a Dios* and Javier Juyó's *La Memoria*).
- Day seven:
  - By this time, students will have shared their findings of the songs, their possible interpretations, and contexts. They will discuss the importance of the arts as vehicles of representation.

Week three:

The last activity of the module focuses on the students' ability to contextualize, interpret, make connections, and reflect on the topic. Each section for the final assignment reinforces students' abilities to comprehend, analyze, and apply the knowledge they have acquired from the discussions and materials. The most important feature of this assignment is that students make specific connections between the topic and their interests as citizens and/or members of a specific community.

- This week, students will work on a project comparing and contrasting commemorations of atrocities in the United States, Colombia, and Argentina. They will receive individual guidance, if necessary, to complete the activity. By the fifth day of this last week, they should have posted their final products so other classmates may provide feedback.

Course Assignment Overviews

Module 6: ¡Basta ya! / ¡No más! / ¡Sin Olvido! Politics of memory after the atrocity

Assignment #1—Week 1

Description

This module explores the meaning and relevance of memory in Latin America after dictatorships or armed conflicts. In this activity, students answer the questions in Spanish or English to better explain their thoughts. The feedback I provide in Spanish helps them build the vocabulary and expressions to discuss the topic.

Objective

- identify the main concepts and ideas surrounding historical memory.

Task

Please answer these questions individually. To start, you will only share them with me. Note that the answers you provide are not right or wrong.

1. In two sentences, how could you define "memory"?
2. In what way do you think memory serves the interests of a person or community?
3. Do you think it is vital for a society to remember positive and negative events? Why?
4. What are the physical forms in which societies represent their memories?
5. Do you consider that you, your family, or community keep the memory of the past alive? Why or why not?
   a. If you can, share how you, your family, or community keep memories of the past alive.
6. What do you consider to be the difference between history and memory? Which of the two is more beneficial for society?
7. Do you consider the United States a country with or without "memory"? Why?

** Before starting, I would like to warn you that some of the topics we will deal with are strong in content and language. If there is something that disturbs you or affects you, do not hesitate to discuss it with me. **

Module 7: ¡Basta ya! / ¡No más! / ¡Sin Olvido! Politics of memory after the atrocity

Assignment #2—Week 1

Description

The reading "¿Por qué es necesaria la memoria histórica?" provides some initial tools to consider how individuals and communities have decided to preserve and communicate memories of difficult, violent, or traumatic pasts. In this activity, students will share some responses from the first task. A group forum helps students find points of reference for their experiences and thoughts about the topic.

Objective

- compare and contrast previous ideas about memory and historical memory
- recognize the difference between memory and history

Task

In the discussion, answer the following questions:

1. Did your definition of "memory" and "history" change after the reading? How so?
2. The authors introduce the terms "resilience," "forgetting," and "democracy" as essential components of historical memory. What's the relationship between these three concepts?
3. What did the reading inform you about how you, your family, your community, and/or your country think about the memory of the past?
4. Share four words with the group that help summarize the importance of memory in this reading.

Procedure

Students will publish their answers in the discussion forum. They will react to at least two of their classmates' responses by acknowledging, agreeing, disagreeing, or complementing them.

Assignment #3—Week 1

Description

Mothers of Plaza de Mayo in Argentina and Mothers of Soacha in Colombia are women-led organizations that keep the memories of their sons and daughters who were assassinated or disappeared by their respective state forces alive. These mothers' stories show the cruelty of violence and their efforts to claim justice and change their societies.

The materials in this section include two readings about the organizations and two videos that explain the mothers' efforts to rescue and maintain their sons' and daughters' memories. First, students will prepare the readings and videos. Afterward, they will participate in Voice Thread, discussing some of the main questions proposed in the activity (see below).

Objectives

- report the central premises of two Latin American organizations of women
- compare the mothers' stories to find commonalities and differences in their struggles

Task

You will read the history behind the Argentine movement of Mothers of Plaza de Mayo and the Colombian organization Madres de Soacha. You will also watch two videos to listen directly to their testimonies and struggles.

I suggest you do the readings before watching the videos so that you have a general idea of who these women are. The testimonies these women provide are sad yet meaningful and powerful. That is why I invite you to LISTEN carefully to what they say. Imagine you are in front of these women, listening directly to their histories. Try not to rush or get frustrated by their accent or testimonies. If that's the case, stop, and try again when you do not feel upset.

Once you finish the readings and the videos, discuss the last three questions of this questionnaire. Remember to respond to at least two classmates by acknowledging their participation, highlighting what you liked about their answers, and asking a question about something you disagree with or do not understand.

    a. What are the similarities and differences between these two organizations?

    b. What actions have the mothers taken to recover and communicate their sons' and daughters' memories?

    c. How has the State responded to their claims? How have their respective societies responded to their claims?

To share with your classmates in the voice thread:

    a. How do the mothers define and understand the concepts of **memory, oblivion, and justice**?

    b. Based on what you have learned in the last few days, how do these terms complement or change your understanding of historical memory?

    c. Is there any case in the United States or the world that makes you think about the mothers' perspectives? (It does not need to be something similar. Think about social catastrophes that would have some connection with the mothers' work or claims.) Use images or other references in your voice thread to talk about this.

Remember the rules for our voice threads: locate yourself in a space with good light, speak loud and clearly, and don't be too brief or too eloquent (7 minutes max.)

Module 7: ¡Basta ya! / ¡No más! / ¡Sin Olvido! Politics of memory after the atrocity

Assignment #4—Week 2

Description

Students will attend a synchronous or asynchronous meeting to complement the information they learned during the first week. At this point, I will carefully explain the historical context of the struggles for memory in Colombia and Argentina. Students can post questions about the content during or after the presentation to clarify some doubts or share information with the instructor and classmates.

Introduction to the Module's Project
A Laboratory for Difficult Memories: Brainstorming

After violent episodes, victims' relatives find a place close to where the catastrophe occurred to mourn and memorialize the event. In many cases, these places are sites ideal for praying, protesting, or asking for significant changes. Unfortunately, in some societies, such spaces of memorialization do not exist due to the catastrophe's persistance, threats from oppressors, or because there is no time or strength left to commemorate.

For the last activity of the class, we will contrast how memory "takes place" in the U.S. and Latin America, specifically Argentina and Colombia. Start thinking about these ideas with your instructor or your classmates:

a. Think about a difficult or traumatic event that communities have commemorated in the U.S. It does not need to be as violent as the examples we have explored in class. It could be a natural or human-made disaster, for example.

b. Find information about the event and identify what these communities demand or hope for by commemorating it. Pay attention to the symbols or objects they use to memorialize the victims. Try to determine how they make other people aware of the event.

Assignment #5—Week 2
Description

Mercedes Sosa's interpretation of *Solo le Pido a Dios* became a hymn in Argentina and Chile. While the song could be considered a plea to God, it appeals directly to people, asking them not to be indifferent to the pain of others. Likewise, Juyó's *La Memoria* provides a series of metaphors about the power and vulnerability of memory. Both songs are cultural productions that help understand how artists think about music's power to reflect the role of memory and justice in society. Students will respond in Spanish using the discussion forums.

Objectives

- identify and explain the metaphors in music about the role of memory in society
- discuss the role the arts play as tools to represent difficult knowledges

Task

Listen to the songs *Sólo le Pido a Dios* by Mercedes Sosa and *La Memoria* by Javier Juyó. Before listening to the songs, read the lyrics and highlight the sections you consider relevant. Then, ask yourself why those sections are essential and keep that information in mind.

While listening to the songs, pay attention to the following details:

- the rhythm and pace of the songs
- the emotion the singers and music display during the interpretation
- the emphasis the singers put in the chorus or any specific section of the songs.

After listening to the songs, answer the following questions in the discussion:

1. How do you think the arts contribute to memorializing and thinking about the past?
2. Do you think these songs are ideal complements for movements such as the Mothers of Plaza de Mayo or Mothers of Soacha? Why or why not?
3. What sections of the songs made you think about the Mothers? What parts of the songs made you think about the difficult memories you are investigating?

Week 3—Final Assignment

Objectives

- examine the main elements that constitute the construction of difficult memories in society

- compare and contrast conceptions about commemoration and social justice in the U.S. and Latin America

Introduction

In the last few weeks, we have tried to understand how historical memory has become one of the primary resources in societies that have suffered traumatic events. We have learned that some societies have confronted their difficult pasts, while others have kept silent about catastrophes that impacted entire communities.

The cases we studied give us a glimpse of how and what victims of violence think about justice, forgiveness, and oblivion. It is time for you to provide an example of what commemoration looks like in the United States and how it connects with the cases we studied in this module.

Task

Instead of writing a reflection or final paper, you will present the findings of your investigation orally. You may use images, slides, or any type of material you choose. Your presentation will be divided into four sections:

- **Contextualization:** Talk about the event, emphasizing when it occurred, where it took place, how it was reported, and what communities were impacted.
- **Commemoration:**
  - **Talk about how the community commemorates the event:** If possible, explain how the commemoration began and what products they created to commemorate the event. Identify if private, local, state, or federal institutions sponsor those initiatives.
  - **Perhaps the event you are interested in does not have any examples of communal commemoration. If that is the case:** look for information about why communities have not decided to commemorate the event. Then, try to establish the obstacles that impede commemoration.
- **Connections:** Discuss how the concepts of historical memory, resilience, and/or justice that you have studied in this module

connect with the event you investigated. Find similarities and differences with the Latin American Madres' efforts to commemorate the past.

- **Reflection:** It is time to provide your take on why the event must be remembered. Why do you think the event is vital for constructing historical memory in American communities? How do you feel knowing that the event is (or is not) commemorated? Finally, what did you learn about this laboratory?

Procedure

- You will have until the end of the week to work on this project. This seems to be an easy project, but don't be fooled!
- You may record yourself via Zoom, Voice Thread, or Kaltura. It is important that, by Friday, you provide the group with a link to your video.
- You have between 10 to 15 minutes to present the results of your work.
- All of you must react to at least five presentations. The reactions consist of:
  - Asking questions
  - Expanding the information, or
  - Discussing something interesting about the presentation

If you have any questions, do not hesitate to contact me.

VoiceThread and Discussion Rubric

	Exceeds Expectations (5)	Meets Expectations (4)	Below expectations (3)	Objectives not met (2–0)
Task	All the activities, including responses, were completed on time.	Most activities, including responses, were completed on time.	Some activities, including responses, were completed on time.	None of the activities were completed on time.
Comments	Excels at providing questions or comments and complements their peers' contributions.	Questions and comments are appropriate and reflect the student's disposition to work with others.	The comments are limited to agreeing with the reflection of their colleagues without elaborating.	The student does not participate in the discussion.
Message	The message is characterized by a careful reflection on the readings and topics. The student considers different perspectives to explain their contribution.	The message has a general reflection of the text based on the readings. However, the student shows some confusion with terms or ideas.	The message summarizes the themes well and approaches the objectives of the activity. However, the response lacks reflection or care.	The message is a summary of the theme.
Language	The student uses grammar and diction clearly and effectively. Their vocabulary to talk about the subject is precise and sophisticated.	Good command of grammar and pronunciation.	The message is understandable, but the student needs more control over grammar and pronunciation.	The answers demonstrate a lack of grammar usage and pronunciation.

Laboratory of Memories Project

	Exceeds Expectations (5)	Meets Expectations (4)	Below Expectations (3)	Objectives not met (2–0)
Organization	The presentation is very clear and detailed. The presentation is informative and organized flawlessly.	The presentation is clear and detailed. The information is linked to the task proposed and information is well organized.	The presentation is somewhat clear but could use more detail. Most information is linked to the questions proposed and information is organized.	The summary is not clear and lacks significant detail. Some information is linked to the questions proposed and information is loosely organized.
Language	The student demonstrates skill, produces meaningful sentences, and uses appropriate vocabulary and structures.	The student was able to produce meaningful messages at an advanced level. The student uses appropriate vocabulary and structures with few mistakes.	The student produced meaningful sentences, although with some difficulty. The vocabulary and structures are basic.	The student's ideas are well communicated, but at times some errors obscure the message they intend to communicate. Be careful with the use of vocabulary and other structures.
Verbal Communication	The student's voice is very confident, steady, strong, and clear; the student consistently uses inflections to emphasize key points or create interest; the student's talking pace and pronunciation are consistently appropriate.	The student's voice is steady, strong, and clear; the student often uses inflections to emphasize key points and create interest; the student's talking pace and pronunciation are mostly appropriate.	The student's voice is generally steady, strong, and clear; the student sometimes uses inflections to emphasize key points and create interest; the student's talking pace and pronunciation are appropriate.	The student's voice is frequently too weak or too strong; the student rarely uses inflections to emphasize key points and create interest, or the speaker sometimes uses inflections inappropriately; the student's talking pace is often too slow or too fast.
Effectiveness	This was an exceptional presentation and extremely effective.	This was a very good presentation and very effective.	This presentation was good and effective.	This presentation was average and somewhat effective.
Collaboration	The student's discussion was on time and they replied to all classmates.	The student's discussion was on time and they replied to the majority of their classmates.	The student's discussion was not on time and they replied to 2–3 of their classmates.	The student's discussion was not on time and they replied to one of their classmates.

Printed in the USA
CPSIA information can be obtained
at www.ICGtesting.com
LVHW011940160324
774454LV00012B/457